# PSYCHOANALYSIS

## The Impossible Profession

## Janet Malcolm

GRANTA

Granta Publications, 12 Addison Avenue, London W11 4QR

First published in the US in 1981 by Alfred A. Knopf Inc.
Paperback editions published by Granta Books, 2004, 2012
This edition published by Granta Books, 2018

Most of this book was first published in the *New Yorker*

A CIP catalogue record for this book is available from the British Library.

1 3 5 7 9 10 8 6 4 2

ISBN 978 1 78378 453 0

Printed and bound by CPI Group (UK) Ltd, Croydon, CR0 4YY

*To my father*

It almost looks as if analysis were the third of those "impossible" professions in which one can be sure beforehand of achieving unsatisfying results. The other two, which have been known much longer, are education and government.

—SIGMUND FREUD,
"*Analysis Terminable and Interminable*" (*1937*)

As psychoanalysts, we are only too aware that our profession is not only impossible but also extremely difficult.

—ADAM LIMENTANI,
*International Journal of Psycho-Analysis* (*1977*)

If two people are repeatedly alone together, some sort of emotional bond will develop between them.

—PHYLLIS GREENACRE,
*Journal of the American Psychoanalytic Association* (*1954*)

The soul God gave me isn't of the sort
That prospers in the weather of a court.
It's all too obvious that I don't possess
The virtues necessary for success.
My one great talent is for speaking plain;
I've never learned to flatter or to feign;
And anyone so stupidly sincere
Had best not seek a courtier's career.

—MOLIÈRE, "*The Misanthrope*," *translated by Richard Wilbur*

# Acknowledgements

I AM DEEPLY INDEBTED TO DANIEL SCHWARTZ, DIRECTOR OF the Austen Riggs Center, who encouraged—no, incited—me to write the article that forms the basis of this book, then patiently read the manuscript to rid it of many errors, and, above all, kept me on course in my writing and thinking through his embodiment, in my imagination, of the ideal of analysis. I am grateful to many other psychoanalysts who generously gave of their time to discuss the profession and the theory of psychoanalysis with me. Thanks also are due to the New York Psychoanalytic Institute for placing its incomparable library at my disposal; to the staff of the library for kindly assisting *The New Yorker's* checking department; to Nancy Franklin, of the checking department, for her outstanding, elegant work; to Elizabeth Kramer for her illuminations of many koans of psychoanalytic theory and practice; to Hartvig Dahl and Virginia Teller for the immense intellectual stimulation and personal kindness I received from them; to Peter Gay for his astute and most valuable criticisms and suggestions; and to Marianka Vynová-Mueller for her assistance beyond the call of duty in the basement of the Albrecht Mueller Rat Man Archive. Above all, I thank and salute, "Aaron Green," the remarkable and lovable man who opened his mind and heart to me and gave this book its life.

# Psychoanalysis:
# The Impossible Profession

# I

AARON GREEN (AS I SHALL CALL HIM) IS A FORTY-SIX-year-old psychoanalyst who practices in Manhattan, in the East Nineties. He has four patients in analysis, who come four or five times a week and lie on the couch, and six patients who come for psychotherapy once or twice or three times a week and sit in a chair. He charges between thirty and seventy dollars per (fifty-minute) hour. He is on the faculty of a local medical school, where he teaches and supervises medical students and psychiatric residents. He is a graduate of the New York Psychoanalytic Institute and a member of the New York Psychoanalytic Society. He came to New York to study at the Institute after getting his medical degree and serving his internship and residency in a New England city.

He is a slight man, with a vivid, impatient, unsmiling face. He has thin dark hair and wears professorial clothes. A herringbone jacket, light-blue oxford shirt, subdued tie, and gray flannel trousers are his customary apparel. He looks Jewish. He lives with his wife and son in a brownstone apartment off Madison, four blocks from his office. The living room of his apartment is furnished with black modern sofas and armchairs, beige carpets, reproductions of modern art, photographs, folk art and archeological objects, and books;

it is spare, extremely neat, pleasant, perhaps a hair studied. His consultation room is a kind of poor relation of his living room. The couch is fifties Scandinavian modern rather than seventies high-tech Italian; the pictures are old MOMA reproductions rather than Fondation Maeght exhibition posters; there are floor lamps instead of track lighting. The lights in the consultation room are kept dim, purposely.

The psychoanalysis that Aaron Green practices is of the most unswervingly classical Freudian sort. His thinking about theory and technique has been shaped by Charles Brenner, the intransigent purist of American psychoanalysis, author of a forbidding *Elementary Textbook of Psychoanalysis* and, with Jacob Arlow, of *Psychoanalytic Concepts and the Structural Theory*, a once controversial, now standard advanced text. Brenner is known for his advocacy of a fanatically meticulous, aseptic analytic technique and for his hard-line theoretical position, which goes from Freud through the ego-psychology triumvirate of Heinz Hartmann, Ernst Kris, and Rudolph Loewenstein to the culminating quartet of himself, Jacob Arlow, Martin Wangh, and David Beres. Green is contemptuous of most recent developments in psychoanalysis, dismissing them as fads. He is unimpressed by the French structuralist psychoanalyst Jacques Lacan, whose impenetrably obscure writings have been gaining increasingly earnest attention here, but whose innovation of reducing the fifty-minute analytic hour to a Delphic seven or eight minutes (or sometimes even to a single oracular *parole* murmured in the waiting room) has yet to be adopted. He is similarly skeptical of the new theories of Heinz Kohut and Otto Kernberg, derived from work with narcissistic and borderline disorders; the stir that Kohut (who is the center of a fervid cult in Chicago) and Kernberg (who works in New York and has a quieter following) have been making within and outside the field fills him with disgust. The English object-relations people (D. W. Winnicott, W. R. D. Fairbairn, Michael Balint, Harry Guntrip, and others), who predate and foreshadow the Kohut and the Kernberg groups, are equally wrong-minded, he feels. When the name "Melanie Klein" is uttered, he closes his eyes and groans softly.

Green is critical of his own work. He feels it is good, but not as good as it will be when he has had more experience. He looks back on past cases with misery and guilt over blunders he has made. When a patient gets better, Green credits the psychoanalytic process; when he doesn't, he blames himself. He has been doing analysis—counting the years of work he did under supervision during his training at the New York Psychoanalytic Institute—for more than a decade. He was in analysis himself, with two analysts, for a total of fifteen years. The first analysis began while he was in medical school and lasted for six years; the second was his training analysis at the Institute, which lasted for nine years.

I met Aaron Green for the first time on a freezing winter day when I went to his office to interview him; I was preparing a report on contemporary psychoanalysis, and his name was on a list of sources that a psychoanalyst friend had given me. I remember that the day was freezing because I remember the agreeable warmth of the low-ceilinged, dimly lit room in which he received me; I felt as if I had come out of a bleak, harsh woods into a cozy lair. This feeling of comfort and relaxation, I now suspect, derived from something besides abundant steam heat. I had sat in other analysts' overheated offices and had felt, if anything, rather chilled. The analysts I had seen so far had dealt with me as they habitually deal with patients on first meeting—courteously, neutrally, noncommittally, reservedly, "abstinently"—and had also shown a certain wariness at being in the presence of a journalist. With Aaron Green, however, things were different from the start. He subtly deferred to me, he tried to impress me. He was the patient and I was the doctor; he was the student and I was the teacher. To put it in psychoanalytic language, the transference valence of the journalist was here greater than that of the analyst.

THE PHENOMENON OF TRANSFERENCE—HOW WE ALL INvent each other according to early blueprints—was Freud's most original and radical discovery. The idea of infant sexuality and of the Oedipus complex can be accepted with a good deal more equanimity than the idea that the most precious and inviolate of entities—personal relations—is actually a messy jangle of misapprehensions, at best an uneasy truce between powerful solitary fantasy systems. Even (or especially) romantic love is fundamentally solitary, and has at its core a profound impersonality. The concept of transference at once destroys faith in personal relations and explains why they are tragic: we cannot know each other. We must grope around for each other through a dense thicket of absent others. We cannot see each other plain. A horrible kind of predestination hovers over each new attachment we form. "Only connect," E. M. Forster proposed. "Only we can't," the psychoanalyst knows.

Freud got on the scent of transference in the late eighteen-nineties, during his early, hit-or-miss treatment of hysteria by the "cathartic method" of Josef Breuer, in which memories of the events believed to have precipitated hysterical symptoms were evoked under hypnosis—and thus presumably defused of their power over the sufferer. In his *An Autobiographical Study*, of 1925, Freud recalls "an experience which showed me in the crudest light what I had long suspected." The experience related to

> one of my most acquiescent patients, with whom hypnotism had enabled me to bring about the most marvellous results, and whom I was engaged in relieving of her suffering by tracing back her attacks of pain to their origins. . . . As she woke up on one occasion, [she] threw her arms round my neck. The unexpected entrance of a servant relieved us from a painful discussion, but from that time onwards there was a tacit understanding between us that the hypnotic treatment should be discontinued. I was modest enough not to attribute the event to my own irresistible personal attraction, and I felt that I had now grasped the nature of the mysterious element that was at work behind hypnotism. In order to exclude it, or at all events to isolate it, it was necessary to abandon hypnosis.

But the "mysterious element" was also present in the method Freud next adopted—of pressing the patient's forehead and urging him to remember—as it was in the culminating free-association method of psychoanalysis proper. Time after time, without any apparent provocation on his side, Freud's women patients (overtly or covertly) fell in love with him. "On the first few occasions, one might perhaps think that the analytic treatment had come up against a disturbance due to a chance event," Freud wrote in his *Introductory Lectures on Psycho-Analysis*, of 1917.

But when a similar affectionate attachment by the patient to the doctor is repeated regularly in every new case, when it comes to light again and again, under the most unfavorable conditions, and where there are positively grotesque incongruities, even in elderly women and in relation to grey-bearded men—even where, in our judgment, there is nothing of any kind to entice—then we must abandon the idea of a chance disturbance and recognize that we are dealing with a phenomenon that is intimately bound up with the nature of the illness itself. This new fact, which we recognize so unwillingly, is known by us as *transference*.

The "painful discussion" could no longer be avoided. "It is out of the question for us to yield to the patient's demands deriving from the transference; it would be absurd for us to reject them in an unfriendly, still more in an indignant, manner," Freud went on in the *Introductory Lectures*. Instead, "we overcome the transference by pointing out to the patient that his feelings do not arise from the present situation and do not apply to the person of the doctor, but that they are repeating something that happened to him earlier. In this way we oblige him to transform his repetition into a memory."

This was easier said than done. In a paper of 1915 entitled "Observations on Transference-Love" (part of a series of papers on analytic technique addressed to his fellow pioneering psychoanalysts), Freud took up in forthright detail the delicate and weird task of persuading a female patient to regard her love for the analyst both as a normal part of the treatment ("She must accept falling in love with her doctor as an inescapable fate") and as something unreal and hallucinatory—an artificial revival of early feelings that has nothing to do with the person of the analyst. Then, in one of those startling and beguiling reversals that characterize his writings, Freud turns on his own argument and says, But isn't *all* love like that? Isn't what we mean by "falling in love" a kind of sickness and craziness, an illusion, a blindness to what the loved person is really like, a state arising from infantile origins? The only difference between transference-love and "genuine" love, he concludes, is the context. In the analytic situation, nothing is permitted to come of the patient's love; it is a situation of renunciation. Both parties must "overcome the pleasure principle" and renounce each other for a higher goal—the doctor for the sake of professional ethics and scientific progress, the patient in order to "acquire the extra piece of mental freedom which distinguishes conscious mental activity—in the systematic sense—from unconscious." Freud describes the temptations for the analyst that are inherent in the situation—especially for "those who are still youngish and not yet bound by strong ties"—with rueful candor:

Sexual love is undoubtedly one of the chief things in life, and the union of mental and bodily satisfaction in the enjoyment of love is one of its culminating peaks. Apart from a few queer fanatics, all the world knows this and conducts its life accordingly; science alone is too delicate to admit it. Again, when a woman sues for love, to reject and refuse is a distressing part for a man to play; and, in spite of neurosis and resistance, there is an incomparable fascination in a woman of high principles who confesses her passion. It is not a patient's crudely sensual desires which constitute the temptation. These are more likely to repel, and it will call for all the doctor's tolerance if he is to regard them as a natural phenomenon. It is rather, perhaps, a woman's subtler and aim-inhibited wishes which bring with them the danger of making a man forget his technique and his medical task for the sake of a fine experience.

From these early, unimaginable transactions between proud, lovesick women and nervous, abstinent analysts the concept of transference expanded beyond the situation of the patient's falling in love with the analyst (or, in the case of a male patient, of bitterly hating him) to embrace every aspect of the patient's relationship to the analyst. As psychoanalysis developed, the transference became at once more central and more complex. By 1936, in *The Ego and the Mechanisms of Defense*, Anna Freud was able to distinguish between the passionate love and hate transferences—what she called the simple "irruptions of the id"—and the more subtle transferences that are the early defensive maneuvers of the ego against the instincts. But such distinctions could not be made in the earliest period of psychoanalysis, to which the "Transference-Love" paper belongs.

In that period, the feverish rush of discoveries that Freud had made in the eighteen-nineties—about dreams, the unconscious, repression, infantile sexuality, the Oedipus complex, free association, transference—was settling into a design of orderly beauty. All the pieces fit, and the whole thing shone. When Freud was invited to Clark University, in Worcester, Massachusetts, in 1909, he gave a lecture series that was an excited celebration of the new science of psychoanalysis. A radiance and a buoyancy run through the Clark lectures (Freud reconstructed them from memory— they had been given extemporaneously—and published them shortly after his return to Vienna), which were to fade from later accounts of the same events. (Compare the Clark lec-

tures with "Analysis Terminable and Interminable," of 1937
—Freud's last, dark, dense, profound paper. It is like comparing a Beethoven bagatelle with a late quartet.) These lectures remain the most concise and lucid account in and out
of Freud's writings of the birth of psychoanalysis; nowhere
is the complicated story more effortlessly told.

Freud begins by asserting that Breuer, and not he, was
the father of psychoanalysis (a statement he was to curtly
retract a few years later). "I had no share in its earliest be-
ginnings," he writes, and he goes on to tell of Breuer's treatment, back in 1880, of a girl called Anna O., who was afflicted with "the enigmatic condition which, from the time of
ancient Greek medicine, has been known as 'hysteria,' and
which has the power of producing illusory pictures of a
whole number of serious diseases." Anna's hysterical symptoms included paralysis of her limbs, disturbed vision, a severe nervous cough, aversion to food and drink, loss of memory (bizarrely, she had forgotten her native German, and
could speak only English), and a tendency to go into states
of what Freud, dropping into French terminology, called *absence.* Unlike other doctors of the time, who believed hysteria
to be a form of malingering and treated its victims with
harshness and contempt, Breuer devoted himself to this beautiful, intelligent twenty-one-year-old girl, sympathized with
her sufferings, and, through "benevolent scrutiny," finally arrived at a means of helping her. He was struck by the way
she muttered words to herself during her fits of *absence,* and
he had the idea of hypnotizing her and—by using the muttered words as a starting point—getting her to relate her
"profoundly melancholy fantasies," which very often cen-
tered on the image of herself at her father's sickbed. These
gloomy musings made the girl feel better—she coined the

term "talking cure" for them—and presently led to the disappearance of her symptoms, after she had been "brought to remember, under hypnosis, with an accompanying expression of affect, on what occasion and in what connection the symptoms had first appeared." For example, one of Anna O.'s most troublesome symptoms—a pathological aversion to drinking water, even though she was horribly thirsty—was dispelled by her recollection of once seeing a little dog belonging to her English lady companion drink water from a glass. The sight had filled her with disgust and anger, which she had politely suppressed; only now, in Breuer's trance, could she express these feelings, and after doing so she asked for water, drank a great deal, and was never troubled by her water phobia again. Gradually, other symptoms disappeared, through other recollections of psychic traumas, and "the treatment was brought to an end."

This account, as readers of Ernest Jones's biography of Freud are aware, discreetly leaves out the disaster that befell Anna O.'s treatment and brought it to an abrupt end. "Freud has related to me a fuller account than he described in his writings of the peculiar circumstances surrounding the end of this novel treatment," Jones reveals, and he goes on:

> It would seem that Breuer had developed what we should nowadays call a strong countertransference to his interesting patient. At all events, he was so engrossed that his wife became bored at listening to no other topic, and before long she became jealous. She did not display this openly, but became unhappy and morose. It was a long time before Breuer, with his thoughts elsewhere, divined the meaning of her state of mind. It provoked a violent reaction in him, perhaps compounded of love and guilt, and he decided to bring the treatment to an end. He announced

this to Anna O., who was by now much better, and bade her good-by. But that evening he was fetched back to find her in a greatly excited state, apparently as ill as ever. The patient, who according to him had appeared to be an asexual being and had never made any allusion to such a forbidden topic throughout the treatment, was now in the throes of an hysterical childbirth (pseudocyesis), the logical termination of a phantom pregnancy that had been invisibly developing in response to Breuer's ministrations. Though profoundly shocked, he managed to calm her down by hypnotizing her, and then fled the house in a cold sweat. The next day, he and his wife left for Venice to spend a second honeymoon, which resulted in the conception of a daughter; the girl born in these curious circumstances was nearly sixty years later to commit suicide in New York.[1]

In a recent study, *The Therapeutic Revolution: From Mesmer to Freud,* two French psychoanalysts, Léon Chertok and Raymond de Saussure, pointedly contrast Breuer's panic in the Anna O. case with Freud's coolness in the face of similar erotic stimulation (the incident of the patient's putting her arms around his neck), arguing the interesting notion that Freud's discovery of transference was (apart from any question of its validity) a *defensive* measure—a kind of "prophylaxis" that depersonalized the relationship and interposed a "third person" between the patient and the doctor, like the duenna-nurse who peers over the gynecologist's shoulder during examinations. "Until Freud's discovery," they write, "psychotherapists had been haunted, whether consciously or not, by the possibility of erotic complications in the relationship. They could thenceforth feel reassured." That Breuer took Anna's sexual feelings toward him personally, whereas Freud discovered transference as a result of the importunities of *his* importuning patient is the difference between ordinary intellect and genius. The difference might also be, as Chertok and de Saussure hypothesize (and it doesn't detract from Freud's genius to do so), the difference between a man of confident sexuality and one who wasn't so sure of his attractiveness—who couldn't believe a woman would find him irresistible and so had to hunt around for some other explanation for her conduct.

Freud heard about the case of Anna O. from Breuer in 1882, and it made a great impression on him, but seven years went by before he ventured onto the path that the frightened ur-psychoanalyst had fled. In 1886, on his return from study in Paris with the great neurologist Jean Martin Charcot, who had convinced him of the psychological etiology of hysteria, Freud set up practice in Vienna as a specialist in nervous diseases. For twenty months, he treated his patients by means of electrotherapy (according to directions in a textbook by Wilhelm Erb) plus baths, massage, and something called the Weir Mitchell rest cure, but with a growing sense of futility. Then, for sixteen more months, he treated them with no less ineffectual hypnotic suggestion. Finally, in 1889, he tried Breuer's cathartic method, and found, as he reported in the Clark lectures, that "my experiences agreed entirely with his." However, it was not long before Freud became dissatisfied with this method, too. Inducing hypnosis was not easy for him—he didn't seem to be good at it—and he could get only a fraction of his patients into the desired trance. To judge from the following account of his attempts to put patients under (it appears in his and Breuer's *Studies on Hysteria,* of 1895), erotic complications were the least of Freud's troubles:

I soon began to tire of issuing assurances and commands such as "You are going to sleep! . . . sleep!" and of hearing the patient, as so often happened when the degree of hypnosis was light, remonstrate with me: "But, doctor, I'm *not* asleep," and of then having to make highly ticklish distinctions: "I don't mean ordinary sleep; I mean hypnosis. As you see, you are hypnotized, you can't open your eyes . . ."

Freud began to wonder whether he could achieve catharsis without hypnosis, and was emboldened to try by an inference he drew from an experiment he had recently witnessed in Nancy, performed by a physician named Hippolyte Bernheim, who was also using hypnotic suggestion to treat hysterics. Bernheim demonstrated that a person awakened from a trance could be induced to remember what had happened during the trance if the hypnotist firmly insisted that he *did* remember, against all his protestations that he didn't. Freud tried similar coercion on his patients, and it worked. "In that way, I succeeded, without using hypnosis, in obtaining from the patients whatever was required for establishing the connection between the pathogenic scenes they had forgotten and the symptoms left over from those scenes. But it was a laborious procedure, and in the long run an exhausting one; and it was unsuited to serve as a permanent technique."

However, the very difficulty and laboriousness of the process led Freud to a crucial insight. This was his postulation of a force within the patient that had originally pushed the pathogenic experiences out of consciousness (Freud called it "repression"), and of its counterpart ("resistance"), which had *kept* them out of consciousness. "All these experiences had involved the emergence of a wishful impulse which was in sharp contrast to the subject's other wishes, and which proved incompatible with the ethical and aesthetic standards of his personality," and thus had to be "repressed," Freud wrote in the Clark lectures. For example, one of his patients (Elisabeth von R.) had repressed the memory of a wish to marry her brother-in-law, which had come to her unbidden at the deathbed of her sister and had so horrified her that she converted it into a hysterical symptom. "Our hysterical patients suffer from reminiscences," Freud wrote in the first Clark lecture. Only when his urging technique forced the memory back into Elisabeth's consciousness could she rid herself of its pathogenic power.

Eventually, by ceasing to badger the patient and allowing him to say anything he liked, Freud arrived at (stumbled on) the psychoanalytic method that has remained unchanged to this day. "Allowing" (Freud's word in the Clark lectures) hardly does justice to the process of free association. In a well-known passage in *The Interpretation of Dreams* (1900), Freud likens the feat of the patient who suspends his critical faculties and says everything and anything that comes into his mind, regardless of its triviality, irrelevance, or unpleasantness, to that of the poet during the act of creation. He quotes from a letter that Schiller wrote in 1788 in reply to a friend who had complained of meagre literary production:

> The ground for your complaint seems to me to lie in the constraint imposed by your reason upon your imagination. I will make my idea more concrete by a simile. It seems a bad thing and detrimental to the creative work of the mind if Reason makes too close an examination of the ideas as

they come pouring in—at the very gateway, as it were. Looked at in isolation, a thought may seem very trivial or very fantastic; but it may be made important by another thought that comes after it, and, in conjunction with other thoughts that may seem equally absurd, it may turn out to form a most effective link. Reason cannot form any opinion upon all this unless it retains the thought long enough to look at it in connection with the others. On the other hand, where there is a creative mind, Reason—so it seems to me—relaxes its watch upon the gates, and the ideas rush in pell-mell, and only then does it look them through and examine them in a mass. . . . You critics, or whatever else you may call yourselves, are ashamed or frightened of the momentary and transient extravagances which are to be found in all truly creative minds and whose longer or shorter duration distinguishes the thinking artist from the dreamer. You complain of your unfruitfulness because you reject too soon and discriminate too severely.

Just as there are few people who can write poems like Schiller, there are few analytic patients who can free-associate easily, if at all. Analysts today don't expect the free-association process to take hold until well into the analysis; in fact, some regard the appearance of true free association as a signal to terminate the analysis. But in 1900 Freud, enchanted by his great discovery (which was nothing less than the "invention of the first instrument for the scientific examination of the human mind," according to James Strachey, the English psychoanalyst and editor of the Standard Edition of Freud's works), underestimated its complexities and contradictions. "A relaxation of the watch upon the gates of Reason, the adoption of an attitude of uncritical self-observation, is by no means difficult," he innocently reported in *The Interpretation of Dreams*. "Most of my patients achieve it after their first instructions."

Free association—"the ore from which, with the help of some simple interpretative devices, the analyst extracts its content of precious metal," as Freud wrote—led to dream interpretation, since the patient's associations often led him to the dreams of the night before. "It came as the first fruit of the technical innovation I had adopted when, following a dim presentiment, I decided to replace hypnosis by free association," Freud wrote in 1914, in *On the History of the Psycho-Analytic Movement*. He went on, "My desire for knowledge had not at the start been directed toward understanding dreams. I do not know of any outside influence which drew my interest to them or inspired me with any helpful expectations." Through associations with parts of a dream, the patient would penetrate its disguises; the associations would lead him from the deceptive "manifest content" of the remembered dream to the deep "latent content," where a wish was invariably lodged. In the *History*, Freud recalled that

> the interpretation of dreams became a solace and a support to me in those arduous first years of analysis, when I had to master the technique, clinical phenomena, and therapy of the neuroses all at the same time. At that period, I was completely isolated, and in the network of problems and accumulation of difficulties I often dreaded losing my bearings, and also my confidence. There were often patients with whom an unaccountably long time elapsed before my hypothesis—that a neurosis was bound to become intelligible through analysis—proved true; but these patients' dreams, which might be regarded as ana-

logues of their symptoms, almost always confirmed the hypothesis. It was only my success in this direction that enabled me to persevere.

From the study of his own dreams during his self-analysis in the late eighteen-nineties, Freud discovered "what an unsuspectedly great part is played in human development by impressions and experiences of early childhood," as he wrote in the Clark lectures. He went on, "In dream-life, the child that is in man pursues its existence, as it were, and retains all its characteristics and wishful impulses, even such as have become unserviceable in later life. There will be brought home to you with irresistible force the many developments, repressions, sublimations, and reaction-formations by means of which a child with a quite other innate endowment grows into what we call a normal man—the bearer, and in part the victim, of the civilization that has been so painfully acquired."

Along with free association and dreams, Freud goes on to cite (we are in the third Clark lecture) a third entrée into the unconscious: the various small "faulty actions," or "parapraxes"—slips of the tongue, misreadings, the forgetting of names, the losing and breaking of objects, and so on—by which we daily betray ourselves. These trivial actions provide clues to unconscious motivation and bolster the psychoanalyst's belief in psychic determinism—the belief that there is nothing arbitrary or haphazard or accidental or meaningless in anything we do.

Freud pauses here to take one of his habitual swipes at the opponents of psychoanalysis, comparing them to patients under the sway of resistance. "We often become aware in our opponents, just as we do in our patients, that their power of judgment is very noticeably influenced affectively, in the sense of being diminished," he writes. This argument puts the reader into a quandary. On the one hand, it offends all his notions of fairness in arguing; to ascribe an opponent's opposition to his going soft in the head is surely the most outrageous of ad-hominem arguments. On the other hand, it cannot be dismissed, either, by anyone who has ever helplessly felt his own power of judgment being sapped by a strong emotion—as who of us hasn't?

Lecture Four begins with the observation that "psychoanalytic research traces back the symptoms of patients' illnesses with really surprising regularity to impressions from their *erotic life*." Freud reflects on the unpalatability of this notion, observing that his colleagues all disbelieved it initially, and that he himself reluctantly "converted" to it only after much clinical experience compelled him to do so. "A conviction of the correctness of this thesis was not precisely made easier by the behavior of patients," he adds. "Instead of willingly presenting us with information about their sexual life, they try to conceal it by every means in their power. People are in general not candid over sexual matters. They do not show their sexuality freely, but to conceal it they wear a heavy overcoat woven of a tissue of lies, as though the weather were bad in the world of sexuality." Just how truly wretched the sexual weather was in Vienna in the eighteen-nineties may be gleaned from the letters that Freud wrote to his friend Wilhelm Fliess between 1887 and 1902. (These came to light after the Second World War and were published in 1950.) In a draft of a paper called "The Aetiology of the Neuroses," which he sent to Fliess in 1893 (enjoining him to keep it away from his young wife!), Freud draws a picture of contemporary Viennese sexual life that is fraught with

Ibsenesque gloom and fatalism. All choices were hopeless: either a young man went to prostitutes and got syphilis and gonorrhea or he masturbated and became neurasthenic; women who married neurasthenic (thus impotent) men became hysterical; women and men who (perforce) practiced coitus interruptus to avoid conception became neurotic. "Society seems doomed to fall a victim to incurable neuroses which reduce the enjoyment of life to a minimum, destroy the marriage relation, and bring hereditary ruin on the whole coming generation," Freud bleakly concluded.

By 1897, Freud had undergone the intellectual revolution that took him from this dour but unremarkable social view of sexual malaise to his radical psychological theories regarding infantile sexuality and the Oedipus complex. Things within proved to be no less grim than those without: If we aren't dashed on the shoals of the psychosexual stages of development (becoming perverts, homosexuals, or obsessional types), we sink beneath the weight of our Oedipal grief. No one leaves childhood unscathed; few reach adulthood capable of love and heterosexual sex. The difference between neurotics and normal people is a matter only of degree, Freud says in the last Clark lecture: we all "entertain a life of fantasy in which we like to make up for the insufficiencies of reality by the production of wish fulfillments." In distinction from the successful man of action who is able to impose his wishes on reality, or the artist who transforms them into works of art, the neurotic escapes from reality through his symptoms. "Today, neurosis takes the place of the monasteries which used to be the refuge of all whom life had disappointed or who felt too weak to face it," Freud writes.

In closing the Clark series, Freud addressed himself to

the question of what happens when, after psychoanalytic treatment, the neurotic's repressed unconscious wishes are set free. Does he become a libertine and rebel? Extremely unlikely, Freud says. In most cases, *"repression* is replaced by *condemning judgment."* The ex-neurotic will now deliberately choose not to do what he has previously murkily not done; his "better" impulses," rather than his unsuccessful (symptom-producing) repressions, will guide him to his renunciations. Or he may "sublimate" the infantile wishes; that is to say, convert their original sexual aim into a culturally and socially valuable end while retaining their basic energy. Or, finally, he may choose to claim some modicum of sexual happiness for himself. Freud here protests (as he continued to do into the nineteen-twenties and -thirties) the too harsh repressions of society. "Our civilized standards make life too difficult for the majority of human organizations," he writes. "We ought not to exalt ourselves so high as completely to neglect what was originally animal in our nature. Nor should we forget that the satisfaction of the individual's happiness cannot be erased from among the aims of our civilization."

BY 1909, FREUD'S UNASSUMING QUEST FOR A CURE FOR nervous disorders ("Anyone who wants to make a living from the treatment of nervous patients must clearly be able to do something to help them," he tartly observed of his own bungling attempts in *An Autobiographical Study*) had improbably flowered into the vast system of thought about human nature—psychoanalysis—which has detonated throughout the intellectual, social, artistic, and ordinary life of our century as no cultural force has (it may not be off the mark to say) since Christianity. (Freud himself preferred to align the psychoanalytic revolution with the revolution of Copernicus and then the revolution of Darwin, saying that the first showed that the earth was not the center of the universe, the second that man was not a unique creation, and the third that man was not even master of his own house.) It was as if a lonely terrorist working in his cellar on a modest explosive device to blow up the local brewery had unaccountably found his way to the hydrogen bomb and blown up half the world. The fallout from this bomb has yet to settle. It isn't even clear whether the original target—the neurotic patient— wasn't overshot; "proof" of the efficacy of psychoanalytic cure has yet to be established, and no analyst claims it.

Soon after the Big Bang of Freud's major discoveries— around the time of the Clark lectures—the historian of psychoanalysis notes a fork in the road. One path leads outward into the general culture, widening to become the grand boulevard of psychoanalytic influence—the multilane superhighway of psychoanalytic thought's incursions into psychiatry, social philosophy, anthropology, law, literature, education, and child-rearing. The other is the narrow, inward-turning path of psychoanalytic therapy: a hidden, almost secret byway travelled by few (the analysts and their patients), edged by decrepit mansions with drawn shades (the training institutes and the analytic societies), marked with inscrutable road signs (the scientific papers)—the road along which Aaron Green is trudging. As for Freud himself, he travelled both routes, extending the psychoanalytic view to literature, art, biography, anthropology, and social philosophy in works such as *Leonardo da Vinci, Totem and Taboo, Group Psychology*, and *Moses and Monotheism*, as well as sticking to the theoretical and clinical core of psychoanalysis.

In the period between 1910 and 1915, by which time a

small band of fellow-workers had formed, Freud published a series of short papers on analytic technique which reflected his growing understanding that "to make the unconscious conscious" was not as simple a business as he had first thought. His work with patients was leading him to new appreciations of the complexity of the task. In a paper called " 'Wild' Psycho-Analysis" (1910), he derides (his own) "long superseded idea . . . that the patient suffers from a sort of ignorance, and that if one removes this ignorance by giving him information (about the causal connection of his illness with his life, about his experiences in childhood, and so on), he is bound to recover." He goes on to mordantly observe that "such measures have as much influence on the symptoms of nervous illness as a distribution of menu cards in a time of famine has upon hunger." In "On Beginning the Treatment" (1913), Freud burlesques the analyst who can't wait to zap the patient with the patient's horrid unconscious wishes: "What a measure of self-complacency and thoughtlessness must be possessed by anyone who can, on the shortest acquaintance, inform a stranger who is entirely ignorant of all the tenets of analysis that he is attached to his mother by incestuous ties, that he harbors wishes for the death of his wife, whom he appears to love, and that he conceals an intention of betraying his superior, and so on!" In this same paper, Freud spells out the various practical arrangements that have remained more or less intact in classical analysis. He recommends that the analyst lease his time by the hour, and that the patient be liable for payment whether he comes or not, adding dryly, "Nothing brings home to one so strongly the significance of the psycho-genic factor in the daily life of men, the frequency of malingering, and the non-existence of chance as a few years' practice of

psycho-analysis on the strict principle of leasing by the hour."
Analysts have tended to follow Freud in this, with a few notable exceptions, such as the late Frieda Fromm-Reichmann,
who couldn't bring herself to charge for missed appointments. ("I feel that it is not the psychiatrist's privilege to be
exempt from the generally accepted custom of our culture
in which one is not paid for services not rendered," she wrote
in her book *Principles of Intensive Psychotherapy*.) Another piece of practical advice offered by Freud that did
not fall on deaf ears was that the psychoanalyst shouldn't be
ashamed to charge substantial fees for his services, that he
should collect payments regularly, and that he shouldn't take
free patients. (Freud had tried free treatment—as he tried
everything—to see how it worked, and reported that it didn't:
"Free treatment enormously increases some of a neurotic's
resistances. . . . The absence of the regulating effect offered
by the payment of a fee to the doctor makes itself very painfully felt; the whole relationship is removed from the real
world, and the patient is deprived of a strong motive for en-
deavoring to bring the treatment to an end." The derisive
popular notion that psychoanalysts hypocritically claim that
their high fee is "good for the patient" or "part of the treatment" may have arisen from a misunderstanding of this passage.)[2] The physical arrangement of analysis—the patient
lying on the couch, with the analyst seated behind him—is
discussed in "On Beginning the Treatment." Freud called the
arrangement a "remnant of the hypnotic method" and said
that he continued it first of all because, frankly, he didn't like
to be stared at all day, and—more to the analytic point—because it kept "the transference from mingling with the patient's associations imperceptibly" and allowed it to come
more sharply into relief as a resistance.

In "Recommendations to Physicians Practicing Psycho-Analysis" (1912), Freud describes the special way of listening to the patient that the psychoanalyst must learn. It is as different from ordinary listening as the patient's free association is different from ordinary talking; in fact, it is a counterpart of free association. "It consists simply in not directing one's notice to anything in particular and in maintaining the same 'evenly suspended attention' (as I have called it) in the face of all that one hears," Freud writes, and he cautions the analyst not to let anything—therapeutic ambition above all—get in the way of the aimless, Zen-like state of desirelessness in which he listens, bending "his own unconscious like a receptive organ toward the transmitting unconscious of the patient." He compares the analyst to the surgeon, "who puts aside all his feelings, even his human sympathy, and concentrates his mental forces on the single aim of performing the operation as skillfully as possible." (Nowhere does this surgical analogy, which Freud repeatedly uses in his writings, seem more inapt than in this paper—the incongruous yoking of the image of the exquisitely relaxed analyst, inclining toward his patient's psyche as a sinuous, long-stemmed plant languorously yields to the law of tropism, with that of the cold, hard surgeon, tensely concentrating his mental forces on the technical job at hand. The incongruity derives, perhaps, from Freud's own struggles to reconcile the unwieldy findings of psychoanalysis with the orderly positivism of the Helmholtz school of science, in which he had been educated. An unfinished early work called *Project for a Scientific Psychology* was his strenuous, doomed effort to give a physiological source to the psychological phenomena he was discovering.)

Freud made other "recommendations" in 1912 that have

since become standard in psychoanalytic treatment: that the analyst should himself be analyzed, that he should not reciprocate the patient's confidences ("The doctor should be opaque to his patients and, like a mirror, should show them nothing but what is shown to him"), and that he must not try to educate or morally influence or "improve" the patient in any way. "As a doctor, one must above all be tolerant of the weakness of a patient, and must be content if one has won back some degree of capacity for work and enjoyment for a person even of only moderate worth." For a doctor to speak of the "worth" of his patients falls strangely on the modern ear. An earlier discussion of the issue, in "On Psychotherapy" (1905), sounds even stranger:

> One should look beyond the patient's illness and form an estimate of his whole personality; those patients who do not possess a reasonable degree of education and a fairly reliable character should be refused. It must not be forgotten that there are healthy people as well as unhealthy ones who are good for nothing in life, and that there is a temptation to ascribe to their illness everything that incapacitates them if they show any sign of neurosis.

As Freud groped his way toward the complexities of ego psychology, he was obliged to modify this simple view of human fallibility—to see that illness and character were not, after all, discrete—but, significantly, he never changed his profoundly amoral view of psychoanalytic therapy. "Transforming your hysterical misery into common unhappiness" (*Studies on Hysteria*) remained the ungarnished program of psychoanalysis, with no frills added of "self-improvement" or "fulfillment," which such revisionists as Alfred Adler, Harry Stack Sullivan, Erich Fromm, and Karen Horney were to covertly offer their patients. Herbert Marcuse, in his "Critique of Neo-Freudian Revisionism" (the epilogue to his book *Eros and Civilization*), icily examines the tone of uplift and the Power of Positive Thinking that pervades the revisionists' writings, and mocks their claim to scientific seriousness. That same atmosphere of the sermonette pervades the writings of today's *nouvelle vague* neo-Freudians, Kernberg and Kohut. Kernberg's "clinical descriptions" of narcissistic patients are like passages from a nineteenth-century novel cataloguing the ethical deficiencies of its villains and villainesses. Kohut adopts a more pastoral tone toward *his* "shallow," "grandiose," "self-centered," "envious," "exploitive," "empty" patients, but his intention seems no less reproving and improving.

In "Remembering, Repeating, and Working Through" (1914), Freud added a new dimension to his repudiation of intellectual knowledge as a mechanism of cure. When he replaced urging by free association, it was still in order to facilitate the backward flow of the patient's thoughts—the "precious metal" Freud sought was the memory of psychic trauma. Now Freud saw that it wasn't necessary to struggle against the patient's resistance to remembering. The doctor needed only to observe the patient's present behavior, since even though "the patient does not *remember* anything of what he has forgotten and repressed, he *acts* it out, without, of course, knowing that he is repeating it." Freud goes on, "For instance, the patient does not say that he remembers that he used to be defiant and critical toward his parents' authority; instead, he behaves in that way to the doctor. . . . He does not remember having been intensely ashamed of certain sexual activities and afraid of their being found out; but he makes it clear that he is ashamed of the treatment on which he is now embarked, and tries to keep it secret from everybody." Freud called this phenomenon the "repetition compulsion," and went on to observe that the task of the analyst is to convert repeating into remembering. The analyst must be prepared "for a perpetual struggle with his patient to keep in the psychical sphere all the impulses which the patient would like to direct into the motor sphere; and he celebrates it as a triumph for the treatment if he can bring it about that something that the patient wishes to discharge in action is disposed of through the work of remembering." Freud is here talking of the impulsive, foolish, even dangerous things that the patient may do outside the analysis while under the sway of wishes that have been activated by the analysis. He notes how much more dangerous analysis is now than it was in the old days of hypnosis: "Remembering, as it was induced in hypnosis, could not but give the impression of an experiment carried out in the laboratory. Repeating, as it is induced in analytic treatment according to the newer technique, on the other hand, implies conjuring up a piece of real life; and for that reason it cannot always be harmless and unobjectionable." Freud proposed a rather inelegant precaution (one that is no longer advocated): that the analyst get the patient to agree to put off during his treatment all important decisions—such as marrying or taking a new job—which he might repent of later.

During the period of the technical papers, Freud was guided in his thinking about repression and resistance by conceiving of the mind in terms of a *spatial* arrangement of the unconscious and conscious states. In the *Introductory Lectures,* proposing a "crude" metaphor, he asks the student to imagine a large entrance hall that opens onto a small, narrow drawing room. In the large hall (of the unconscious), mental impulses "jostle one another" as they try to get past the guard who stands on the threshold of the drawing room, which Freud named the preconscious. The fate of most of these impulses is to be immediately repelled by the guard or, should they slip by him and get into the drawing room, to be dragged back. (The latter are the *repressed* unconscious thoughts.) The few impulses that *are* allowed into the drawing room are not yet conscious, and may or may not become so, depending on whether or not they "succeed in catching the eye of consciousness." Freud located this "eye" at the far end of the preconscious drawing room. The significant border relationship in regard to repression and resistance was not the one between the preconscious and the conscious but the one between the preconscious and the unconscious. This "topographic" model of the mind was derived from Freud's concept of how dreams are formed, and it remains at the heart of psychoanalysis. ("The property of being conscious or not is in the last resort our one beacon light in the darkness of depth psychology," Freud wrote in 1923 in *The Ego and the Id*.) However, it proved not to provide a strong enough theoretical structure to carry the increasing weight of clinical discovery; as time went on, and Freud did more and more analyses, the topographic model began to creak, and finally—on the issue of unconscious guilt—it broke down. To deal with the fact that some patients didn't get well—in fact, seemed to *worsen*—as the unconscious became conscious, Freud devised a new model of the mind, which offered a way of grappling with this perplexity, and which changed the analyst's view of what his task was. Previously, the analyst had conceived of himself as a kind of medium bringing messages from the realm of the unconscious to the reluctant ear of consciousness—as an intermediary between the patient's buried passions and his overt morals. In the Clark lectures, for example, Freud (in another of his "crude analogies") likened repression to the measures that would be taken if someone in the university lecture hall began to laugh and shout and make such a nuisance of himself that the lecturer had to stop speaking. Three or four strong men in the audience would then have to put the unruly fellow out and wedge their chairs against the door to prevent his return—as in psychic life unacceptable wishes are expelled from consciousness and a barrier of repression is mounted against them. However—Freud went on with the analogy—putting the unruly fellow out might only make matters worse; enraged by his expulsion, he might stand outside the door and shout and bang his fists against the panels and altogether make more trouble than he made when he was in the room. (Repression is always a failure.) In that case, Freud whimsically proposed, Dr. G. Stanley Hall, the president of Clark University, would have to go out and speak to the man, get him to promise to behave himself, assure the lecturer and the audience of the transgressor's good intentions, and get him readmitted to the hall. This, Freud concluded, "presents what is really no bad picture of the physician's task in the psycho-analytic treatment of the neuroses."

In the situation of "negative therapeutic reaction," which impelled Freud to construct a new model of the mind, this scenario took an unexpected turn. Everything happened as described—the barricade of chairs was removed, the chastened miscreant was allowed back in the auditorium, peace and quiet were restored—but the lecturer still couldn't speak! Dr. Hall's efforts had evidently been for nothing; it appeared that the man making so much noise wasn't the cause of the lecturer's incapacity at all. They had got the wrong man! The culprit unnerving the speaker was a man standing outside the window singing religious hymns—a man nothing like the unshaven bum who had pounded on the door, but a man of unutterable refinement, a colleague of Stanley Hall's! What Freud was beginning to realize was that his tidy equating of the unconscious with unbridled instinct and of the conscious with morality wasn't workable. There appeared to be *unconscious* morality as well, and consequently, as he wrote in *The Ego and the Id,* "we land in endless obscurities and difficulties if we keep to our habitual forms of expression and try, for instance, to derive neuroses from a conflict between the conscious and the unconscious."

The new "structural theory" accounted for the new element by conceiving of the mind in terms of three psychic agencies: the ego, the id, and the superego, which stand for reason, passion, and conscience, and whose fate it is to be locked in perpetual conflict. In this view, the neurotic is a person whose ego has become weakened by the conflict with its internal enemies as well as by its responsibilities as the mind's emissary to external reality. (The psychotic is someone whose ego has abdicated from this responsibility—as it does nightly in normal people in the psychosis known as dreaming.) The analyst comes to the aid of the beleaguered ego and joins forces with it against its internal enemies. Invariably, the cause of the trouble, the start of the debility, is traced back to childhood—to a particular, fateful, universal experience called the Oedipus complex. The complex describes the shattering, by fear of castration, of a small boy's dream of making love to his mother, and the formation of the superego as a permanent memorial to his dread. "The paradoxical proposition that the normal man is not only far more immoral than he believes but also far more moral than he knows" (as Freud wrote in *The Ego and the Id*) arises from this dire early experience. Freud's association of morality with castration anxiety—"the little lover" of four or five gives up his ambitions toward his mother *fast,* and forever, when "more or less plainly, more or less brutally, a threat is pronounced that this part of him which he values so highly will be taken away from him"—led him to the inescapable conclusion that women, to whom the worst had already happened, must be less moral than men. "I cannot evade the notion (though I hesitate to give it expression) that for women the level of what is ethically normal is different from what it is in men," Freud wrote in "Some Psychical Consequences of the Anatomical Distinction Between the Sexes" (1925). "Their superego is never so inexorable, so impersonal, so independent of its emotional origins as we require it to be in men. Character traits which critics of every epoch have brought up against women—that they show less sense of justice than men, that they are less ready to submit to the great exigencies of life, that they are more often influenced in their judgments by feelings of affection or hostility—all these would be amply accounted for by the modification in the formation of their superego which we have inferred above." He added, "We must not allow ourselves to be deflected from such conclusions by the denials of the feminists, who are anxious to force us to regard the two sexes as completely equal in position and worth; but we shall, of course, willingly agree that the majority of men are also far behind the masculine ideal, and that all human individuals, as a result of their bisexual disposition and of cross-inheritance, combine in themselves both masculine and feminine characteristics, so that pure masculinity and femininity remain theoretical constructions of uncertain content."

33

The female Oedipus complex runs an opposite course from the male one. While the boy is frightened out of his love affair with his mother by the threat of castration, the girl is impelled into hopeless love for her father by pique with her mother "for having sent her into the world so insufficiently equipped." "No human individual is spared such traumatic experiences," Freud wrote of the Oedipus complex in *An Outline of Psycho-Analysis* (1940). However, "the whole occurrence, which may probably be regarded as the central experience of the years of childhood, the greatest problem of early life, and the strongest source of later inadequacy, is so completely forgotten that its reconstruction during the work of analysis is met in adults by the most decided disbelief. Indeed, aversion to it is so great that people try to silence any mention of the proscribed subject, and the most obvious reminders of it are overlooked by a strange intellectual blindness."

While belief in the Oedipus complex is universal among psychoanalysts, there is wide disagreement about whether it is indeed the central experience of childhood and the greatest problem of early life. There are schools of analytic thought that hold earlier experiences to be more crucial. The Kleinians, for example, put the action as far back as the first year of life. They see the first faint stirrings of guilt in the mewling and puking of six-month-olds—or, rather, they reconstruct it from the analyses of children and adults—and place the formation of a moral sense at around nine months, when a baby enters what they call "the depressive position." This Blakean state reflects the baby's appalled realization of what he is doing to his mother as he nurses at her breast— the "hole" he is leaving in her as he sucks—and his wish to make reparation. It marks, in D. W. Winnicott's phrase, "the change-over from pre-ruth to ruth." The regular Freudians dismiss the Kleinian reconstructions as crazy and fantastic (as if their own reconstructions of the castration complex described perfectly ordinary, everyday events). Where an analyst stands today in relation to "pre-Oedipal" or "pregenital" experience is a measure of his orthodoxy. The more orthodox the analyst, the more certain he is that the buried child unearthed in each adult analysand is a four- or five-year-old reliving and reënacting the Oedipal drama; and the more avant-garde the analyst, the more certain he is that the child is a maimed infant reëxperiencing some lack or some trauma in his early rearing. The orthodox school doesn't deny that significant mental events take place during infancy, but insists on the primacy of the Oedipal period. Conversely, to the Kleinians and the rest of the avant-garde (the object-relations schools) the events of the Oedipal period are pallid and inconsequential in comparison with the cliffhanging psychodramas of infancy.

Freud's structural theory, with its epilogue of the super-ego, gave the Oedipal scenario its final form, but it didn't introduce the Oedipus complex. Freud had happened on that back in the eighteen-nineties while coming to terms with his disconcerting realization that his patients' stories of childhood seduction, on which he had confidently erected his theory of the etiology of the neurosis in childhood trauma, were largely untrue. The chief innovation of the structural theory was the way its new terminology changed the attitude of the analyst toward the patient's resistances. In his new capacity as the ally of the ego in its struggle against the id and the superego, the analyst (paradoxically) became an even more passive agent in the therapeutic relationship. In the beginning, the analyst all but shook the patient to get him to remember traumatic events; then there came a period of more subtle struggle over the patient's insufficient observance of the fundamental rule of saying whatever comes to mind; and finally a culminating condition of total laissez-faire. Under the new dispensation, the manner in which the patient (unconsciously) defends himself against the analysis becomes itself a focus of the analysis, since the patient's defenses repeat and reflect his characteristic resistances, or "defense mechanisms," as Anna Freud called them in her housewifely ordering of the new material, *The Ego and the Mechanisms of Defense* (1936). In contemporary psychoanalysis, how the patient disobeys the fundamental rule is at least as interesting to the analyst as what comes out when he obeys it. The study of his disobedience is "ego analysis" and that of his obedience "id analysis," and, as Freud said in "Analysis Terminable and Interminable," analytic work "is constantly swinging backward and forward like a pendulum" between the two. The patient's transferences are similarly classified according to their ego or id origins. Passionate love for or hatred of the analyst is a repetition of early instinctual impulsions. More subtly unjustified feelings about the analyst are reversions to early defenses of the ego against threatening primitive id impulses. The defenses, Anna Freud points out, are harder to get at than the impulses, because while the "irruptions of the id" make the patient uncomfortable and ashamed—he is only too glad to dissociate himself from them by accepting the idea that he is repeating something from childhood—the defenses against them are familiar, comfortable, unobjectionable, "ego-syntonic" ways of being, and are thus difficult to see as transference rather than as "real."

The patient's difficulty on this score is paralleled by the analyst's difficulty in maintaining himself as a mirror for the patient's self-scrutiny. The analyst is, after all, a real person, with real qualities and peculiarities and emotions. Since Freud's establishment of the psychoanalytic situation as we now know it, psychoanalysts have been wrestling with (in some cases, escaping from) its radical unlikeness to any other human relationship, its purposeful renunciation of the niceties and decencies of ordinary human intercourse, its awesome abnormality, contradictoriness, and strain. Analysts have been as restive under and resistant to the rigors of the situation as patients have—particularly analysts of a certain benignity and expansiveness of temperament. Freud himself seems never to have totally grasped (or chose to overlook) the dire implications of his great therapeutic instrument. He conducted therapy as no classical Freudian analyst would conduct it today—as if it were an ordinary human interaction, in which the analyst could shout at the patient, praise him, argue with him, accept flowers from him on his birthday, lend him money, and even gossip with him about other patients.[3] Sandor Ferenczi, one of Freud's circle of early analysts, was a still worse offender than the Master. In his biography of Freud, Jones reprints a letter that Freud wrote to Ferenczi in 1931 playfully admonishing him to stop kissing his patients—which in its jocularity is as interesting for what it reveals about Freud's free-and-easy attitude toward therapy as for the evidence it furnishes of Ferenczi's far-outness. "Now picture what will be the result of publishing your technique," Freud wrote. "There is no revolutionary who is not driven out of the field by a still more radical one. A number of independent thinkers in matters of technique will say to themselves: Why stop at a kiss? Certainly one gets further when one adopts 'pawing' as well, which, after all, doesn't make a baby. And then bolder ones will come along who will go further, to peeping and show-ing—and soon we shall have accepted in the technique of analysis the whole repertoire of *demi-viergerie* and petting parties, resulting in an enormous increase of interest in psy-choanalysis among both analysts and patients. . . ."

Among Freudian analysts today, there is fairly uni-versal agreement about what constitutes analytic behavior and what doesn't. The analyst as far as possible confines him-self to listening to the patient and (sparingly) offering him his conjectures—which are called "interpretations"—about the unconscious meaning of his communications. He does not give advice, he does not talk about himself, he does not let himself be provoked or drawn into discussions of ab-stract subjects, he does not answer questions about his family or his political preferences, he does not show like or dis-like of the patient, or approval or disapproval of his actions. His behavior toward the patient is as neutral, mild, color-less, self-effacing, uninterfering, and undemanding as he is able to make it, and as it is toward no one else in his life —with the paradoxical (and now absolutely predictable) result that the patient reacts with stronger, more vivid and intense personal feelings to this bland, shadowy figure than he does to the more clearly delineated and provocative fig-ures in his life outside the analysis. On this paradox—on the patient's quickness to overfill the emotional vacuum cre-ated by the analyst's reticence—the analysis is poised, and it may as easily founder as take off. If the patient sees the an-alyst as a cold, callous person of limited intelligence and unbounded tactlessness, he may decide to quit the analysis. In fact, Freud originally felt that positive feelings toward the analyst at the start of treatment were a necessary pre-condition for it. Although this is no longer accepted (numerous patients have stuck out analyses with analysts they disliked), analysts continue to search themselves for what may have been their own contribution to the debacle of discontinued, aborted, or failed treatment. Perhaps it wasn't a patient's negative-transference reactions so much as his obscure perception of the analyst's unkindly, if not outright sadistic, disposition toward him that caused him to flee the analysis. For to the complication of transference must be added that of countertransference; i.e., the analyst's inappropriate reactions to the patient, based on his own unconscious misassociation of him with significant figures in his own past. (In its original, limited meaning, countertransference referred to an obstruction to the analyst's understanding of the patient, which the analyst had to strive to overcome. In recent years, countertransference has been expanded to embrace *all* the feelings of the analyst toward the patient, with special attention to those that are deliberately—if unconsciously—elicited by the patient and thus properly belong in his dossier rather than in the analyst's.) And to *that* complication must be added the treacherous and unresolved (unresolvable?) question of analytic "reality." For implicit in the idea of transference as distortion is the assumption of some true, or truer, state of things that is being obscured. If the patient's "menacing illusion" (as Freud called it in *An Outline of Psycho-Analysis*) of being in love with the analyst is just that—an illusion, which the analyst must "tear the patient out of," showing him "again and again that what he takes to be new real life is a reflection of the past"—then how is one to regard the "reality" to which the patient is returned? What is the nature and who is to be the judge of the "real relationship" between patient and analyst? Freud never much interested himself in this question.

His discovery of the illusory relationship was, after all, the news, and the actual relationship between doctor and patient was not. But as time went on it became increasingly evident that in psychoanalysis doctor and patient stand in a relationship markedly different from the relationship that exists between doctor and patient in medical practice, and analysts have been increasingly preoccupied with (and divided on) the subject of the "non-transference relationship." The lengthening duration of analysis is a factor in this new interest: analysis as a kind of weird avant-garde experiment that you lend yourself to for a couple of months (as the early patients did) is quite a different proposition from the eight- or ten-year analyses that are nowadays commonplace. (When analysis changed from a symptom-curing therapy to a character-changing therapy, as the shift from id to ego psychology caused it to do, it naturally required more time.) A modus vivendi of some sort must be established between patient and analyst, tolerable to both, if this singular and unprecedented association is to last the course, to say nothing of whether it will benefit the patient. "With due respect for the necessary strictest handling and interpretation of the transference," Anna Freud wrote in 1954, "I feel still that we should leave room somewhere for the realization that analyst and patient are also two real people, of equal adult status, in a real personal relationship to each other. I wonder whether our—at times complete—neglect of this side of the matter is not responsible for some of the hostile reactions which we get from our patients and which we are apt to ascribe to 'true transference' only."

Anna Freud's plain speaking occurred at an analytic symposium where she discussed a paper called "The Widening Scope of Indications for Psychoanalysis," by the New York analyst Leo Stone, with whose humanistic view of the analytic relationship she heartily concurred. A few years later, Stone was to elaborate this view in his classic study *The Psychoanalytic Situation* (1961). At the symposium, he was content to simply express his fear that analysts' overzealous playing of their roles as silent, ungratifying, unknowable beings might subvert the very process it was intended to set in motion. Early in the paper, Stone reveals the sort of person (and analyst) he is as he looks with a kind of sorrowing wonder at the flourishing psychoanalytic scene of New York in the nineteen-fifties (today wistfully referred to as "the heyday of psychoanalysis"), when "scarcely any human problem admits of solution other than psychoanalysis." Stone goes on to ruefully note that "by the same token, there is an almost magical expectation of help from the method, which does it grave injustice. Hopeless or grave reality situations, lack of talent or ability (usually regarded as 'inhibition'), lack of an adequate philosophy of life, and almost any chronic physical illness may be brought to psychoanalysis for cure." What Stone finds most disquieting about this overestimation is its implicit "loss of a sense of proportion about the human condition, a forgetting or denial of the fact that few human beings are without some troubles, and that many must be met, if at all, by 'old-fashioned' methods: courage, or wisdom, or struggle, for instance; also that few people avoid altogether and forever some physical ailments, not to speak of the fact that all die of illness in the end." Stone goes so far as to offer the startling suggestion that "if a man is otherwise healthy, happy, and efficient, and his rare attacks of headache can be avoided by not eating lobster, for example, it would seem better that he avoid eating lobster than that he be analyzed."

In *The Psychoanalytic Situation*, Stone argues for the necessity of "framing" the stormy primitive drama of transference and countertransference in a placid relationship of two adults: one a doctor of manifest good will and reliability, the other a patient of comparable maturity and responsibility—insofar as he comes to the sessions, pays the bills, and takes the analyst's unconventional behavior as a "technical instrumentality" rather than as a personal attack. *Within* the transference, of course, the patient may (and almost invariably does) wallow in his sense of injury and deprivation, rejection and outrage. But a part of him should always "know" that these feelings are not to be altogether trusted. This capacity of the patient for detachment and self-observation Stone characterizes as "a benign split of the ego" (into observing and experiencing parts), which he considers essential for the working of the analytic process. His concern is that the analyst's unrelentingly analytic behavior may subvert the process by shaking the faith of the patient's observing ego in the analyst's benignity and tipping the balance in favor of the experiencing ego's delusion of malevolence. "Whereas purely technical or intellectual errors can, in most instances, be corrected, a failure in a critical juncture to show the reasonable human response which any person inevitably expects from another on whom he deeply depends can invalidate years of patient and largely skillful work," he writes. In wry protest against the overliteral and trivializing application of Freud's "mirror principle," Stone remarks, "I doubt that the evolution of the transference neurosis is often seriously disturbed by the patient's knowing whether one takes one's vacation in Vermont or Maine, or indeed (let me be really bold!) that one knows something more about sailing than about golf," and he adds, "I think that it *is* not seldom disturbed by a persistent or repetitive arbitrary refusal to answer such questions, after sufficient speculative fantasy, if there is no more *specific* or *adequate* reason than a general principle that the patient must not know anything about one, or that the analyst does not answer questions." (Kohut puts the matter very succinctly in a footnote in his book *The Analysis of the Self* when he says, "To remain silent when one is asked a question is not neutral but rude.") Stone mordantly notes, "The enthusiastic and engaging assertion of an older colleague many years ago that his patient would have developed the same vivid transference love toward him 'if he had been a brass monkey' is, alas (or perhaps fortunately!), just not true. For *all* patients, to the degree that they are removed from the psychotic, have an important investment in their real and objective perceptions; and the interplay between these and the transference requires a certain minimal, if variable, *resemblance*."

To his delicate disentanglement of the strands of transference from those of "the real relationship" Stone adds the complication of a kind of metatransference, which he calls "the primary transference," or "the primordial transference." This has to do with the unconscious meaning that the patient attaches to the psychoanalytic situation itself, which derives, Stone hypothesizes, from his craving for the omnipotent parent of early infancy. This craving is universal and can be activated by doctors, politicians, clergymen, and teachers as well as by analysts. Stone draws an interesting (and, for his argument, telling) distinction between the meaning of the primary transference generated by the physician and that generated by the analyst. While the physician's direct physical and emotional ministrations correspond to those of the "omniscient, omnipotent, and unintelligible" mother of the earliest period of infancy, the analyst's activities resemble (in unconscious reverberation) the not so agreeable ones of the mother in the months when the infant is learning to talk and to separate from her—"that period of life where all the modalities of bodily intimacy and direct dependence on the mother are being relinquished or attenuated, *pari passu* with the rapid development of the great vehicle of communication by speech." It is in this state of "intimate separation," or "deprivation in intimacy," that analysis is conducted, deriving its mutative power from the tension between verbal closeness and emotional distance. Stone believes, however, that the earlier, gratifying mother must not be totally eclipsed by the later, frustrating one—that the analyst's "physicianly vocation" must meld with his analytic one if the analytic process is to develop and flourish.

This brusque summary of Stone's exquisite essay is comparable to a "college outline" of *The Golden Bowl*. Stone's plea for humaneness and flexibility and common sense is encased in the most subtly reasoned, profoundly erudite, and awesomely "difficult" of meditations on a complex subject. Other analysts, before and after Stone, have remonstrated against analytic rigidity, but none with Stone's authority and sincerity. In its comfortable commingling of abstruse technical and metapsychological concepts with ordinary human wisdom, *The Psychoanalytic Situation* recalls the writings of Freud—and, indeed, among psychoanalysts Stone inspires the sort of reverence that few but Freud himself have inspired. (That Stone is almost completely unknown outside the profession is curious and unfortunate.)

Stone's attractive humanistic view of the analyst's role is currently shared by all but a small minority of analysts. The leader of the opposition is Charles Brenner. Brenner has none of Stone's elegance of expression and incandescence of literary persona, but he is a worthy foeman. His austere position has an icy beauty. In an article entitled "Working Alliance, Therapeutic Alliance, and Transference" (1979), Brenner challenged the whole notion that transference and "the real relationship" can be separated. "Therapeutic alliance" and "working alliance" are terms coined by the late Elizabeth Zetzel and the late Ralph Greenson, respectively, to denote the positive adult relationship in which the transference is framed. To Brenner, all such separating and "framing" is suspect. He sees the "working alliance" or the "therapeutic alliance" as a kind of shady side deal that the analyst offers the patient to gain his compliance—a deal that looks kindly and humane on the surface but in fact robs the patient of the full use of the analytic instrumentality. "Suppose an analyst were to fall asleep during a session, or to forget an appointment with a patient. Should he apologize, explain, and discuss the reasons for his action with his patient?" Brenner asks in his book *Psychoanalytic Technique and Psychic Conflict* (1976). He gives this rather magnificent answer:

> Many analysts would say he should . . . and their arguments for doing so are persuasive. Yet I believe the better course to follow is the usual one of encouraging a patient to express *his* thoughts and feelings about what has happened. Only in that way can one learn whether a patient has taken his analyst's mistake as a slight that has offended and angered him, or as a sign of weakness that allows him to feel superior and even triumphant, or as a welcome excuse for anger, etc. A conscientious analyst will natu-

rally regret such a mistake, he will certainly try, through self-analysis, to discover his unconscious reasons for having acted as he did, but he will be well advised to maintain an analytic attitude even to such an event, and not to assume what it must mean to his patient without hearing what his patient has to say. It is presumptuous to act the analyst, unbidden, in a social or family situation. It is a technical lapse to be other than an analyst in one's relation with an analytic patient.

Several years ago, Brenner and Stone jointly led a seminar at the New York Psychoanalytic Institute in which just such nice points of technique were debated. "Should the analyst express sympathy to a patient whose father has just died?" was one question that was put to the leaders. Stone said that he, of course, *would* express sympathy. Brenner said that he, of course, *wouldn't*. Recently recalling this incident, a younger woman analyst of somewhat romantic leanings declared, "Charlie is a very kind man. He might not *say* anything to the patient, but I'm sure he would let him know somehow, probably with his eyes, how sorry he was." She has missed Brenner's point. In the "Working Alliance" article, Brenner returns to this eventuality, and gives this unexpected and unarguable reason for analytic neutrality even in the face of death:

It is true enough that it often does no harm for an analyst to be thus conventionally "human." Still, there are times when his being "human" under such circumstances can be harmful, and one cannot always know in advance when those times will be. As an example, for his analyst to express sympathy for a patient who has just lost a close relative may make it more difficult than it would otherwise be for the patient to express pleasure or spite or exhibitionistic satisfaction over the loss.

This is taking respect for individual experience and generosity of spirit toward human frailty very far indeed.

# 2

"WHEN I RECEIVED MY LETTER OF ACCEPTANCE FROM the New York Psychoanalytic Institute, it was as if I had been given an injection of adrenaline, amphetamine, and heroin. I have seldom in my life felt so triumphant. I knew that my life was going to be the way I wanted." Aaron Green said this to me one Wednesday morning in his consultation room, where he and I had taken to meeting weekly at the same hour, as if for therapy. The empty couch looked out on the room with a meaningful air. "I'm not any old shabby foam-rubber sofa," it seemed to say. "I am *the couch*." Aaron sat in a big, sagging olive-green upholstered chair near its head—his habitual seat, a sort of nest padded with accustomed objects: the lamp table on the right strewn with books, scientific journals, letters, pencils, notebooks, a mug of tea; the glass-topped table on the left piled with paper towels (the couch's antimacassars, changed for each occupant) and also holding a telephone, a small round clock, a drug company's appointment calendar, and a vase of decaying chrysanthemums. It put me in mind of a chronic invalid's chair. I sat across from him in a smaller easy chair, and between us, on a hassock, lay my small, attentive-looking Japanese tape recorder. "I had hated medical school," Aaron continued. "It was dehumanizing and brutalizing, and when I was an intern and resident in B—— I learned what horrible places hospitals are—how the patient's needs are trampled underfoot and everything is done for the staff's convenience. When I got into the New York Psychoanalytic, I felt I had come in out of the cold. I had applied to other institutes, but this was the one I desperately hoped to get into—the oldest, largest, most renowned analytic institute in America, the institute of Hartmann, Kris, Loewenstein, Jacobson, Greenacre, Isakower, Bak, Arlow, and Brenner. The one thing that marred my happiness was the prospect of going into analysis again. I didn't see why I had to. I felt I was already perfectly well analyzed."

Freud's recommendation that the analyst himself be analyzed has become an inflexible and central fact of analytic education. The "candidate," as the student is called, is assigned a "training analyst," with whom he has an analysis that—at least in theory—is no different from ordinary therapeutic analysis, though certain subtle differences are inevitable. In a grim voice, Aaron went on to tell me of a traumatic event that had marked his arrival in New York from B——.

"When I was told the name of my training analyst, I was somewhat mollified by the fact that I had drawn one of the plums of the New York Psychoanalytic's roster—a very eminent older woman analyst, now deceased, who was a writer and theoretician of international renown. I was frankly flattered by the assignment—feeling it to be connected to my own superior attributes—and arrived at the first session nervous but cocky. I sat down (it is the custom for

4 8

candidates to have a few preliminary sessions sitting up with their prospective training analyst) and we began to talk, and about fifteen minutes into the session—after I tell you what happened, you will imagine what those fifteen minutes had been like—this small, stout, benign-looking older woman suddenly banged her hand on her desk in exasperation and said, '*You are a maddening person! You are like a gadfly!*' She glared at me with anger and dislike. I had been weaving and dodging and interrupting and cutting into her questions with counterquestions. But I hadn't realized how irritating I was being, so when that raw aggression suddenly came flying across the room I was absolutely stunned by it."

"What did you do?"

"Nothing. I was scared. I was afraid I'd get into trouble. That the Institute would see me as a troublemaker. I had had trouble in medical school. I was a very abrasive person. But I didn't want trouble with this woman, so I became humble and conciliatory. At the end of the hour, I asked meekly when the analysis proper would begin. When would I start lying down on the couch? And it was then that she showed her true quality. She said—this impressed me, I will always admire her for it—'Forgive me for bursting out at you like that, and go to another analyst. An analysis should not start with a scene. I am not the right analyst for you. Go to someone else.' Now, that's being a *mensch*. No, she shouldn't have burst out at me like that. But *who* had the courage to face up to what had happened? Not me. I was too frightened. I would have been willing to work with her to avoid trouble."

"Did you get another woman analyst?"

"No. They assigned me a man. At first, I was contemptuous of him. I thought him a dull mediocrity. I found him pedestrian. I regarded his work as hack, textbook stuff. Well, it wasn't hack, it wasn't textbook. His work turned out to be of extremely high quality. My second analysis turned out to be much more thorough, much more profound than the first. But I didn't know that at the time. My initial attitude was 'Who are you? I've never heard of your name, even in the literature. You're not famous.' You see, my first analyst *had* been famous. He was a very brilliant and charming old man—an Austrian Jew of the first generation of analysts after Freud—who had come to this country during the big exodus of European analysts in the thirties. He didn't keep the analytic incognito very much. He was a good deal more casual about it than my second analyst, and was much more demonstrative, expressive, and supportive. *His* analyst had been Sandor Ferenczi, and he idealized him. There was a bust of Ferenczi in his consultation room, together with one of Freud, who had analyzed Ferenczi. I could thus trace my analytic lineage back to Freud. You smile, and you should. It's a preposterous notion. It's the most primitive kind of family romance—my parents are aristocrats, I'm descended from royalty, all that sort of stuff. I know that now. But I didn't then, and you'd be surprised by the number of people in and out of establishment psychoanalysis who hold to these childish fancies about their royal descent."

I asked Aaron what he meant by "establishment" psychoanalysis. He explained that in this country the establishment is formed of the institutes that are recognized by the American Psychoanalytic Association, which came into existence in 1911, three years after the International Psycho-Analytical Association was organized by Freud in Europe. The regulations and standards of the American are stricter and stiffer than those of the International, which oversees the analytic institutes and societies of the rest of the world. Aaron believes that American psychoanalysis is a great cut above psychoanalysis elsewhere in the world; he is contemptuous of what he calls the laxness and sloppiness of English, European, and South American analysis. There are other people, naturally, who are unimpressed by American analysis and are critical of the American Psychoanalytic Association's iron hold over the profession. The most controversial of the American's regulations is the one that, in effect, requires members to be medical doctors. The rule was laid down in 1923 in the belief that alignment with the medical establishment would give the struggling new profession the respectability it needed. It gave it that, but debate continues on whether too much wasn't sacrificed by this strategy—whether too many good people who are unwilling to go through medical training aren't being lost to analysis. Some of the greatest names in psychoanalysis were laymen—Anna Freud, Erik Erikson, Ernst Kris, to name the most celebrated. The International leaves the question to the discretion of the individual institutes, and most do not require that their members be doctors. Freud himself was opposed to the medical requirement, arguing (in a pamphlet called *The Question of Lay Analysis*, written in 1926 on the occasion of a lawsuit by the Austrian government against a non-medical colleague, Theodor Reik) that training in the care of bodies has little bearing on the treatment of souls. Philip Rieff, in *The Triumph of the Therapeutic* (1966), points with bitter malice to what he sees as the evil consequences of the medical requirement:

> More often than not, the contemporary candidate for training in one of the institutes now comes straight out of

a medical school with precisely the wrong kind of education, for which a reading of Freud's case histories and various other courses in the development and structure of psychoanalysis cannot compensate. The early psychoanalysts were educated men when they gathered around Freud; the contemporary psychoanalyst is not an educated man when he leaves the institute. . . . By default, the institutes have become what most of their students ardently desire them to be: trade schools preparing them for accreditation and the good life in some suburb, without night calls from troublesome patients.[4]

Non-doctors who wish to practice psychoanalysis in this country get their training at what Aaron (with unabashed snobbery and an admitted total lack of justification) calls the "fly-by-night" institutes. These include institutes founded by revisionists, such as the Karen Horney Institute and the William Alanson White Institute, as well as those set up specifically to accommodate non-doctors, such as the National Psychological Association for Psychoanalysis, founded in 1946 by Reik, who had emigrated here. The situation is a messy, incoherent one, difficult for the person who is looking for an analyst to make his way through. And this is to say nothing of the back street of dubious and outright fraudulent therapies beckoning to the person in desperate straits.

Within the establishment, in addition to the New York Psychoanalytic Institute, New York has the N.Y.U. Psychoanalytic Institute (formerly the Downstate Institute), peaceably founded in 1949 by Sandor Lorand, of the New York Psychoanalytic, and the Columbia University Center for Psychoanalytic Training and Research, painfully wrested from the New York Psychoanalytic in 1944 by Sandor Rado, in a savage schism whose scars are apparently still borne by both institutes. Aaron's attitude toward the N.Y.U. Institute is that of an older sibling toward a younger brother: affectionate, tolerant, a bit condescending toward the boy's evident immaturity, and admiring and envious of his dash and style and charm. For Columbia, the no-good son, he has nothing but bitterness and scorn.

"But the schism was years ago," I said. "What's the matter with them now?"

Aaron frowned, and said in a low, dark voice, "They're sharp dressers."

I laughed. "Is that all?"

"Isn't that enough?" Aaron said. He laughed, too.

"Do they tell you how to dress at the New York Psychoanalytic?"

"No. But let me tell you a story. One time soon after I graduated, I wanted a sports jacket, and went to Abercrombie & Fitch. I immediately saw a soft-shouldered black-and-white-herringbone tweed jacket and thought, That's it! That's the one! So I bought it, and when I wore it I thought, Fantastic! I felt great in it, I enjoyed it, it corresponded to my adolescent idea of what good dressing was. Two years later, I met with two colleagues—a man and a woman—whom I regularly joined for mutual supervision. I was wearing my herringbone jacket, and when the other man came in—he was ten years older than me—he was wearing an almost identical herringbone jacket. The woman turned to him and said, 'What a nice jacket!' and he said, 'Thank you, I just bought it at Brooks Brothers. Yes, I think it's nice, too.' There I sat in the same jacket, making self-satiric gestures of Hey, look at me! But they went right on talking about *his* jacket. Finally they noticed me—and my jacket—and my colleague laughed and said, 'But, you know, everyone at the New York Psychoanalytic wears this kind of jacket.' So then I understood why I had felt so great about my jacket. I began to look around the Institute and, sure enough, the jacket was all over the place."

"So they don't give a course on how to dress like an analyst."

"They don't have to. You do it by keeping your eyes open—or closed, as I did."

We returned to his early training at the New York Psychoanalytic. "When I started, I was eager to do the course work," he said. "I had taught myself a little theory in an undisciplined way, and now, I thought, I would learn the whole corpus of psychoanalytic theory from the great teachers of the greatest analytic institute in the world. I didn't attach much importance to the supervised casework I would be doing. I felt that I was already a good psychotherapist—I had been at the top, or close to the top, in my residency—and I thought I just needed more practice. And I looked on the training analysis as a loathsome, unnecessary encumbrance. So I came to analytic training with values that were the exact *opposite* of those of the training institution in which I was enrolled. The New York Psychoanalytic (like most institutes) sets the greatest store by its training analysis. Second to that, it values the supervised casework—a one-to-one relationship about another one-to-one relationship. And pretty far down below those two is the book learning. Now, after several years of training, my values, by some strange coincidence, have reversed and become those of the Institute. The courses turned out to be disappointing. There were a few exceptions, taught by good teachers, but mostly they were boring discussion classes, in which I had to sit and listen to my fellow students—who knew even less than I did. The classes were at night, from eight-thirty to ten, three times a week. Analytic institutes are night schools; the faculty and the students—most of whom are already working psychiatrists—see patients during the day. I would arrive after a day's hard work at the hospital and sit there tired and bored and irritated. My training analysis opened my eyes and gradually changed me. I realized that my first analyst had not been rigorous or ruthless enough. His technique hadn't been good. The troubles I'd had in medical school—I'd started analysis at the end of my second year—would probably have been compounded if I hadn't been in analysis; he helped me get through all kinds of confusions and despairs. But it was the second analysis that changed me. I'm not so belligerent and abrasive anymore, so touchy and angry."

I said, "How do you know it was the analysis that changed you, and not simply the fact of getting older?"

"That's a very common and firmly held idea," he said. "The idea that what happens in analysis would have happened anyway—that people 'naturally' change as life goes on, and analysts take credit for changes they aren't responsible for. I've had thoughts like that myself about my analysis, and have had to stop myself. I've had to remind myself of how rigidly determined our lives are—how predictable and repetitive, how encrusted and hardened, how resistant to change. If we changed as easily as it's claimed, there wouldn't be people going into analysis at forty and fifty; they would all have changed 'naturally' by then into wise, mature, moderately contented people. A person who goes into analysis in his twenties, as many people are doing today, can't see this as well as a person who goes into analysis later on, after his life has become hopelessly, repetitively unsatisfying, after he has seen himself make the same mistake over and over again, after he has come to feel how trapped he is and to understand how little freedom he has. The young person whose life hasn't taken a course yet can deceive himself into thinking that his life has unlimited potential, though in fact it is already limited and determined. I made that mistake earlier, but I'm old enough now to have a sense of how my life would have gone if I hadn't had analysis."

"What would have been different about your life?"

"It would have been extremely constricted, full of bitterness and depression. To some extent, I know that because it still is," Aaron said with a rueful smile. "You see, I haven't changed all that radically. I don't think basic character structure ever changes. We're not that malleable. But one of the ways I became impressed by the changes occurring in me was through the appearance of substitute symptoms. As I gave up certain character traits, I developed acute symptoms. I had read about that happening—Freud writes about it—but I never thought it would happen to me. Well, it was happening. As I grew less nasty and pugnacious and argumentative —as I began more and more to say to myself, 'Hell, you don't have to do that anymore'—I grew more and more anxious about things I had never been anxious about before. Like being in crowds and sitting in the balcony at the theatre. I also developed a speaking anxiety, which I still have, and which really troubles me. It gets in the way of my teaching and prevents me from speaking at congresses. I was invited to speak at a meeting of the American Psychoanalytic Association—I was to be one of the discussants of a paper on a subject of special interest to me: Freud's dual-instinct theory—and I had to refuse. I just couldn't do it. The mere thought of being on that stage at the Waldorf terrified me. I feel flawed and humiliated by this symptom. It's one of the things I may have to go back into analysis about."

"But is it such a serious flaw? Is it even a symptom?" I asked. "Don't we all have something we don't do well or can't do at all?"

"My immediate reaction to that is to say, 'Look, if I'm going to have a flaw, let it be in an area that doesn't interfere with my professional ambition'—which, of course, is nonsensical."

"Since ambition is the problem?"

"Right. There's no question about it. Ambition is the problem. But I think you'd be surprised by what the ambition is about. It isn't just getting out there and killing my father. That's just part of it. There are other things, too. Well, I'll be frank. It's the desire to be a beautiful woman. You find all kinds of surprises in analysis."

"Somehow, that doesn't surprise me about you," I was interested to hear myself say.

"Well, it surprised me! It bothered me, I can tell you."

# 3

THE NEXT WEDNESDAY, I TOLD AARON ABOUT MY MEETing the night before with three people from the Institute. This was the second time I had met with this trio—two male analysts in their fifties and a woman analyst in her sixties —in the woman's handsomely appointed Park Avenue apartment. The meetings were in response to a telephone call I had made to the Institute, asking for information about its curriculum, entrance procedures, faculty appointments, and so on, and requesting permission to sit in on a few classes. It was soon clear that the three analysts, who were members of the powerful Educational Committee, by which the Institute is largely ruled, had been sent out to meet and fend off the press. After each of the evening meetings, which were long, strained, and tedious, I felt the stirrings of an old childhood sense of anxiety, obscure wrongdoing, and resentment.

"The more I think about it, the more I think there's something very queer about the way they meet me in threes," I said to Aaron.

"They're policing each other," he said. "They're saying to each other, 'You keep me from saying anything wrong, and I'll do the same for you. We're in this together.'"

"But what is it all about? What are they hiding? What could there be to hide in an analytic institute?"

"I don't know exactly. But I suspect that this kind of peculiar, suspicious, guilt-ridden behavior has something to do with the training analysis and its special difficulties. Analysts learn to do analysis by being analyzed themselves—a rather remarkable method of professional training. It's as if a surgeon learned to do surgery by being operated on. And yet the training analysis isn't exactly like the regular therapeutic analysis, either. An analysis ends when the patient resolves his transference neurosis—when he finally accepts the fact that the analyst is *not, not, not* going to fulfill the wishes the patient had as a child toward his parents, that it just isn't going to happen that way, that he must renounce these wishes toward the analyst and fulfill them in his own life, in his work, in his attachments, through his children. In other words, that he is an adult and must put away childish things. Which is *horribly painful*. O.K. Now, imagine the situation of the candidate when his analysis ends. Instead of going his way like the ordinary analysand, he joins the profession of his analyst—joins the very institute of which his analyst is a member, and begins to make his way up in the hierarchy his analyst has already reached the top of. As time goes on, the wishes that the candidate has had to renounce and sublimate—but that are always there—are powerfully reactivated. He begins to dare hope that maybe he *will,* after all, be admitted into the parental bedroom, that he *will* be treated to the secrets of the parents, that he *will* find out what they 'do' in there, that he *will* be able to form alliances with one or another of them. Not everyone feels like that—some people drop out of the institute world and go their own way—but the majority, like me, for whatever infantilely motivated reason, hope that they will get into that bedroom: that they will become training analysts."

"But not everyone makes it."

"Not everyone makes it. Our institute is large, and the places in the inner sanctum are limited. Many of those who don't make it—who see others accepted into the bedroom while they are passed over—become bitter. They are the reason for the discontent, antagonism, backbiting, and factionalism of our institute, for the constant danger of schism. As for the ones who do make it, their behavior is like that of uneasy, shifty-eyed 'good children' who have got into favor with their parents at the expense of their siblings. They have made it into the bedroom and are keeping the other children out, and they feel guilty and defensive because they're afraid they didn't get in there fairly."

"What about you? Are you going to get into that bedroom?"

"I don't know. I have certain inhibitions—neurotic in nature, I know—about pushing myself into places. The Oedipal rivalries, fears, guilts are still operative. They're not anywhere near as strong as they were before my second analysis, but they're still there, and they take their toll."

"Why do you feel you have to push? Why don't you assume you'll naturally rise in the hierarchy because you're good at the work?"

"Oh, I'm very good at the work. I'm better than most people in my year—there's no doubt about that."

"Then why do you have to push? Why don't you just rise?"

"Right. That's the question. Why aren't they tapping me on the shoulder and letting me in? The fact is that the people who are appointed training analysts aren't always the best people available. There are others who are just as good, and maybe even better, who are not chosen."

"And you are afraid that this will happen to you—that you will be passed over?"

"Yes. I'm not politic. I don't socialize much with analysts. My friends are mostly academics and artists. When I'm invited to analysts' parties, I often refuse. My wife, who is a sculptor, isn't part of the society that the analysts' wives form, and she feels out of place at these affairs. The analysts' wives all know each other, they serve on the Institute's Hospitality Committee together, they all but play mah-jongg together."

"So you don't like analytic society?"

"It bores me."

"What about the younger people, the colleagues on your own level?"

"They bore me, too. It's the same thing. They talk about their houses in the country, the schools their children go to, their trips in the summer—all that. I don't feel comfortable with them. I recognize this as an old childhood trait. I've never felt 'in' anywhere—not in school, not in college, not in medical school, not in psychiatric training—and now I'm playing it out in relation to the analytic community. Everyone's analysis unearths a central fantasy, and mine is that of an outsider looking into the bedroom: feeling excited and scared, getting aroused, trying to figure out what is going on, but not having to get involved, not having to risk anything. There are many ways of playing out this fantasy. I could have become a Peeping Tom, for one extreme possibility, but I became a scientist instead—a psychoanalyst, a person who gets to know another person very intimately but doesn't have to get involved with him. I'm very much a Jew—another kind of outsider. So if you ask me if I want to get into the inner sanctum of the New York Psychoanalytic—well, *yes*, I do, well, *no*, I don't. I have all kinds of fantasies about what goes on in the inner sanctum, most of which aren't true. They couldn't possibly be true." Aaron laughed at his fantasies.

"Don't things always look better from the outside?" I said.

Aaron agreed. "I used to have a symptom. I used to have social anxiety before going to parties. Parties, you know, are highly instinctualized things. Well, the symptom fell away during my analysis, and now I go to parties, and they're so mundane."

"The best parties are the ones you're not invited to."

"That's right."

"When you do get into the inner sanctum, you'll find that all they talk about is their houses in the country, their children's schools, their wives' yoga classes. . . ."

Aaron smiled and said, "You know, in actuality, I've been treated very nicely by the administration. I've had appointments to minor committees, I've been invited to do various things. Just last week, someone called me up and said I was being proposed for a minor administrative office. I said O.K.—though I probably won't get it, because I'm young and unknown. I'm forty-six years old and I'm young. What kind of a profession is this?"

"Do you feel like a kid in relation to the older analysts?"

"Sometimes. Look, you felt it, too, when you compared yourself to a child in front of threatening grownups after you'd met with the Educational Committee people. Which was partly your own psychology coming out—and it's partly *my* psychology coming out, too. I can imagine that, theoretically, there are people younger than I who feel on the level of equals with Them—who are not cowed and intimidated. But only partly. Because there's no doubt that the organization is hierarchical and that the people in charge do not extend an attitude of invitation and incorporation to the younger generation and to the people on the periphery. They *are* exclusive, and all analytic institutes aren't like this one."

"During my meeting with the Educational Committee people, I was always aware that they were three and I was one. There was the feeling of 'against' throughout the evening."

"That is the way they come on with the students, and even, to some extent, with the general membership. I experienced that feeling of 'against' during training. Everyone felt it. We all felt like children. Thirty-five-year-old children! There's a student organization at the Institute now—there's even a national organization of analytic candidates and recent graduates, called CAPE—but there were only faint rumblings about organizing when I was a candidate. I remember once one of my classmates—a very fiery, radicalized fellow, who has since moved to the suburbs and become dull and rich—was haranguing a group of us about organizing, when one of the more authoritarian people on the Educational Committee came into the room. He listened, and then, looking at my classmate as if he were some unpleasantness, said silkily, 'Why an organization? The important thing is to say whatever comes into your mind.' I thought, Son of a bitch! *But. But.* He was right. The motives of student organizations are nothing if not transferential."

"The kids getting together against the parents."

"Right. The student organization is kid stuff in the truest sense of the term. That son of a bitch was right. The Educational Committee never came out with any official pronouncement about the student organization. About how it would interfere, how it would be extraneous—at best a waste of time, at worst a resistance. They never said that—it would have been foolish of them to say it—but I believe that that was their attitude. Let the children play. Analytic education is inescapably an infantilizing experience. Interesting, isn't it? That a profession which gears itself so much to progressive maturation should conduct its education as an infantilizing experience."

"The Educational Committee people told me that from twenty to twenty-five percent of the candidates don't graduate, and that most of these are asked to resign. How did you feel about the threat of expulsion when you were a candidate?"

"I didn't feel it as a threat, exactly. But the possibility was always there. I had several friends who were asked to resign."

"After a long time in training?"

"Yes, sometimes after many years."

"What does it mean when someone is dropped?"

"I don't know. These things are shrouded in mystery and a tremendous amount of secrecy—secrecy that is observed not only by the Institute but by the person dropped. In general, either people founder on their casework or they are unanalyzable. Character also counts. There was a man in my class who had a terrible character. He was slick, sharp, he lied, he wasn't *nice*. It enraged me to see him at the Institute and to think that he would be practicing analysis. Well, one day he wasn't there anymore, and I was enormously relieved and glad that he had been found out and booted."

"So the parents are omniscient after all."

"Hardly. The place is run like a candy store."

"What do you mean?"

Aaron squirmed in his chair and grimaced. "They're so casual. They're so unprofessional. They're like the people in the British House of Lords, who would meet in the evening and run England. I look around me and wonder, Do I want to be connected with these people for the rest of my life? Can I fulfill myself among them? Am I going to be happy? Or will I be bored and stultified and trapped? You should excuse that I, a psychoanalyst, put things as naïvely as that, but that's the way I think about them. I feel I'm being sucked in and taken over. I feel scared and out of control. I had this feeling with this kind of intensity once before in my life

—the first time I fell in love. The Institute has a strong gravitational pull. When you spend all day alone with patients—which is to say *alone*—the company of colleagues becomes a great source of solace and reassurance and of stimulation. Some analysts spend almost every evening at the Institute; there are psychoanalytic widows and orphans. I ask myself, Do I want to live like that—like a man hopelessly entangled with a voracious, dull mistress? Obviously, it's not *just* boredom and stultification that I fear. It's getting involved, it's having to put my narcissism on the line, it's getting bruised. I've seen so many colleagues get bruised. A colleague somewhat senior to me—a man I like very much—recently suffered a small but painful, and I'm afraid typical, public humiliation. He presented a proposal at one of our general business meetings—it had something to do with the renovation that is going on in our building—which got ignominiously tabled. Not because it wasn't a good idea but because it had got caught up—as so many issues recently have got caught up—in the factionalism of the Institute. His eminently sensible and reasonable proposal became another battleground for the struggle between the ins and the outs. All kinds of recriminations, with implications of improper behavior, began to come out. It was fascinating and horrifying for us younger members (of forty-five) to look on as our elders made cruel, slanderous attacks on each other."

"What was it about?"

"It was about rugs and chairs. A member of the Renovation Committee knew of someone—the wife or the sister-in-law of another member—who was a decorator and might get things cheaper. And this was the chance the other side was looking for to jump in and criticize the committee—accusing them of bad planning, of irresponsible allocation of money—and even, finally, to question the whole renovation and the morality of spending money on decoration when it could go for things like pensions for the workers at the Institute. But none of this was the real issue."

"What was the real issue?"

"The real issue was that there is a clique of people at the Institute who fill all the important posts and decide who is to become a training analyst, and there is another clique of people who don't have power and who want it. That's what practically every controversy at our institute is about. It used to trouble me—until I thought about other professions and realized that it's no different anywhere else. The neighbors do it, too! The *goyim* do it! This kind of hierarchy and infantilization exists in every other profession. It's in law, in business, in science, in education. There are Oedipally significant positions in every profession, and when people are up for them it creates a crisis that infantilizes them—causes grown men to squabble like kids about trivial things. I remember a few years ago when my older brother was in one of these crises. He was then assistant headmaster of a boys' private school in N——. The head of the school, who was one of those legendary great schoolmasters, was up for retirement, and my brother was in an agony of indecision about whether or not to put himself up for the position in competition with people from the outside. Freud wrote about this very trenchantly in *Moses and Monotheism*. Things happen in life, he said, which correspond so closely to infantile fantasies or infantile experiences that they cause the infantile fantasies or experiences to dominate adult life. We're constantly reacting to the evocative power of reality. In my brother's case, there was, in addition, a horrible sharing of unconscious fantasy. The older man saw the succession as the younger generation coming to cut off his member, and the younger man, who wanted the position, saw it in terms of cutting off the older man's member—thus his indecision. So they were very much in sync with each other in this Oedipal drama. Which exists only on a fantasy level. Because the fact is, it's a job. *It's just a job!* So is being a training analyst at the New York Psychoanalytic. That's the funny thing about it all. Why can't adults deal with these things in terms of objective realities?"

"But if the job were seen for what it is—for the poor thing it is—who would want to do it?"

"That's just it. What are the sources of motivation and pleasure? The sources of motivation and pleasure are *infantile wishes.*"

# 4

THE TREATMENT CENTER OF THE NEW YORK PSYCHO-analytic is characterized in the Institute's catalogue as "an outpatient psychiatric clinic," but it would be more accurate to call it a clearinghouse for the cases on which candidates learn to do analysis. People looking for low-cost analytic treatment come to the New York Psychoanalytic building, at 245 East 82 Street—a shabby five-story structure of a kind of timorous Art Deco aspect (the thirties Nebbish style?)—where they are interviewed by one of a voluntary staff of analysts and are usually found wanting:

eighty-nine percent of the people who come for interviews (referred by New York Psychoanalytic members or by psychiatrists or social workers) are turned away.

Cases suitable for starting analysts are not easy to come by, the head of the Treatment Center, an analyst named George Gross, told me as I sat across from him in his gloomy, decrepit office on the fourth floor of the Institute, and as he struggled to open a drawer in his enormous desk. Gross is a dark, heavyset man in his early fifties, of a grudging, not easy courtesy, who has a way of investing commonplace facts with aliveness and interest. The right sort of case, he explained, has to be both suitable for analysis and not too hard for an inexperienced practitioner. Some narcissistic disorders, for example, are too hard for a student. "I have one such case here in my desk," Gross said, struggling again with the drawer. Giving up on the narcissistic disorder, he went on, "We look for patients whose object relations are not so insecure that they cannot form therapeutic alliances. In narcissistic and borderline patients, that capacity is impaired. We consider the classical psychoneuroses—obsessional cases, hysterics—very promising. We know more today about criteria for analyzability than we did in the past, and we have a high success rate. Our crude criterion for success is whether or not the patient stays in treatment. We divide applicants into two categories: acceptable—which includes high-risk-high-gain cases—and unacceptable. There are no surprises —we haven't had a surprise since 1974. When a case in the high-risk category fails, we are not surprised, and when a case in the acceptable category succeeds we are not surprised, and we screen out psychotics. To avoid self-fulfilling prophecy, the student analyst doesn't know whether his patient is high-risk or not. Nor does he get the interviewer's comments and impressions; he gets only neutral descriptive material. We don't take patients who can afford thirty dollars or more an hour. The fee is arranged according to income, and the average today is seven dollars and nine cents an hour. Patients have paid as little as ten cents an hour. Analyses are done in the candidate's office, not here, unless the candidate doesn't have an office, and then we let him use a room here. Most candidates are already practicing psychiatrists. Patients are seen five times a week. The candidate meets once a week with his supervisor to discuss the case, and every six months he is supposed to turn in a summary of his work to that point. Candidates sometimes have trouble turning in those summaries, and we have to remind them. Another problem a candidate sometimes has is with his patient's initial feeling that the candidate is inferior to the older, established analysts."

Gross gave the drawer one more futile tug, and then spoke with quiet pride of the Institute's refusal both of federal reimbursements and of money from private foundations. He said that the faculty is not paid (Gross's job as the administrator of the Treatment Center is the only paid position in the Institute), that supervisors are not paid, that most of the Institute's income is from members' dues (six hundred dollars a year, from about two hundred members), and that analysts can be found at the Institute on weekends fixing venetian blinds and painting chairs. All this is to avoid any trace of outside influence or interference. "We want to remain absolutely independent, we want no one to tell us what to do, and we are slowly, inexorably going bankrupt," Gross said.

At the beginning of his second year of training at the New York Psychoanalytic, Aaron Green received his first case

—a twenty-two-year-old woman—from the Treatment Center. It was a case he now regards with a mixture of horror, pleasure, amusement, puzzlement, self-criticism, and self-satisfaction. "For the first two years of this analysis, I was in agony over it," he recalled. "I cursed the people at the Treatment Center for giving me such a case. I felt totally incompetent and impotent. I dreaded the time of day when her hour came. The analysis lasted seven years, and today I'm rather proud of it. The patient came into analysis a very unhappy young girl with some very troublesome hysterical symptoms, and she left with all the symptoms gone and married to a dentist. But it took me a long time to realize that I wasn't failing with her.

"I remember when she first came into my office—a short, plump, self-conscious girl, who giggled and gave vapid, inconsequential answers to the questions I asked her. We had a few sessions sitting up, and then one day I said, 'Why don't you lie down on the couch?' She giggled and walked over to the couch and arranged herself on it gingerly, with a lot of tugging at her skirt, and went on talking in her inane, girlish, monosyllabic way. This kept up for three or four sessions. Then one day she walked in and didn't *get* on the couch, she *threw* herself on it. She bounced up and down and began to *rail* at me. 'You don't *do* anything for me,' she said. 'You just sit there and don't *do* anything. You don't tell me anything. What kind of business is this? Why don't you *do* something for me? Why do you just sit there?' She went on and on, berating me for my coldness and passivity and indifference to her sufferings—and that was the true beginning of the analysis. But I didn't know it. I sat there cowering under her anger and irked with her for not knowing that what I was doing as I 'just sat there' was classical Freudian analysis. I found her in every way disappointing. I had expected a patient who would free-associate, and here they had sent me this banal girl who just blathered. I didn't understand—I was so naïve then—that her blathering *was* free association, that blathering is just what free association is. Worse than that, I thought I had to instruct her on the nature of her unconscious. I would laboriously point out to her the unconscious meaning of what she said and did. Only after years of terrible and futile struggle did it dawn on me that if I just listened—if I just let her talk, let her blather—things would come out, and that this was what would help her, not my pedantic, didactic interpretations. If I could only have learned to shut up! When I finally did learn, I began to see things that Freud had described—to actually see for myself symptoms disappearing as the unconscious became conscious. That was an incredible thing. It was like looking through a telescope and realizing that you are seeing what Galileo saw.

"But for the first two years that case seemed like a personal misfortune. I wanted to throw her back at the Institute and say, 'What? You gave me *this* for a first case?' She was so nasty and unpleasant. She was so uncoöperative and unappreciative. If I heard her say it once, I heard her say it a thousand times: *'So what?'*—in a nasty, sneering voice. *'So what?'* I felt demeaned, put down, furious, frustrated, impotent. My fury often caused me to act in unanalytic ways toward her. I'm ashamed of that. I would do many things differently now. But the interesting thing—the incredible thing—is that what I did didn't matter. She sneered and scoffed at everything I said, but she came faithfully five times a week, month after month, year after year, and the analysis bubbled along in spite of her belligerence and mistrust and my innocence and ignorance."

"You say that just 'letting things come out' helped her," I said. "That sounds like the old cathartic method."

"Yes, yes," Aaron said. "That old stuff that Freud and Josef Breuer wrote about in *Studies on Hysteria* hasn't really changed. Analysis is still cathartic. We're still trying to 'transform neurotic misery into common unhappiness' by setting in motion a process whereby motivation gets expressed directly, rather than going off sideways into symptoms. Freud and Breuer called this 'abreaction.' We no longer use that term, and we have a more refined knowledge of the kinds of obstruction that the mind puts up against the threat of change, but the process is essentially the same. In the case of this girl, when I finally learned to shut up, stuff began to spew out of her—stuff that was barely on the fringes of her consciousness but that caused her to change just by being brought out. In the popular imagination, the analyst is an authoritarian, dominating figure who has rigid control over a malleable, vulnerable patient. What this case forcibly impressed upon me is that the reverse is true—it is the patient who controls what is happening, and the analyst who is a puny, weak figure. Patients go where the hell they please. All the analyst can do is say, 'If you'll deign to listen to me for a moment—if you could just divert your attention to this particular place instead of that one—you may see that . . . et cetera, et cetera.' That's all he can do. In this case, all I could do was every now and then direct the patient's attention to what she was doing in her attempts to keep that stuff from spewing out—something she preferred not to watch. That's called 'the analysis of the resistance,' which doesn't mean that you shake your finger at the patient and say, *'You're resisting!'* That's the worst thing you can do, and I'm afraid I sometimes did do it in the first years of that case. The right way is just to point out to the patient how he keeps himself from thinking certain things and feeling certain things, so that he becomes self-conscious and the evasion doesn't work so automatically. That's all. That's the analyst's scalpel. He can't open up his patient's mind and reach in and start tinkering. The only thing he can do is tell the patient, 'Look there,' and most of the time the patient doesn't look. But sometimes he does, and then his automatic behavior becomes less automatic."

I had read a writeup of the young woman's case which Aaron had prepared for the American Psychoanalytic Association as a prerequisite for certification and membership, and had found it baffling, irritating, boring, insulting to women, and self-damning. In its unrelenting pursuit of sexual matter and meaning, it brought to mind the Dora case, in which Freud often conducted himself more like a police inspector interrogating a suspect than like a doctor helping a patient. "Aha!" Freud would say to poor Dora, an attractive and intelligent eighteen-year-old girl suffering from a nervous cough, migraine, and a kind of general youthful malaise. "Aha! I know about you. I know your dirty little secrets. Admit that you were secretly attracted to Herr K. Admit that you masturbated when you were five. Look at what you're doing now as you lie there playing with your reticule—opening it, putting a finger into it, shutting it again!" I sensed some of the same badgering and needling quality in Aaron's case history. I asked him whether his own behavior might not have provoked some of the girl's belligerence and antagonism.

"My analytic behavior was not everything it should have been," he agreed. "I was very unschooled and very intent on getting analytic procedure down pat. I come out of that writeup looking pedantic and constricted, and there is some truth to that impression. There is some truth to Leo Stone's characterization of the beginning analyst as a rather ludicrously rigid and unyielding person. I take full responsibility for the excruciating and ill-advised things I did in that analysis. She was often 'right,' and I was often 'wrong.' And for all that, for all my oafishness and pompousness, her basic attitude toward me—the transference—was quite unaffected by what I said and did, had its own rhyme and reason, went its own way. My unanalytic behavior muddied the water, made the transference harder to discern and point out convincingly to the patient, but it didn't *create* the transference. If I had been St. Francis of Assisi, she would have said '*So what?*' no less frequently and sneeringly."

I mentioned a paper I had read by Ralph Greenson on "the non-transference relationship," in which the author relates a number of horrendous stories about rigid beginning analysts. In one of these cautionary tales, a beginning analyst comes to his supervisor and tells him about an oddly unsatisfying session he has had with a patient who came in with his head swathed in an enormous bandage. Following strict analytic technique, the young analyst made no comment on the bandage, and silently waited for the patient to start free-associating. No associations came: the patient was struck absolutely speechless by the analyst's unbelievable insensitivity and inhumanity. In another example (this one appears in Greenson's book *The Technique and Practice of Psychoanalysis*), an anxious young mother tells her candidate analyst how desperately worried she is about her ailing baby.

The analyst says nothing. His silence and lack of compassion cause the patient to lapse into a miserable, tearful silence of her own. Finally, the analyst says, "You're resisting." The patient quits the analysis, saying to the analyst, "You're sicker than I am." Greenson, concurring with this opinion, advises the candidate to seek further analysis.

"Yeah," Aaron said. "I know those stories of Greenson's. They are very heartrending and affecting, and completely off the mark. If you look at them closely, they just don't hold up. In the case of the mother with the sick baby, it wasn't the analyst's lack of 'compassion' that caused the patient to break off treatment—it was his poor analytic technique. There are a hundred things he could have said to her other than 'You're resisting' which would have been helpful, which would have led somewhere, but which would have been neutral. The job of the analyst isn't to offer the patient sympathy; it's to lead him to insight. It was the same thing with my first case. The trouble wasn't my lack of compassion for the patient but my lapses from analytic neutrality. It isn't that I should have accepted the presents she brought me—though maybe I could have refused them less priggishly—but that I should have analyzed the motive that lay behind the gift-giving in a more rigorous and thoroughgoing manner."

"But what *about* that priggishness?" I asked. "Can you leave it out of account? Greenson says that it's important for the patient to distinguish between his transference reactions to the analyst and his realistic perceptions of him. He says of the woman with the baby that her reactions to the analyst were 'realistic.' "

Aaron shook his head. "That's taking such a crude and simplistic view of analysis—and of life," he said. "It perpetuates the myth that what goes on in the analysis is different from what goes on in real life. It gives analysis an 'as if' quality. It says the transference isn't real. But the transference *is* real—as real as anything out there. And, conversely, 'the real relationship'—whatever that is—is not exempt from analytic scrutiny. If the analyst comes into the session and insults the patient, and the patient says 'So it's true! You really hate me!' and the analyst says 'Yes! I really hate you!' does this mean that all the patient's irrational and fantastic ideas about the angry parent of childhood are now *negated?* Are now not to be investigated? Now fall outside the pale of analytic scrutiny?

"I remember a seminar I once attended that was led by a brilliant and flamboyant Hungarian analyst named Robert Bak. The issue under debate was the nature of transference, and I raised my hand and asked rhetorically, 'What would you call an interpersonal relationship where infantile wishes, and defenses against those wishes, get expressed in such a way that the persons within that relationship don't see each other for what they objectively are but, rather, view each other in terms of their infantile needs and their infantile conflicts? What would you call that?' And Bak looked over at me ironically and said, 'I'd call that life.'

"In both analysis and life, we perceive reality through a veil of unconscious infantile fantasy. Nothing we say or do or think is ever purely 'rational' or 'irrational,' purely 'real' or 'transferential.' It is always a mixture. The difference between analysis and life is that in analysis—in this highly artificial, extreme, bizarre, stressful, in some ways awful situation—these infantile fantasies come into higher relief than they do in life, become accessible to study, as they do not in life. The purpose of analysis isn't to instruct the patient on the nature of reality but to acquaint him with himself, with the child within him, in all its infantility and its impossible and unrepudiated and unrepudiatable longings and wishes. Terms like 'the real relationship' and 'therapeutic alliance' and 'working alliance' simply obscure and dilute and trivialize the radical nature of this task."

"So you share Charles Brenner's dislike of those terms, and his uncompromising view of analytic technique."

"I do. I think that Brenner's uncompromising—you might even say fanatically pure—way of doing analysis permits you to find things out that you would not find out under a less rigorous procedure. It also, paradoxically, gives the patient more freedom than he has under the more relaxed analytic techniques. Ruthless and authoritarian though it seems, strict analytic neutrality is the more libertarian alternative. When you temper the rigors of analysis with judicious doses of kindliness and friendliness, you are taking away some of the patient's freedom, because *you* are deciding what is best for him. But doing analysis in Brenner's pure and undeviating way is very hard. It demands a great deal of the analyst, and puts him under a tremendous strain. No one likes to hurt people—to cause them pain, to stand silently by as they suffer, to withhold help from them when they plead for it. That's where the real wear and tear of analysis lies—in this chronic struggle to keep oneself from doing the things that decent people naturally and spontaneously do. One hears a lot about the abstinence that the analytic patient has to endure, but the abstinence of the analyst is more ruthless and corrosive. The 'working alliance' and the 'therapeutic alliance' and the 'non-transference relationship' are all what Brenner calls resistive myths—myths that analysts who are unable to tolerate analytic abstinence have invented to justify their lapses from neutrality. They say, 'Oh, I don't have to act analytically now. This is the therapeutic alliance, this is non-transference'—as if they were stepping into some no-man's-land where all bets were off and the analyst and the patient could assume a relationship different from the one of analysis proper. But there is no such neutral zone, there is no 'other' relationship, there is no honest way of escaping the pain and stress of doing analysis.

"Let me illustrate with an incident from my practice. I once arrived fifteen minutes late for an appointment with a patient. I was appalled by my oversight and apologized profusely to the patient. Now, the analysts of the lenient sort would say, 'You did the right thing. It's good to admit it when you've made a mistake; it's good to show the patient you're only human. It's an empathetic response. It strengthens the therapeutic alliance. It makes him feel you're on his side.' And so on. But I knew I should *not* have apologized. I knew I should have waited to learn what the patient's response to my lateness was, instead of rushing in with my apology. In my self-analysis of the lapse, a rather vicious analyst joke came to mind, which goes like this: A new woman patient comes to a male analyst's office, and he says, 'Take off your clothes and get on the couch.' The woman gets undressed and lies down on the couch, and the analyst gets on top of her. Then he says, 'You can get dressed now and sit in that chair.' She does so, and the analyst says, 'O.K. We've taken care of my problem. What's yours?' It's a silly joke, and a vicious one, but it gets at something fundamental. In that situation of being late, I acted like the analyst in the joke. I put my own interests before those of the patient. I felt guilty about my lateness, and by apologizing I was seeking forgiveness from the patient. I was saying to him, 'Let's take care of my problem—never mind about yours.' "

# 5

T HE SECOND PATIENT AARON RECEIVED FROM THE TREAT-
ment Center was a refined, cultivated woman, eager to
do the analytic work, appreciative of Aaron, extremely pleasant and interesting to be with, and very good-looking. As he
had cursed his luck with the first patient, he couldn't believe
his good fortune in having drawn the second. She was the
most gratifying of patients. She made literary allusions, and
understood the ones he made. She worked on a magazine
and had an impressive-sounding circle of literary acquaint-
ances. As he had dreaded the sessions with the first patient,
he looked forward to the ones with the second. He was daz-
zled by her, a little in love with her. After two years, the
analysis ground down to a horrible halt. It was a total failure.
"I was blinded and lulled by her charm," Aaron recalled
ruefully. "I fell down badly on the job. Instead of pointing
out to her the nasty, harsh things I should have pointed
out, I exchanged literary references with her. I didn't see
the trap I had fallen into until it was too late. In the first
case, where the patient gave me no pleasure whatever, to put
it mildly, I was able to hew to my course and be of some
help to her. In the second case, I failed the patient utterly."

"Are you suggesting that the more congenial a patient,
the harder it is to analyze him or her?"

"In this case it was."

"So personal relations are an encumbrance in analysis."

"Freud says they are, in several places in his writings.
There is the well-known passage in 'Recommendations to

Physicians' where he compares the analyst to the surgeon, 'who puts aside all his feelings.' Then there's the passage in a letter to the analyst Oskar Pfister in which Freud chides him for being 'overdecent' and insufficiently ruthless to his patient, and counsels him to behave like the artist who steals his wife's household money to buy paint and burns the furniture to warm the room for his model. I like to tell the residents I teach a story I heard from one of my teachers at the Institute—obviously apocryphal—about the artist Benvenuto Cellini, which makes the same point. Cellini was casting a statue, and he needed some calcium for his bronze alloy. He couldn't find any around the studio, so he picked up this little boy and threw him into the pot for the calcium in his bones. What was the life of a little boy to the claim of art?"

I thought of George Orwell's "Reflections on Gandhi," in which he objected to the side of Gandhi's nature that permitted him to do the moral equivalent of throwing the boy into the pot in the name of a higher ideal. To Orwell, there was no higher ideal than the humanistic one. "The essence of being human is that one does not seek perfection, that one *is* sometimes willing to commit sins for the sake of loyalty, that one does not push asceticism to the point where it makes friendly intercourse impossible, and that one is prepared in the end to be defeated and broken up by life, which is the inevitable price of fastening one's love upon other human individuals," Orwell wrote, with moving irascibility. To the notion that the ordinary man is a failed saint Orwell retorted, "Many people genuinely do not wish to be saints, and it is probable that some who achieve or aspire to sainthood have never felt much temptation to be human beings."

I remembered a talk I had had with an analyst I'll call Gregory Cross—a man of saintlike dedication to his calling, whose eyes shone with zeal as he spoke of his work and of his aspiration to give ever more precise interpretations to his patients. We sat in his consultation room one evening after the last patient had left. The room had the harsh and anguished modernity of the rooms in the paintings of Francis Bacon; in its motel-like detachment from the things of this world, it was like analytic abstinence itself. The couch was a narrow foam-rubber slab covered with an indifferently chosen gold fabric; over its foot, where the patient's shoes rested, a piece of ugly black plastic sheeting was stretched. The room was like an iconoclast's raised fist; this analyst's patients didn't come here to pass the time of day, it told you. Cross himself looked like the gnarled, tormented stubs of men that Bacon paints. You felt that he didn't sit down to meals but furtively gulped his food, like a stray animal; you fancied that his wife had left him years ago, and that for several days he hadn't noticed she was gone. He was a man without charm, without ease, without conceit or vanity, and with a kind of excruciating, prodding, twitching honesty that was like an intractable skin disorder. He told me of his love of Freud. He said that he read and reread the Standard Edition, finding constant inspiration and refreshment in the Master. But he confessed that when he had first encountered Freud's writings, as a psychiatric resident, he couldn't understand what they were all about. He just couldn't crack the surface. He had become interested in psychoanalysis through the simple social-revisionist writings of Karen Horney, and it wasn't until his training analysis that he was able to break through the resistance to true psychoanalysis which he felt that most people put up. He said that now he sat all day in his chair—from eight in the morning to seven at night—listening to patients, leaving the room only to go to his own analyst. To understand his patients better, he wanted to know himself better—to delve into himself more deeply—and so he had gone back into analysis, as Freud had counselled analysts to do in "Analysis Terminable and Interminable." Cross spoke in a soft, low, deliberate, somewhat monotonous manner. He was one of the most serious and sincere and austere men I have ever met. As we talked, I felt chastened by his thorny sincerity and gravity, and felt difficult things in me coming out to meet the difficulty of his nature. Everything he said was very simple (he used no jargon) and yet somehow veiled, as are the utterances of poets and holy men. I asked him to recommend books and papers. The other analysts I had talked to all told me to read this book, to read that paper. Gregory Cross dismissed my request. He looked at me kindly and seriously and said, "It will come out of yourself." When I got home and played the tape of the conversation, Cross's words were completely unintelligible. So I have invented him after all, I thought.

I remembered another evening talk, this one in the Fifth Avenue apartment of a woman analyst I'll call Greta Koenig —an older Middle European émigrée with a fresh, smiling face and a simple, gentle, earnest manner. We sat around a coffee table laden with pastries, little rolls, cheeses, fruit, chocolates, and bottles of liqueur, and as my hostess pressed delicacies on me she talked of female orgasm. She sliced *Dobos Torte* onto translucent old flowered porcelain and re-marked thoughtfully that a clitoral orgasm may be accompanied by feelings in the vagina and thus, properly speaking, can be called a vaginal orgasm. I felt a strong urge to laugh. As if reading my thoughts, Greta Koenig smiled and said, "It used to be very difficult for me to talk about such things. I used to have to force myself to talk about them to patients.

But the analyst must talk about the genitals. There is no way around it, and now there is nothing I can't talk about." She spoke of her unequivocal devotion to the Institute and to psychoanalysis. She and her husband (also an analyst) are in the inner circle of the Institute. Her entire life was taken up with psychoanalytic concerns: during the day she saw patients, at night she went to meetings at the Institute, and when she and her husband went out to dinner or entertained at home it was always with analysts. Other people fall away, she explained. There is less and less to talk about with people on the "outside," who don't look at things the way analysts do. "We never seem to tire of one another's company," she said with wondering satisfaction. She told me that she never lied to patients, never talked about herself, and never had physical contact with them. She showed me her consultation room, which led off the front hall of the apartment: a pleasant, orderly room, of a faintly European stamp, but without much character. It wasn't as insistently impersonal as Cross's room, but it calmly kept its owner's secrets, respectfully guarded the patient's right not to know.

A third soldier of Freud I had met, who now came to mind as another exemplar of psychoanalytic transcendence, was Hartvig Dahl. That is his real name. Most of the other analysts I talked to asked me not to use their real names, in order to preserve their analytic incognito with patients. But Dahl is an analyst without patients. He is a psychoanalytic researcher—a member of a small, scattered group of analysts who work mostly alone and mostly without the respect or interest of their patient-seeing colleagues. The reason for their lowly status derives from the nature (and history) of psychoanalysis itself. Its therapeutic and scientific functions have traditionally been viewed as inseparable; the therapeutic encounter is seen as the laboratory of the science of psycho-analysis. Accordingly, each practicing analyst is a scientific investigator, each case an experiment yielding corroboration or elaboration or interesting refutation of established theory, each patient a sort of unwitting laboratory animal. The non-practicing analytic researcher doesn't fit into this self-contained dual-purpose scheme of things, and is felt to be superfluous and a little déclassé.

Hartvig Dahl is the New York Psychoanalytic Institute's grudging concession to the claims of "pure research"; he is a sort of *shabbas goy* to the orthodox membership. (The once nastily anti-Semitic characterization of psychoanalysis as "the Jewish science" is today good-humoredly accepted by analysts as an accurate comment on the great predominance of Jews in the profession, and on the parallel between Talmudic and analytic hermeneutics.) Hartvig Dahl doesn't look like the other New York Psychoanalytic analysts. When I first met him, in his office at the Downstate Medical Center, in Brooklyn, he was wearing faded jeans and a work shirt, and at subsequent meetings (in warmer weather) he wore shorts and running shoes. He is an extraordinarily tall man, in his mid-fifties, who came here sixteen years ago from Seattle, where he had studied psychoanalysis at a training-center branch of the San Francisco Psychoanalytic Institute. He has the flavor of the American West about him, and there adheres to him something of the poignancy of the rough-hewn, morally fine Americans in Henry James's international novels who find themselves embroiled with outwardly soigné, morally piggish Europeans. But when I first met Dahl I was put off and bored. I couldn't understand what he was up to—much of it depended on a knowledge of higher mathematics, which I didn't possess—so I dismissed it out of hand. He gave me a batch of his published papers, and the first one I looked at, entitled "The Measurement of Meaning in Psychoanalysis by Computer Analysis of Verbal Contexts," so alarmed me with its charts and graphs that I fled the meeting as if pursued by a swarm of bees. In my own defense, I submit this extract from it:

WORDS CORRELATED [p <.05, N=25 analytic hours] WITH
EACH OF FOUR SELECTED WORDS

Each of four selected words and the words with which it significantly (p ≤ .05, N = 25 hours) correlated.

A few months later, I happened to come across the rest of the papers that Dahl had thrust into my unwilling hand, and idly leafed through one of the less horrible-looking ones. I found myself reading it with growing excitement; though dauntingly titled "Countertransference Examples of the Syntactic Expression of Warded-Off Contents," it was clear and fascinating. It told of a rather commonplace discovery that Dahl and his co-authors—Virginia Teller, a Ph.D. in linguistics, and the psychiatrists Donald Moss and Manuel Trujillo—had made while reading transcripts of a tape-recorded analysis, and of a most extraordinary inference that they had drawn from it. The discovery, familiar to all users of tape recorders, was the fact that people who sound all right when you are talking to them are actually speaking in a most peculiar fashion, as a verbatim transcript of their words will disclose. What the tape recorder has revealed about human speech is something like what the photographer Eadweard Muybridge's motion studies revealed about animal and human locomotion; no one had ever seen the strange positions that Muybridge's camera caught and froze, and no one had ever heard what the tape recorder pointed out about the weirdness and sloppiness of human speech. Dahl and his colleagues, instead of simply "allowing for" the difference between the spoken word and the transcript, as everyone before them had done, went on to take a closer look at the syntactical peculiarities that the transcript threw into relief, and it dawned on them that these peculiarities were no accident but had a hidden purpose: they were a devious way of expressing unacceptable wishes and feelings. The tool for the unmasking of these covert communications was Noam Chomsky's transformational-generative grammar, in which Virginia Teller was well versed. From the tape under study, a number of the analyst's interventions were extracted and scrutinized for "hostility or seductiveness, approval or disapproval of the patient's behavior, as well as excessive assertions of authority." The findings were devastating. Ten interventions were held up as illustrations of ten different "syn-*tactics*" (as Dahl called these covert communications), through which the analyst did the psychological equivalent of pinching, kicking, and twisting the arm of the hapless patient. Here is the first example and the authors' commentary:

> "YOU KNOW, THIS IS THE WAY IT HAS ALWAYS BEEN PRE-
> SENTED, IN TERMS OF NEGATIVES. YOU KNOW, IT WAS NOT
> BAD, IT WAS NOT THIS, IT WAS NOT THAT."
>
> Consider the phrase ". . . it has always been pre-
> sented. . . ." This is an instance of the agentless passive—
> a passive-voice sentence with no underlying subject. . . .
> The analyst could have said, "You have always presented
> it in terms of negatives," but instead said, "it has always
> been presented"—a form which makes it impossible to
> determine who has done the presenting. The analyst has
> effectively eliminated the patient in a manner which seems
> quite inappropriate to the dyadic situation. In short, we
> seem to have uncovered psychological murder by syntax.

At our next meeting, in Dahl's agreeably book- and paper-cluttered office, he stated his firm belief in the necessity of tape-recording analytic sessions for research purposes. "Otherwise, we have no data," he said. "Now we have only analysts' subjective accounts of what they *believe* went on— accounts that are simply restatements of the hypothesis about the patient that the analyst ended up accepting. Science doesn't consider that good enough. In other sciences, hearsay accounts are not admissible as data." Having a body of raw data and making it publicly available, Dahl feels, is the first step toward the validation of the claims of psychoanalysis to be a science. He believes that the analyst's apparently "intuitive" inferences of a patient's unconscious motives must be shown to derive from objective rules and laws—i.e., that what a patient says during an analytic session (the "data" of psychoanalysis) will compel the same interpretation from any and every analyst listening to him. He has dedicated his life to making a contribution to this most difficult demonstration, which he feels will not take place in his lifetime. His devotion to, and belief in, psychoanalysis derives from his own experience of analysis, which he credits with "giving me a second chance to grow up." "My analyst's analyst was Menninger, whose analyst was analyzed by Abraham, whose analyst was no one. Which makes me an orphan," he said, with a smile. After graduating from the San Francisco Institute, Dahl practiced analysis in Seattle for four more years and then came East to train in research. Analytic work hadn't suited him—it was an ordeal for him to sit all day, to be silent and passive. He said that he got restless, bored, and itchy. He told me of a turning point in his relations with the New York Psychoanalytic, to which he had been unenthusiastically admitted on his arrival here. The Institute had invited the celebrated Otto Kernberg to come and speak on his theory of object relations, and Dahl had been named one of the two discussants of the presentation. The other discussant was Charles Brenner. "Brenner did something very nice," Dahl recalled. "He let me talk first. Usually, the more important discussant speaks first, and then everyone leaves; by putting me first, Brenner assured me of an audience. That was very decent of him. I did a hatchet job on Kernberg. I had done my homework, and I crushed him, and everyone knew I had. After that, I became socially acceptable. People who had dismissed me as a computer nut started being nice to me. All kinds of people started noticing me, inviting me to parties."

We left Dahl's office and went a few floors up, past the animal-experimentation section of the hospital, to a bleak little warren of rooms where a keypunch machine, recording equipment, and the tapes, transcripts, and notes of a six-year analysis that Dahl had conducted and tape-recorded a few years ago were kept. Dahl introduced me to Virginia Teller, a pretty young woman of reserved friendliness and calm and confident orderliness, who was sitting at an empty desk analyzing a sentence. Dahl has attacked his recorded analysis (1,204 sessions) on many fronts, and his attention has finally come to rest on a single session: the fifth hour of the analysis. Through intensive linguistic and logical analysis of the verbatim transcript of this hour, Dahl and Teller are attempting to lay bare the mental processes of analysts as they listen with "closely hovering attention" to a patient's utterances and find themselves forming hypotheses about their unconscious meaning. For embedded in the transcript, like a message written in invisible ink, are innumerable, unmistakable traces of the patient's unconscious motives. Invisible to the naked eye as such, they come into glaring view under the special linguistic and logical microscopy devised by Dahl and Teller for their singular demonstration of the existence of the unconscious. What every analyst implicitly "knows" about his patient Dahl and Teller are attempting to explicitly show with their textual analyses.

Dahl proposed that I listen to Session Five as a preliminary to studying the annotated transcript. He said that any other hour of the analysis would have served his purposes as well, but that Session Five happened to be a particularly rich hour—a kind of microcosm of the whole analysis, like the overture of an opera in which all the themes are announced. At the time of its recording, however, Dahl recalls, the session hadn't struck him as particularly significant; only in retrospect, after the analysis was over, could he make out the fifth hour's prophetic character. He seated me in a small room borrowed from some vacationing sex researchers, threaded a tape into a large recording machine, showed me how to start and stop the tape, and left the room. I paused before turning on the machine, a little awed by what I was about to do: eavesdrop on a patient's confessions to his analyst. I remembered Freud's admonition in the first of his *Introductory Lectures*: "You cannot be present as an audience at a psycho-analytic treatment. You can only be told about it; and, in the strictest sense of the word, it is only by hearsay that you will get to know psycho-analysis. . . . The talk of which psycho-analytic treatment consists brooks no listener." I turned on the machine, and listened for fifty minutes to a young man's halting, rambling soliloquy describing ordinary trivial events and expressing commonplace thoughts and feelings. It was like listening to a boring, self-absorbed acquaintance. Freud had been right: an outsider eavesdropping on an analytic session gets almost nothing from it; he is like an eavesdropper on a conversation (or monologue) in a foreign language. Only later, on reading the annotated transcript of the hour, did I laboriously decode the secret messages from the unconscious that the patient had wafted toward his analyst years before, and which Dahl, following Freud's instructions about loose, desireless, undirected listening, had "intuitively" grasped. In Session Five, Dahl spoke only twice. He sounded impressive—like an older, wiser, more benign and authoritative version of himself. When I told him of this impression, he laughed, and said, "I was pretty impressed with myself, too." He said that he deliberately spoke very little in the first years of the analysis so that no one could say he had "suggested" anything to the patient. In the later years of the analysis, he talked more. (Another precaution Dahl took was to enlist the supervision of the eminent New York Psychoanalytic Institute analyst Jacob Arlow, with whom he met weekly throughout the analysis.) The analysis developed along the standard Oedipal lines that classical analyses of mildly neurotic patients are expected to follow. Only a relatively small part of the total analysis has been transcribed; transcription is costly, and the funding from public and private foundations that Dahl depends on for his research is modest and unreliable. He has been working on Session Five for three years now. He thinks he is on the verge of a major breakthrough. His belief in science—his conviction that "the world is an orderly place"—keeps him at his task, in resolute pursuit of knowledge that analysts have trouble grasping and that scientists in other fields have little interest in acquiring.

# 6

WHEN I TOLD AARON OF MY IMPRESSIONS OF PSYCHO-analysts as a species of near-saint, he gave me one of the looks that he uses whenever someone or something he considers "unscientific" comes under discussion. But presently, as if in unconscious, grudging acquiescence, he began to speak of two analysts who had sinned against the mores of the analytic community, had traduced its ascetic ideal, and had been savagely punished for their transgression. Their sin was to marry a patient. Or, rather, as Aaron caustically explained (since analysts have been known to marry patients before), their sin was to be prominent, powerful, renowned analysts—leading lights of the analytic world—who married patients. If some nonentity should marry a patient, Aaron said, he would merely be frozen out of the referral network and allowed to sink into even greater obscurity in the institutional world. But if a former president of the American Psychoanalytic Association marries a patient, if a member of the Educational Committee of the New York Psychoanalytic Institute marries a patient, if a training analyst marries a patient, if a brilliant theoretician marries a patient—all of which is what happened here—then he must be ruthlessly dealt with, hurled from his high place, stripped of his honors, and have his head stuck on a pike as an example to others who might be tempted to forswear their analytic vows.

These events occurred years ago, and Aaron had heard about them only at tenth hand. He wasn't sure that the stories he had heard were accurate in their details—in the version he told me, Analyst X had begun to go out with his patient shortly after her analysis had ended, while Analyst Y had got into a messy triangle during the analysis—but there was no question about what happened when the relationships became known to the leaders of the Institute. The transgressors were instantly disciplined: they were removed from the roster of training analysts, they were divested of their various functions in the ruling structure, they were dismissed from their teaching posts. Their careers in the higher reaches of establishment psychoanalysis were over. They eventually left the city; one of them died a few years ago. The scandal rocked the analytic community, and has become a part of its mythology. Like children watching in fascinated horror as a sibling is caned for something the watchers themselves have done many times in their imagination, analysts talk in hushed tones about the downfall of X and Y, some agreeing with the harsh implacability of the Institute's position, others feeling that justice should have been tempered with mercy.

I said, "The first analyst was punished for something he did *after* the analysis. Isn't that taking things very far?"

Aaron sighed and said, "From patients' second and third analyses we now know things about the 'aftereffects' of analysis which make the line between what is 'in' and what is 'outside' our work a good deal more tenuous than was previously supposed. In the early days of analysis, people were very casual about things that we're very careful and nervous about today. In fact, they did things we would consider crazy today. They didn't know what we know about the transference. They didn't know its dangers. They were like Marie Curie, who didn't know about the dangers of radium, and who got leukemia from handling it casually."

Freud's own well-known case of transference-burn was Dora, who did not kindle his affections so much as trash his therapeutic ambitions by walking out on the analysis after three months. "Her breaking off so unexpectedly, just when my hopes of a successful termination of the treatment were at their highest, and her thus bringing these hopes to nothing—this was an unmistakable act of vengeance on her part," Freud laments at the end of the case history, adding, "No one who, like me, conjures up the most evil of those half-tamed demons that inhabit the human breast, and seeks to wrestle with them, can expect to come through the struggle unscathed." Freud's characteristic propensity for turning crushing defeat to brilliant intellectual advantage is exemplified by the Dora case, for in ruminating about the causes of his failure he came up with his first full-blown formulation of the concept of transference. His brief allusion to transference in *Studies on Hysteria*—in regard to a patient who wanted to kiss him because of a "false connection" she had made between him and a man she had wanted to kiss years before—shows at what a murky and unformed stage his discovery then was. In a postscript to the Dora case history, Freud makes the leap from vague intuition to confident hypothesis, and to some historians of psychoanalysis this is where the chief significance of the paper lies. But there is a curious lacuna in the various accounts Freud gives of his discovery of transference—a strange silence concerning the circumstances under which he made his first rueful public acknowledgment of its powerful presence. In all these accounts Freud conveys the idea that it was the erotic importunities of his women patients that caused him to postulate the presence of a universal phenomenon that would explain the behavior he was convinced he had not provoked. Yet from the evidence of the postscript one would gather that it was, rather, Freud's rage, frustration, and disappointment over Dora's defection that were the fulcrum of his momentous discovery. Chertok and de Saussure's notion of the "prophylactic" function of the concept of transference may apply to the negative example of Dora as well as to the positive one of the importuning woman: it offers protection against the mortification of therapeutic failure just as much as it does against the temptation of sexual involvement. In "forgetting" Dora's role in the discovery of transference, was Freud wreaking a vengeance of his own on the feckless girl who, as he saw it, had given him a servant's fortnight's warning of her intention to quit the analysis?

This is not the only mystery in the Dora case. There is something rum about the whole paper—something unsatisfactory and unsatisfying. You read it with a growing sense of irritation, confusion, disorientation, and ennui, alternating with excitement. Something nags at you as you read, like a forgotten word, and something seems familiar about your impatience and boredom: it is the impatience and boredom produced by other people's dreams. As Freud taught us, what one thinks of as a dream—i.e., what one remembers and reports—is only a façade behind which an intimate truth is hidden. Through what Freud called "the dream-work," the latent "dream-thought" is transformed into the "manifest dream." This "work" is undone by analysis: the dreamer, by allowing his mind to wander freely in connection with various parts of the dream, is inexorably led to the meaning of the dream, to the *wish* at its heart.

If we regard the Dora paper—whose purported intention was to show how dream interpretation is used in analysis, and which revolves around two dreams of Dora's—as if it were itself a dream, and submit it to the special scrutiny that Freud devised for teasing the repressed out of the manifest, much of its mystery (and boredom) dissolves. That Freud all but openly (if unconsciously) invites us to do so—that the paper bristles with covert meanings and well-placed clues to them—seems more and more evident when one tries to crack its code rather than merely to read it. The first intimation that there is more here than meets the eye is Freud's choice of name for his patient. "But we *know* why Freud chose the name Dora," the well-versed reader of Freud will protest. And it's true that in *The Psychopathology of Everyday Life* (1901) Freud uses his choosing of the name Dora to illustrate the concept of psychic determinism—the notion that nothing is accidental. He writes that when he was considering what pseudonym to give the girl, to his surprise only one name out of the hundreds of possible names occurred to him: his associations led him to his sister Rosa's nursemaid, a girl whose name was also Rosa but who had taken the name Dora to avoid confusion with her mistress. Freud reports the "incredulity" with which he greeted this plebeian association, followed by his philosophical acceptance of the classless ways of the mind. But there is reason to think that Freud stopped associating too soon—that if he had followed his first instinct of recoil from the nursemaid, if he had not settled for her but had forged on past her, he would eventually have arrived at the name whose potent allusiveness and compelling symbolism were the cause of its insistent, all-effacing primacy in Freud's mind. Who could Dora be but Pandora? The case rattles with boxes; you practically trip over one wherever you turn. There is a jewelry box in the first dream (which Freud wastes no time in connecting with the female genitals); there are two boxes in the second dream, whose respective disguises (of key and railroad station) Freud quickly penetrates; and there is the above-mentioned reticule, which Dora pokes her finger in and out of.[5] Another veiled allusion to the authoress of all our ills glimmers out of Freud's discussion of the primitive antithesis between fire and water, with which he inaugurates his interpretation of Dora's (as he believed) masturbation-induced enuresis. In a paper written some thirty years later, called "The Acquisition and Control of Fire" (1932), Freud elaborates his notion of the connection between fire and micturition in the primitive mind, and argues that this atavism is present in the Prometheus myth, signalled by the penis-like fennel stalk in which Prometheus carried his stolen gift to mankind. The point (for the present argument) is the connection between Prometheus and Pandora. She was created to punish man for Prometheus' theft. She was formed of clay and water and endowed with great beauty and a bad character ("a shameless mind and deceitful nature," according to Hesiod). Epimetheus, disregarding the warning of his brother Prometheus, took Pandora into his house as his wife, and it was there that she opened the fatal jar, or box, and let out all the evils and plagues that man had previously been free of, shutting the lid only in time to contain delusive hope. (Note the echo of Freud's complaint about the "half-tamed demons" released by the work of analysis.)

Numerous commentators on the Dora case have been unpleasantly struck by the tone that Freud adopted toward his patient—a good-looking, intelligent, but rather pathetic eighteen-year-old, who was brought in by her father to the forty-four-year-old neurologist and paterfamilias, and who confidingly related a sad story of exploitation, molestation, and betrayal by the grownups around her. But instead of giving her the fatherly concern and compassion that she expected—and that today's practitioners of adolescent psychiatry would naturally extend to someone so young and troubled—Freud treated Dora as a deadly adversary. He sparred with her, laid traps for her, pushed her into corners, bombarded her with interpretations, gave no quarter, was as unspeakable, in his way, as any of the people in her sinister family circle, went too far, and finally drove her away. The association of Dora with Pandora helps explain Freud's strange behavior. If Freud's countertransference invested Dora with all the seductiveness and dangerousness of Eve, if he saw her not as the messed-up little Viennese teen-ager she was but as Original Woman, in all her beauty and evil mystery, it is no wonder that he treated her as he did. Freud was no freer of the capacity for overestimation than the rest of us are, and perhaps less so. His idealizing transference to his friend Wilhelm Fliess is regarded as crucial to the discoveries of the nineties. The scales eventually fell from Freud's eyes about Fliess—after he had made use of him in the way that a patient "uses" his analyst through the transference. His discoveries made, Freud dropped their unwitting catalyst as he had dropped Breuer and was to drop Jung. Dora served something of the same purpose. Her power over Freud's imagination spurred him to his feats of ratiocination about her unconscious and, more significantly, created the tense, irritating, subterranean drama that gleams out of the paper.

Freud describes a scene in the middle of the analysis where he comes upon Dora in the waiting room hastily concealing a letter she has been reading. He naturally insists that she tell him what was in the letter. After a great show of reluctance, she finally confesses that the letter is from her grandmother, who has written to urge her to write more frequently. Freud finds this uninteresting and irrelevant, and concludes that "Dora only wanted to play 'secrets' with me, and to hint that she was on the point of allowing her secret to be torn from her by the doctor." If that indeed was what Dora was doing—and another analyst might have been less incurious about the grandmother—she could not have found a more willing and eager playmate. Freud's eagerness to tear secrets from his patient (what is the Pandora myth at bottom but a parable of defloration?) is amusing to read in the light of the laborious protestations of innocence he makes throughout the Dora paper. In its opening pages, he declares:

> In this case history . . . sexual questions will be discussed with all possible frankness, the organs and functions of sexual life will be called by their proper names, and the

pure-minded reader can convince himself from my description that I have not hesitated to converse upon such subjects in such language even with a young woman. [To defend myself] I will simply claim for myself the rights of the gynecologist—or, rather, much more modest ones—and add that it would be the mark of a singular and perverse prurience to suppose that conversations of this kind are a good means of exciting or of gratifying sexual desires.

Later in the case, after dragging a fellatio fantasy out of the girl, Freud assures the reader—who, he feels, must be astonished and horrified by "my daring to talk about such delicate and unpleasant subjects to a young girl"—that "it is possible for a man to talk to girls and women upon sexual matters of every kind without doing them harm and without bringing suspicion upon himself, so long as, in the first place, he adopts a particular way of doing it, and, in the second place, can make them feel convinced that it is unavoidable," and that "the best way of speaking about such things is to be dry and direct." Today's more sophisticated analysts have no compunction about admitting the stimulation they feel when a patient talks about sex; it is regarded as one of the ordinary occupational hazards of the work. In his innocence (and given his time), Freud was probably more stimulated by his conversations with Dora than today's more wary and (given our time) jaded practitioners would be. Indeed, Freud's unconscious personal motives [6] invest the Dora paper with the powerful and irritating hold on the imagination of analysts which it has held since its publication in 1905, as "Fragment of an Analysis of a Case of Hysteria," five years after Dora slammed the door. (Freud kept delaying publication, fretting over something.) Behind its surface lesson of how to do dream analysis lies a more fundamental preoccupation. Behind the (manifest) scientific report on a doctor's search for the causes of a patient's hysterical symptoms lies a (latent) primitive drama of a man's struggle with himself—a struggle that everyone and anyone who does analysis experiences in relation to each and every one of his patients. "Might I perhaps have kept the girl under my treatment if I myself had acted a part, if I had exaggerated the importance to me of her staying on, and had shown a warm personal interest in her—a course which, even after allowing for my position as her physician, would have been tantamount to providing her with a substitute for the affection she longed for?" Freud asks after Dora's defection. He answers his rhetorical question by primly asserting, "I have always avoided acting a part, and have contented myself with practicing the humbler arts of psychology." But in his postscript Freud acknowledges that his slowness to take in and interpret Dora's transference from Herr K.—the friend of the family whose sexual attentions at once frightened and excited her—to himself was the cause of her abrupt leave-taking. But surely Freud's association of himself with Herr K. was not all on Dora's side; he himself wanted to do the things with Dora that Herr K. had tried to do. The part that Freud was anxious at all costs to avoid acting was that of the lecher, the—horror of horrors!—father who seduces his own daughter. The prurient interest that Freud attributes to others was his own. His harshness and coldness to Dora was his way of throwing cold water on his own far from cold feelings toward her. Ernest Jones, in his biography of Freud, marvels at how "quite peculiarly monogamous" Freud was, and writes, "Of few men can it be said that they go through the whole of life without being erotically moved in any serious fashion by any woman beyond the one and only one. Yet this really seems to have been true of Freud." But was it? The man who taught us to look into our hearts to find that we are interested in little else *but* sex was surely not exempt from his own discovery. Jones fails to distinguish between the desire and the deed. One might say that Freud's remarkable monogamy was, on the contrary, a direct consequence of the erotic arousal he experienced in his daily work. As the first analyst, he was the first to have to grapple with the passions that the unique analytic relationship unleashes in *both* participants, and on his days off he was not apt to chase girls. The Pandora's Box that Breuer opened with Anna O. and fled, Freud steadfastly remained to face. In the Dora paper, Freud sets down—with what Leo Stone has called his "inspiring frankness"—the dialectic of fantasy and reality, passion and reason, freedom of feeling and constraint of behavior by which the analytic situation is ruled. Behind the apparent "innocence" of Freud's sexual wishes toward Dora lies a profound and skeptical knowledge of himself and of his motives and of the danger of his creation. He knew he was playing with fire, but he had the Promethean audacity to persist in his dangerous game of therapy. In the Dora paper, Freud illustrates the double vision of the patient which the analyst must maintain in order to do his work: he must invent the patient as well as investigate him; he must invest him with the magic of myth and romance as well as reduce him to the pitiful bits and pieces of science and psychopathology. Only thus can the analyst sustain his obsessive interest in another—the fixation of a lover or a criminal investigator—and keep in sight the benign raison d'être of its relentlessness.

And, finally, he must let the patient go. Dora's abrupt leave-taking was an extreme but standard version of the ending of analysis. All analyses end badly. Each "termination" leaves the participants with the taste of ashes in their mouths; each is absurd; each is a small, pointless death. Psychoanalysis cannot tolerate happy endings; it casts them off the way the body's immunological system casts off transplanted organs. Throughout its history, attempts have been made to change the tragic character of psychoanalysis, and all have failed. In the forties, for a notable instance, the Chicago-based émigré analyst Franz Alexander, following the lead of Sandor Ferenczi, proposed a happy ending for analysis in the form of a "corrective emotional experience," which enjoyed an enormous vogue. What this "experience" came down to was nothing much—some sort of guarded and antiseptic kindliness and reassurance from the analyst, a form of what is called "supportive" therapy today. Instead of reliving the same old sorry Oedipal drama on the couch, the patient would get a new deal, would find things to be not so bad this time around.[7] The hard-line Freudians savagely fought the soft-hearted Alexandrians, and by the late fifties had defeated them. Today, another Chicago analyst, Heinz Kohut, has come up with another revision of psychoanalysis which seeks to blunt its hardness and coldness, and again the profession has been polarized. In the context of this history, the punishment of the two New York Psychoanalytic Institute analysts takes on a larger meaning. It represents a theoretical posture as well as a moralistic one; it concerns the dogma of the psychoanalytical movement as well as the mores of the profession.

I asked Aaron if he could imagine himself doing what the two analysts had done.

"What do you mean 'imagine'?" Aaron said. "I've had such thoughts many times."

"So the temptation is there, but it must be resisted."

"I don't know about resisted. No. Analyzed."

"But you wouldn't do what they did."

"Analyzed," Aaron repeated. "Analysis says nothing about what one ultimately does. Analysis provides one with the greatest possible freedom regarding what one does. There have been many times when I've entertained fantasies of dating and marrying patients and having sexual intercourse with them. These are common countertransference reactions. Yes, I have had these fantasies. Every other analyst has had them, too, and they're not the issue. The issue is whether the analyst is in an emotionally desperate situation that prevents him from analyzing his reactions and causes him to do something dire. These two men—as far as I can understand the rumors and the myths—were men whose marriages were breaking up in middle age. They were men in desperate straits. Analysts who sleep with their patients are usually people in desperate psychological straits. It isn't the attractiveness and seductiveness of the patient; rather, it's that the analyst is in horrible shape in his own life and turns to the patient for help. People who seduce their own children are people in dire emotional circumstances who turn to their children to feel better about themselves—with tragic consequences."

"So when you analyze your feelings about a patient before choosing not to sleep with her, you already know you won't, the way a father knows he won't sleep with his daughter," I said. "Aren't you being disingenuous when you say you just analyze yourself and your fantasies, not knowing where the analysis will lead? Since you already know it won't lead anywhere? Why not just accept that limitation on your behavior? Those two analysts evidently broke the incest taboo."

Aaron nodded a sort of reluctant agreement and said, "'I feel lucky that I've never been in such a situation. There have been beautiful young patients who have fallen in love with me in an erotic transference—one feels the instinctual tug of this kind of thing—but that's par for the course, that's not what the issue is. The issue is that one of those men had been president of the American Psychoanalytic Association and the other was equally important. There are several ways one can look at their act. One can regard it as an instance of human frailty—the act of men in middle age tempted to grab at an opportunity for more joy from life, aware of what the consequences will be if they go against the mores of their tribe but deciding to do it anyway. Seen in these terms, a certain heroic and tragic quality adheres to their choice. But let me give you another scenario, a less sympathetic one but just as probable. Here are two men who are idealized and idolized. Wherever they go in psychoanalytic circles, people say, 'Look, there goes So-and-So.' They are figures of the most enormous renown and prestige; they generate dazzle and glamour. And they figure, as they say in Yiddish, *'Der Reb meg'*—'The Rabbi is allowed.' That's less sympathetic, but it corresponds to their positions. There is certainly the possibility that they were intoxicated by their own renown and by the idolatry directed at them. You can carry it a step further. Take a person who has an underlying sense of guilt, an abiding feeling of moral deficiency, whose guilt is so strong that he has to do something self-destructive —what about his reaction to being idolized, idealized, lionized, worshipped? Carry it one transformation further. What about the surgeon who doesn't wash his hands before doing an operation? What about the surgeon who doesn't sew the patient up properly? That's malpractice. What these men did may be considered malpractice."

"How so?"

Aaron got up and said, "Phyllis Greenacre has written very trenchantly on this subject. I'll read you what she wrote." He took a bound volume from his bookcase and leafed through it until he found his place. "This is from a paper called 'The Role of Transference' that appeared in the *Journal of the American Psychoanalytic Association* in 1954," he said, and read:

> I cannot in the least agree with the remark of a quite eminent analyst, repeated to me several times, that so many analysts overstep the boundaries of the transference— even in grossly sexual ways—that therefore the best thing to do is to say nothing about these incidents. It is only by discussing these possibilities (rather than by punishing the offenders) and by emphasizing their dangers to students and among ourselves that we can really develop our science to the research precision which must be aimed at in each clinical case. . . . The carrying through into a relationship in life of the incestuous fantasy of the patient may be more grave in its subsequent distortion of the patient's life than any actual incestuous seduction in childhood has been. . . . The power of the unconscious is such that it "gets back" at those who work with it and treat it too lightly.

# 7

ARON WAS APPOINTED TO THE MINOR ADMINISTRATIVE office at the Institute for which he had been proposed. He told me of his feeling of anxiety on the day he got a telephone call from the president of the Institute. He had affected not to care, but the thought of being passed over was afflicting, and when the president told him he had been appointed he was enormously relieved. Though he considers the office unimportant, he says he would have felt terrible if he had lost out. "It took on a transferential meaning for me," he said. "The minute I heard the president's voice on the phone, I started to tremble. My heart was beating too fast. I was in a bad state of anxiety. All this for a menial administrative job!"

The problem of unresolved transference in professional analytic societies is freely and frequently discussed in the analytic journals. In my leafings through the journals, I had come across numerous papers on the subject, and been struck by the extraordinary tension and bad feeling that pervade analytic organizations. "Envy, rivalry, power conflicts, the formation of small groups, resulting in discord and intrigues, are a matter of course," the Dutch analyst P. J. van der Leeuw wrote in 1968, adding wistfully, "We expect fulfillment from the relationships between ourselves, and are so often disappointed. I have the impression that there are few true friendships among our members. Only now and then do our interrelationships develop into real friendship." Jacob Arlow bluntly observed in 1972, "The tensions emanating from the division of colleagues into two categories of analysts—training analysts and just plain analysts—intrude themselves into the organizational and scientific life of the institutes." Arlow went on to attribute "the nagging feeling of discontent which pervades many colleagues who are not appointed training analysts" to the shared fantasy of the analytic community that the training analysis is a "prolonged initiation rite" whose natural culmination is admission to the ranks of the elect.

When I expressed some of my surprise to Aaron that analysts, who are supposed to be wiser and more reflective than the rest of us, conduct their organizational life in such a demented manner, he shook his head in vigorous disagreement.

"Analysts aren't wiser and more reflective than other people," he said. "They're no different from other people."

"But they've been analyzed. Doesn't that give a person some edge, a little extra power over his emotions and impulses?"

"Very little," Aaron said. "And such small edge as analysts have they exercise in only one situation in life—namely, the analytic situation. In that most unnatural, highly artificial, stressful situation, the analyst's small advantage of self-knowledge and self-control comes into play. But when you take him out of his consultation room, his advantage recedes and he becomes just like everyone else—he begins to act just like other people."

"This is ironic," I said. "The analyst works with his patients to get them to behave more rationally and reflectively, and remains irrational and unreflective himself."

"But that *isn't* what the analyst works to achieve with his patients. This is a popular myth about analysis—that it makes the patient a clearer thinker, that it makes him wise and good, that people who have been analyzed know more than other people do. Analysis isn't intellectual. It isn't moral. It isn't educational. It's an operation. It rearranges things inside the mind the way surgery rearranges things inside the body—even the way an automobile mechanic rearranges things under the hood of the car. It's that impersonal and that radical. And the changes achieved are very small. We live our lives according to the repetition compulsion, and analysis can go only so far in freeing us from it. Analysis leaves the patient with more freedom of choice than he had before—but how much more? This much: instead of going straight down the meridian, he will go five degrees, ten degrees—maybe fifteen degrees if you push very hard—to the left or to the right, but no more than that. I myself have changed less than some patients I've analyzed. Sometimes I get discouraged about myself. Sometimes I worry about myself. A few weeks ago, I did something that still bothers me and worries me. My wife and I were having dinner with some friends in SoHo. We were lingering at the table, drinking wine and laughing a lot, and the conversation turned to analytic fees. Someone—these friends weren't analysts—started making jokes about them. Now, fees are a subject that I'm very sensitive about, for a number of reasons. First of all, because the whole subject of money is a charged one for me. I frankly want more money than I have, and I'm envious of analysts who are rich, yet I can't bring myself to do what's necessary to increase my income—that is, to beg for referrals. That, at any rate, is how it looks to me—the whole business of younger analysts sidling up to older colleagues at parties and meetings, like mendicants clutching at the robes of the nobility, and saying with apparent nonchalance, 'Oh, I have some free hours.' That's how it's done, and it seems degrading to me, and I can't do it. So I have unfilled hours, and am bitter. But there's something else that makes me sensitive to jokes about analytic fees. I have a patient whose analysis has all but revolved around the paying of the fee. At one point, this apparently simple practical matter took on such acute significance for him that he didn't pay me for eight months. Yes, *eight months!* And I allowed it to happen: he didn't pay, and I continued to see him week after week, month after month, following the thing out strictly analytically. I consider it one of the most heroic things I have ever done as an analyst, and it was tremendously successful. One day, he came in and handed me a check for everything he owed. But lately he's stopped paying me again. We're going through it all once more, and I'm tense and worried about it, so when they started making jokes about fees at the dinner party I wasn't disposed to laugh, and I began very earnestly and seriously to explain to them how very important these things are. But they went on making their jokes—it was a lively party; we had drunk a lot of wine—and finally I committed the grossest social faux pas. I lashed out with the most boorish, pontificating, morally outraged tirade—embarrassing to everyone there, and most of all to me. There I was: an analyst—mature, reflective, well analyzed (more or less)—acting just like a person. Worse." He laughed bitterly.

Aaron's self-flagellating mood continued during our meeting, weaving itself into our conversation whenever an opening offered itself. The subject of treating psychotics came up, and Aaron said he didn't like to work with them. "It bothers me sometimes," he said. "The reason is that I'm not very generous. I'm self-absorbed. I'm interested in my own ideas, my own worries, my own pains, my own pleasures. It's hard for me to give very much. The people who work well with schizophrenics are people whose center of gravity is a bit displaced, who can make another person the center of their lives, who are endowed with an unusual measure of intuitiveness and sensitivity and kindliness. Ferenczi was such a person—his empathy reached the magnitude of genius, and he was a man of great personal kindness. My first analyst was such a person, and Leo Stone is another. These qualities enable them to withstand the strain of working with very sick patients, and—when they are treating neurotics—allow them to dispense with the rigor of analytic technique a little more easily. *They can afford to do it.* Whereas others, like me, who are not so kind, not so sensitive, not so intuitive, require more graphic demonstrations of data in order to be sure about what they're doing and where the patient is. As for schizophrenics, it takes a special kind of person to work with patients who demand so much, and most analysts don't treat them, for all kinds of reasons. My own reasons—of selfishness and self-absorption and incapacity for immersion in another person—are probably the very reasons that drew me to psychoanalysis itself. I was attracted to psychoanalytic work precisely because of the distance it would create between me and the people I treated. It's a situation of very comfortable abstinence. A situation of *not* getting involved with the other person, of *not* taking responsibility for the other person's behavior, but only for one's own. Psychoanalysts talk quite frankly about the defensive comfort of analytic silence, passivity, and neutrality. It fits in with certain profound motives. Psychoanalysts, moreover, are voyeurs: they're at the window watching what's going on in the bedroom, getting very excited, but not jumping into the fray. The defensive and instinctual motives that go into becoming an analyst are innumerable, and not pretty. They're cowardly, they're primitive. As if—I rush to add—all human behavior didn't have these roots. But these motives are certainly at the bottom of the desire to be an analyst. To say 'I've become an analyst because I'm interested in the mind' or 'because I want to help people' is hardly adequate, and no self-respecting analyst would ever settle for that, ever."

And yet apparently the work of analysis, for all its comfortable distance and non-involvement, is oddly unpleasant and agitating. Analysts are plagued by doubt and anxiety. "The gestalt of the profession is guilt," Aaron said. "Guilt over not understanding the patient. Analysts always suspect themselves of not being in control of the plethora of material coming out of the patient. They are being paid and trusted to perform a therapeutic service, and they are in the dark about certain things about the patient. There may be a rattlesnake under that rock, and they don't see it. This kind of thing is devastating, and it's chronic. Everybody worries about it. It's talked about, in an extremely guarded way, whenever analysts get together in small groups. It's in these small groups that the ambiguities and self-doubts come out. You don't hear about them at the meetings of the American Psychoanalytic Association or of the International.

"There are some analysts who, when they talk in public about their patients, talk with the most tremendous confidence and assurance, and draw the most profound admiration and envy. One such is Otto Kernberg. When Kernberg talks about a patient, he talks as if he understood him inside and out, backwards and forwards, with relatively little effort, and he is just dazzling. Dazzling, brilliant, impressive, and"—Aaron paused to bang his fist on the arm of his chair for emphasis—"*unconvincing*. There's the rest of us, crushed under the ton of bricks we call our ambiguity about our patients, which we drag about with us day after day, and there's Kernberg, who gets up on a rostrum and talks about his cases as if they were nose jobs. Once, I heard him talk about his use of countertransference in a case. He told about an image that floated into his mind as the patient was talking. The image derived from a movie he had seen in which a man murders his mistress in a particularly bloody and sadistic manner. Kernberg related that he pushed it out of his mind. Then, two weeks later, something came up in the patient's associations about his hatred of his wife, and Kernberg remembered the image. 'I realized that I should not have pushed it out of my mind,' Kernberg said. 'I should have taken it as factual material, and had I done so I would have saved the patient ten sessions of work.' I sat there and thought, Christ, how many sessions have gone by when *I* haven't caught something—ten, twenty, fifty, a hundred? And here's Kernberg worrying about ten sessions that he could have saved the patient. He had screwed up, and ten sessions had been wasted. And I was so envious that Kernberg could feel accountable for missing something and costing the patient ten hours, while I dragged my ass for God knows how long before I finally understood something about a patient. I recently thought back to Kernberg's speech —I heard it five years ago—and I thought what foolishness to think that making an interpretation ten sessions earlier would be the equivalent of making it ten sessions later. As if nothing else had taken place, and the delay hadn't had its own reason and logic, and the patient wouldn't be readier to hear it and the analyst readier to make it. If you try to understand the patient in the overwhelming fullness of his individuality and idiosyncrasy, you will not have the easy time of it that Kernberg has had with his schematic methods.

You will feel discouraged, guilt-ridden, depressed, lost, confused, and deluged by the quantity of data and by its ambiguity and complexity. You will suffer back pain, indigestion, headache, fatigue—all the afflictions the flesh is heir to —because of the guilt you constantly feel about not understanding the data. And this isn't even to speak of the other kind of guilt that analysts feel over the pain and frustration they regularly inflict on the people they analyze. Analysts keep having to pick away at the scab that the patient tries to form between himself and the analyst to cover over his wound. That's what the patient keeps trying to do—it's what's called resistance—and what the analyst won't let him do. The analyst keeps picking away at the scab. He keeps the surface raw, so that the wound will heal properly."

"It's unhealthy work you do," I said.

"You mean like dealing with bacteria in a bacteriological laboratory?"

"If you like. You get infected yourself."

Aaron nodded. "You get infected yourself. Nobody talks about that except in the realm of jokes. You detoxify it by making jokes about it. That's the defensive aspect of joke-telling. People tell jokes, you know, about how crazy psychoanalysts are—they've had analysis themselves, right? Or: Analyst says to another analyst, 'How are you?' and the other analyst says, 'I wonder what he meant by that.' That kind of joke about the psychopathology of analysts has hidden in it a profound statement—namely, that it's work that drives people crazy. Yes, it's unhealthy work."

# 8

A T OUR NEXT MEETING, I CONFESSED TO AARON THAT I sometimes got tired of hearing him talk—that I rather resented always listening to him and never talking about myself.

"There it is," Aaron said, with an ironic gesture of his hand.

"Is that how you feel with your patients?" I asked.

"*And how!* In one of the nicest things that Kohut's done, he writes about wanting to shout at the patient who ignores him and treats him as if he were a mere sounding board, 'But what about *me?* Aren't you interested in *me?*' He goes on to counsel analysts working with such a patient not only to accept their feelings of anger and frustration but to accept the patient's self-involvement as well—to understand that the patient has the right to be more interested in himself than in the analyst. Kohut's legitimizing of *all* of the patient's behavior was an important contribution. Analysts have to tolerate all kinds of unpleasant feelings. I'm glad you're experiencing something of what we go through. The uncomfortable emotions that the patient evokes in the analyst should not only be borne but be examined for what they may reveal about the *patient*.

"I had a patient once who made me horribly sleepy. I couldn't understand it at first. She was by no means a boring person. She associated well, and she was someone I liked and respected—a very fine, a truly *good* person. So it just didn't seem possible that this almost suffocating sleepiness could be a reaction to her personally. I thought it must be the time of day I saw her—but that couldn't be, because she had different hours on different days. I thought it might be the result of staying up too late, so I drank black coffee. But the sleepiness persisted, and finally it dawned on me what it was all about. I realized that the patient had developed an erotic transference to me and was defending herself against it by making herself uninteresting and dreary—as she had done throughout her childhood with her father, and as she was doing in adult life with the men with whom (for some strange reason) she could never get into any sort of satisfying lasting relationship."

"But the sleepiness was *your* symptom," I said. "She didn't really *make* you sleepy."

"But she did. That's the beauty of it. That's where countertransference can be of such enormous clinical usefulness. It's not a simple business. You have to carefully pick apart the various strands. You have to distinguish between what your reactions to the patient are telling you about his psychology and what they are merely expressing about your own. In this case, it was necessary for me to distinguish between the usual queasiness I feel when a woman patient develops an erotic transference to me and the peculiar boredom that her behavior toward me elicited. The feeling of queasiness has to do with my anxiety about seduction: here's this person in my charge who trusts me and has developed intense childlike feelings toward me— called the transference—and here I am stimulated, and also scared, because you don't *do* that sort of thing. The sleepiness was something else. It really had nothing to do with me personally. It was evoked in me, as it had been evoked in her father and then in the men in her adult life. I was simply reacting to her as they had reacted to her and as anyone would react to her.

"It was unconscious, of course, and extremely subtle. Her free association seemed to be full of the richest and deepest analytic material. Actually, it was empty. It was shallow and hollow, and I was bored because of what was missing—namely, the sap, the juice, the eroticism that is in everything and that makes for life and interest, that keeps us awake and alive."

"What did you do about it?"

"Whenever I had a chance, whenever it appeared in the analytic material, I would point out to her that she was trying to get away from sexual interaction with me. For instance, when she came into the room she wouldn't look at me. She would sort of sidle past me and scrunch down on the couch with her head turned toward the wall. I pointed this out to her. Once, I happened to come into the building as she was coming in, and we rode up in the elevator together. I could see that it was agonizing for her to be so close to me. She went into a kind of panic over the incident. Well, I brought it out into the open and referred to it whenever an opportunity presented itself. I was now attuned to her defensive maneuver and watched for it. And slowly the whole issue of her sexuality and her relationships with men and her attitude toward her father began to emerge. She began to *remember* rather than *act out* her vengeful coldness and sexlessness toward her father. And I, of course, stopped being sleepy."

The conversation turned back to Kohut. Aaron elaborated on his divided view of the celebrated Chicago analyst —as an important contributor to analytic technique and as a misguided theoretician. "There used to be certain patients whom many, if not most, analysts found difficult, if not impossible, to treat, now known as patients with narcissistic pathology," he said. "These people had always been around —they had different labels—and analysts were always uncomfortable with them. Some of them would idealize the analyst to such a preposterous degree that the analyst felt obliged to remonstrate, to say, 'Look, I'm not that way. I'm not what you think I am. I'm just an ordinary human being.' Others would treat the analyst like dirt, would refuse to recognize him as a person, would simply use him as someone who was there only to listen. These patients would reduce the analyst to saying furiously, 'Look, you're ignoring someone who is *here*. Why are you ignoring me?' Then Kohut came along and said, in effect, 'Don't treat these transferences differently from any others. Don't disabuse the patient who idealizes you. Don't reprove the person who ignores you. Let these transferences develop. Don't cut them short through premature interpretation. You will be better able to tolerate your anger and frustration at being treated as a non-person and your discomfort at being idealized if you understand that these are manifestations of the patient's pathology rather than attempts to subvert the analytic process.' This was a good thing to say. It needed to be said.

"Unfortunately, Kohut didn't stop there. From applying general psychoanalytic principles to narcissistic transferences he went on to inventing a whole 'psychology of the self,' as he calls it. In trying to account for what had happened to narcissistic patients to make them so, he generalized about what happens in everyone's development, and what he has come up with is, to my mind, very dubious. It revises psychoanalytic theory where no revision is warranted, and it introduces assumptions that simply clutter up basic theory. The more postulates you make, the less their explanatory power becomes.

"Last year, Kohut published a paper in the *International Journal* that caused quite a stir. It's called 'The Two Analyses of Mr. Z.,' the first of which Kohut had done before he made his discoveries—before he became a Kohutian—and the other afterward. I read it with utter amazement. The first analysis, which he calls a 'classical analysis,' just didn't make sense. In the second, 'Kohutian' analysis, he finally did what any one of us 'classical' analysts would have done in the first place. His description of the first analysis reads like a caricature of analysis, while the second analysis is made to seem rich and profound, subtle and empathic, humanistic and humane. But the Kohutians rapturously hold up the paper as certification of the Second Coming. You ought to see the coterie that has formed around him. They think that his is the true psychoanalysis—that he has introduced something radical and revolutionary, and that psychoanalysis is going to have to assimilate it. It's what the people around Adler and Jung were saying in the twenties, and what those around Franz Alexander were saying in the forties. Psychoanalysis has waves of this kind of thing, and it serenely lets them wash over itself, because eventually they all subside. Who talks about Franz Alexander today—except those who want to put down his 'corrective emotional experience,' or to deny, as the Kohutians are at constant pains to do, that they are offering more of the same? The people I respect—yes, people like

Arlow and Brenner—just don't write and talk the mawkish way Kohut and his disciples do. The Kohutians are desperately trying to not pull away from psychoanalysis. They try to tone things down. They try to be as unprovocative as possible when they write in the journals and speak at scientific meetings. But underneath you sense the revolutionary fervor, the belief in the New Messiah."

"Have you ever seen Kohut?"

"I've heard him talk twice, but his public appearances are rare. Like a good messiah, he keeps himself further and further away, sequestered from the masses. When he's invited to speak, he sends his emissaries, his true disciples. I hate it all, I'm contemptuous of his 'self psychology,' and yet I respect Kohut's contribution to technique. Whenever I read his clinical discussions, my therapeutic technique improves. It's true. His descriptions of narcissistic transference phenomena help me to recognize them when they appear and to deal with them more evenhandedly than I might do otherwise. He reminds me of my obligation to the patient, which is to think analytically about everything he says and does."

"So what do you have against him?"

"The same thing I have against all the revisionists of psychoanalytic theory. It always comes down to the same issue —the issue of the drives. At the last fall meeting of the American Psychoanalytic, in the Waldorf, Kohut made a brief, charismatic appearance. His disciple Paul Ornstein, from Cincinnati, had given a speech spelling out the Kohutian line and holding up 'The Two Analyses of Mr. Z.' as if it were the miracle of the loaves and fishes. Then Kohut himself appeared, like God or Lenin come down from heaven. The ballroom was filled to the rafters with the faithful and the curious. People were literally dangling from balconies and wedged together in doorways and on staircases. So finally this slight, white-haired man, dressed in a nondescript gray suit, appeared and talked for forty minutes. He didn't say much, but he betrayed it all in one sentence. *'What if man is simply not an animal?'* he asked rhetorically at the end of his homily. Meaning 'Let's forget the drives. Let's forget that sex is the source of all human motivation. Let's forget that we're nasty, beastly, aggressive, infantile. Let's forget that we're determined. Let's forget that we're *driven* organisms.' Freud's hypothesis of the drives has never been acceptable to the public, or palatable even to many within psychoanalysis itself. There has been a persistent attempt to whittle away at the radicalism of psychoanalytic theory—to make it less harsh and less damaging to man's traditional sentimental idea of his nature. That's why I like Brenner so much. Brenner is willing to draw radical inferences, to take things to their extreme, to go all the way. I believe that Brenner's view will prevail, because, for all its apparent harshness and reductionism, it contains a more profound and complex and interesting statement about human nature than any of the revisionist views do. To say 'Man is not an animal' is to say nothing that banal people haven't always said. To say that our essential humanity resides in precisely that part of our nature which is most instinctual, primitive, and infantile—*animal*—is to say something radical."

# 9

AT OUR NEXT MEETING, AARON AND I GOT INTO A DIScussion of "analyzability," a technical term coined to express the idea of some innate capacity (or incapacity) for being analyzed, which would account for the fact that some people swim when thrown into the choppy waters of analysis, while others have to be dragged, coughing and spitting, to shore. If one could detect and head off the "unanalyzables" before they went into analysis, much futile effort, wasted money, bitter disappointment, and even tragedy could be averted. But to date no Geiger counter of analyzability has been devised, and, as Joan Erle and Daniel A. Goldberg wrote in 1979, in a paper called "Problems in the Assessment of Analyzability," "what seemed relatively straightforward at first became increasingly complicated."

The complications began with the "widening scope" of which Leo Stone wrote in 1954, which admitted to psychoanalytic treatment patients who were much sicker than the ones Freud had originally treated, and which ushered in modifications of analytic technique that the needs of these patients seemed to demand. This new situation raised questions that are still being debated: What should the nature of the modifications be? How far can you modify analytic technique and still call what you are doing analysis? *Is* analysis (modified or plain) always the best treatment for everyone? On the third issue, the English analyst Adam Limentani wrote in 1972:

In psychoanalytic circles, there is a tendency to ignore the fact that in certain appropriate cases mental suffering can be alleviated and psychotherapy facilitated by a large variety of means, not always available twenty, or possibly ten, years ago. Even if we paid no attention to the competition coming from esoteric cults and from other approaches, such as touch therapy, hypnosis, sensitivity training, existentialism, etc., it is the duty of the modern psychoanalytic consultant to make positive recommendations for individual psychotherapy, for group or community therapy, and for active resocialization when indicated, rather than thinking of such therapeutic interventions as *faute de mieux,* i.e., once psychoanalysis has been ruled out.

The attitude that Limentani deplores was subtly implicit in the "Widening Scope" paper, where Stone advocated spreading the wealth of psychoanalysis beyond the safe-bet hysterics and obsessionals to the dicey psychotics and "borderlines" (as patients have come to be called who are more severely afflicted than ordinary neurotics but are not mad. The designation remains controversial). "From my point of view," Stone wrote, "psychoanalysis remains as yet the most powerful of all psychotherapeutic instruments, the 'fire and iron,' as Freud called it." While granting that "the difficulties increase and the expectations of success diminish in a general way" as the outer reaches of psychological disorder are approached, Stone insisted that "there is no absolute barrier" and that "the 'borderline' patient under certain special conditions may be a better patient in the long run, for all of the intrinsic difficulties, than the hysteric." In fact, Stone went on to say, "It is basically a greater error to use psychoanalysis for trivial or incipient or reactive illnesses, or in persons with feeble personality resources, than for serious chronic illnesses when these occur in persons of current or potential strength."

What Stone was suggesting—that the complexity and unpredictability and mystery of the human personality may reduce such categories as "borderline" and "schizophrenic" and "hysteric" to near-meaninglessness—was corroborated by the results of a ten-year study of "analyzability" published by Erle in 1979. The study was of forty patients selected by the Treatment Center between 1967 and 1969 and analyzed by candidates under supervision. (The cases were "easy" neurotic disorders, suitable for novice work; Aaron's first case was among them.) In the opinion of the judging committee, only forty-two percent of the patients were thought to have been in any way "involved in a psychoanalytic process," although sixty percent were deemed to have received therapeutic benefit. This on-the-face-of-it peculiar distinction (if the patient has benefitted from his analysis, why split hairs about whether he is "analyzable"?) has pervaded psychoanalytic thought since its earliest days. That the analyst is out for bigger game than simply making the patient feel good is one of psychoanalysis's oldest and most firmly held beliefs. And that the analyst may unwittingly be treading on his own toes—may be subverting the analysis by making the patient feel too good—is a danger that continues to enliven the pages of the analytic journals. Here is a recent (1972) example of this concern, from a paper on transference by Brian Bird:

> One of the most serious problems of analysis is the very substantial help which the patient receives directly from the analyst and the analytic situation. For many a patient,

the analyst in the analytic situation is in fact the most stable, reasonable, wise, and understanding person he has ever met, and the setting in which they meet may actually be the most honest, open, direct, and regular relationship he has ever experienced. . . . Taken altogether, the total *real* value to the patient of the analytic situation can easily be immense. The trouble with this kind of help is that if it goes on and on, it may have such a real, direct, and continuing impact upon the patient that he can never get deeply enough involved in transference situations to allow him to resolve, or even to become acquainted with, his most crippling internal difficulties. The trouble, in a sense, is that the direct nonanalytical helpfulness of the analytic situation is far too good! The trouble also is that we as analysts apparently cannot resist the seductiveness of being directly helpful.

In 1918, Freud was already worrying about the helpfulness that Bird describes. In a paper called "Lines of Advance in Psycho-Analytic Therapy," he sternly wrote that "any analyst who out of the fullness of his heart, perhaps, and his readiness to help, extends to the patient all that one human being may hope to receive from another commits the same economic error as that of which our non-analytic institutions for nervous patients are guilty." He went on:

Their one aim is to make everything as pleasant as possible for the patient, so that he may feel well there and be glad to take refuge there again from the trials of life. In so doing, they make no attempt to give him more strength for facing life and more capacity for carrying out his actual tasks in it. In analytic treatment, all such spoiling must be avoided. As far as his relations with the physician are concerned, the patient must be left with unfulfilled wishes in abundance. It is expedient to deny him precisely those satisfactions which he desires most intensely and expresses most importunately.

Twenty years later, in "Analysis Terminable and Interminable," Freud cites a case of "spoiling" of his own, which impelled him to take a historic step. The patient was the famous "Wolf Man," about whom Freud had written at length in a paper called "From the History of an Infantile Neurosis" (1918)—a rich young Russian who, as Freud described him, "had come to Vienna in a state of complete helplessness, accompanied by a private doctor and an attendant." Freud continued:

> In the course of a few years it was possible to give him back a large amount of his independence, to awaken his interest in life and to adjust his relations to the people most important to him. But there progress came to a stop. We advanced no further in clearing up the neurosis of his childhood, on which his later illness was based, and it was obvious that the patient found his present position highly comfortable and had no wish to take any step forward which would bring him nearer to the end of his treatment. It was a case of the treatment inhibiting itself: it was in danger of failing as a result of its—partial—success.

Freud gave the Wolf Man an ultimatum. He told him that he would treat him for exactly one year more, and no longer. "At first he did not believe me," Freud writes, "but once he was convinced that I was in deadly earnest, the desired change set in. His resistances shrank up, and in these last months of his treatment he was able to reproduce all the memories and to discover all the connections which seemed necessary for understanding his early neurosis and mastering his present one."

Freud's deviation from analytic passivity into active intervention has been codified and incorporated into analytic practice under the term "parameter"—a usage first employed by Kurt Eissler in a paper of 1953, in which, invoking the example of Freud, he cautiously advocated the use of commands, directives, and advice in certain special situations to avoid stalemate. Parameters being by nature minor, almost negligible, deviations from analytic neutrality, they have never aroused much controversy, or even much interest, in the psychoanalytic community; they are like a baseball player's darting off base and scurrying back before the throw. It is another matter with the more far-reaching modifications advocated first by Ferenczi, then by Alexander, then by the British object-relations school, and now by the various American object-relations theorists. These modifications derive from complex and disparate theories about what patients suffer from, how they became ill, and what should be done to help them, and they continue to polarize the profession. But implicit in even the most avant-garde position is a belief in a basic experience called psychoanalysis—a belief in its unique efficacy with mental suffering and in the (homeopathic) idea of curing suffering with suffering. To do its profound and searing work on the soul, analysis must be an ordeal. ("Cruel though it may sound, we must see to it that the patient's suffering, to a degree that is in some way or other effective, does not come to an end prematurely," Freud wrote in "Lines of Advance in Psychoanalytic Therapy.") And at the heart of the ordeal (of classical analysis, that is; the romantic new versions offer other forms of pain) is the "transference neurosis," described by Freud as an artificial illness that the analysis itself brings into being. It takes the form of the patient's obsessive interest in the person of the analyst. As Hans Loewald wrote in 1971, it is "the patient's love life—the source and crux of his psychic development—as relived in relation to a potentially new love object." He continued:

> It cannot be too unusual for patients—I certainly remember it from the time I was a patient on the couch—to experience, at least at times, being in analysis as an illness, insofar as it is a regressive and unsettling experience, not dissimilar to the passions and conflicts stirred up anew in the state of being in love which, from the point of view of the ordinary order and emotional tenor and discipline of life, feels like an illness, with all its deliciousness and pain.

In the final volume of Proust's *Remembrance of Things Past,* the Narrator, sitting in a little library waiting to go in to a recital, is flooded with illumination after illumination about love, art, memory, and time. All the pieces of the puzzle of his experience suddenly come together for him, and he emerges from his reverie ready to undertake the task of writing the magical book that the reader holds in his hand and will soon have to part from. Proust's conviction about the awesome impersonality of love—of its perverse independence of its objects—is the very conviction that the analysand gains on achieving what Loewald calls "the higher psychic organization," which permits him to relegate his love and hatred of the analyst to the rubbish heap of all his past loves and hatreds, and (should he care to pursue the painful matter further) "place" it in the long-gone but never dead days of his parents' well-meaning, disastrous early dealings with him and with each other. Another resemblance between the Proustian and the Freudian views (aside from the shared belief in the power of the unconscious) is reflected in the very circumstance of the Narrator's culminating epiphany. The scene Proust describes has its psychoanalytic counterpart in the phenomenon of the "good analytic hour," described by Ernst Kris in a celebrated paper of 1956, entitled "On Some Vicissitudes of Insight in Psychoanalysis." This hour, which comes only rarely, if at all, in the course of an analysis, "seems as if prepared in advance. . . . All seems to click, and material comes flowing . . . as if prepared outside of awareness." Writing of one such session, Kris recalls, significantly, that "the mood of the patient, the atmosphere in the room was heavy. . . . A mood of skepticism, and even defeatism, mirrored the reluctance originally attached to the scene, of which the good analytic hour was a belated reflection." So, too, did Proust's Narrator have to pass through the Slough of Despond before finding his way to the kingdom of art. Just before his radiant revelation in the library, he had come to the despairing realization that he would have to renounce his lifelong ambition of becoming a writer—that he had nothing to say!

Aaron told me about some of his own past wrestlings with the conundrum of analyzability. He spoke of an early analytic patient with whom he had fumblingly struggled and failed. "She was one of the few patients I've ever had whom I really didn't like. I felt that nothing she did—as a wife, as a parent, as a friend, even as a patient—had any redeeming virtue or value. Her parents had treated her overtly well but fundamentally shabbily, and she grew up to be a shabby person: cruel, exploitative, destructive, cold, false. There was nothing in her upbringing that would have helped her become a decent person. She couldn't trust anyone, and she had false relations with everyone—even with me, her analyst. I hated that patient and condemned her. I would sit there appalled and outraged by what she told me. I remember discussing her case with a group of colleagues with whom I met for mutual supervision, and how appalled and outraged *they* were. 'Look,' they'd say when I told them about one of her gratuitous acts of cruelty to her children. 'Look, you've got to say something to her. You can't let her go on being cruel to innocent children.' But I didn't listen to them. I said nothing to her. I was trying to do analysis."

"And she wasn't analyzable?"

"She wasn't analyzable. For no other reason than that she was so false. I never engaged with that, I never challenged that, and I should have, though she might not have remained in treatment as long as she did. *Or* I should have done what my colleagues urged me to do: given her advice, complimented her on some things, bawled her out a little about others, supported and nurtured her. I find myself doing more and more of that now with my psychotherapy patients. But that's hardly analysis—and in those early days I very much wanted to do analysis."

"So you imposed it on people for whom it wasn't the right treatment?"

"Yes. In my defense—I guess I do feel somewhat defensive about this—let me say that there was a theoretic rationale for trying to do analysis with people who were quite sick. There's a whole literature on the subject of the limits of applicability, and I was following out the position that says interpretive techniques can be extended to borderline and narcissistic disorders, and even used on psychotics. This is the position Arlow and Brenner take in their book on ego psychology, and I know of a number of analysts who have been able to do successful analytic work with very sick patients. But it didn't work out at all well for me. I pursued that experiment of doing analysis with borderlines and severe narcissistic characters for about five years, and they were rather terrible years. I used to dread going to the office, and I was tense and bored for much of the day. Then, as time went on and these patients sort of fell away, other patients came along who were better integrated and more suitable for analysis, and now the work is no longer so gruelling and upsetting. Working with very disturbed patients is painful. Of course, one becomes a psychiatrist by first working with very, very sick patients and only gradually moving on to less sick ones. Then, when one does analysis with a healthy patient, it's easy, like cutting butter."

"So analysis is for the healthy?"

"It works better for the healthy. But I haven't seen anything in general medicine where that wasn't the case. The healthier the patient, the better the treatment."

We talked about what patients suffer from. Many analysts believe that today's analytic patient is a different animal from the one Freud saw and devised psychoanalysis for. In a paper called "Current Psychoanalytic Object Relations Theory and Its Clinical Implications," published in 1975, Leonard Friedman writes, "The uncomplicated good hysterics, or even the exclusively obsessive-compulsive patients for whom our classical analytic technique was developed, are for many analysts now a memory—for many more, they are cases they have only read about." Aaron is suspicious of this view, feeling it to be shaped by ideological bias; its proponents, he says, seek to justify changes in classical theory and technique by saying that the patient has changed. His own experience tells him otherwise. "That first patient of mine was a classic hysteric," he said. "The case could have been done in 1900. Or 1100."

# IO

IN LIMITING HIS ANALYTIC CASELOAD TO "HEALTHY" NEU-rotic patients, Aaron Green is following a tradition that goes back to Freud. Robert Waelder, in his book *Basic Theory of Psychoanalysis* (1960), magisterially states the closed-shop view of psychoanalysis:

> One does not see how psychoanalysis, by making the un-conscious conscious, could teach such individuals [psy-chotics] to feel what they had never felt and never had come near to feeling.
>
> The restriction of psychoanalytic therapy to psycho-neuroses and related conditions was expressed by Freud many years ago in these words: "The field in which analytical therapy can be applied is that of the trans-ference-neuroses, phobias, hysterias, obsessional neuroses, and, besides these, such abnormalities of character as have been developed instead of these diseases. Everything other than these, such as narcissistic and psychotic condi-tions, is more or less unsuitable." If our present examina-tion of the conditions, a quarter of a century later, did not lead to a different answer, it is due to the fact that these limits of psychoanalysis are not the consequence of in-adequate knowledge and likely to be expanded when knowledge expands, but that the very nature of the psy-

choanalytic process makes it the key that fits the neuroses but does not fit other disorders.

But as far back as the nineteen-twenties, this limiting view of psychoanalysis was being challenged by Freud's colleague, ex-patient, and good friend Sandor Ferenczi, who simply refused to give up when the key didn't fit and, if necessary, kicked down the door. "I have had a kind of fanatical belief in the efficacy of depth-psychology, and this has led me to attribute occasional failures not so much to the patient's 'incurability' as to our own lack of skill—a supposition which necessarily led me to try altering the usual technique in severe cases with which it had proved unable to cope successfully," Ferenczi wrote in 1931, in a paper called "Child Analysis in the Analysis of Adults." He went on:

> It is thus only with the utmost reluctance that I ever bring myself to give up even the most obstinate case, and I have come to be a specialist in peculiarly difficult cases, with which I go on for very many years. I have refused to accept such verdicts as that a patient's resistance was unconquerable, or that his narcissism prevented our penetrating any further, or the sheer fatalistic acquiescence in the so-called "drying-up" of a case. I have told myself that as long as a patient continues to come at all, the last thread of hope has not snapped.

Ferenczi distinguished (though not as sharply as later writers were to do) between the cases that founder because the analyst has fallen into one of the traps—of hypocrisy, cruelty, insincerity, insensitivity—that perpetually lie in wait for the unwary practitioner of analysis, and those that fail because the patient is suffering from some malady too deep and intractable to respond to ordinary analytic therapy. Such cases, Ferenczi felt, demand modifications of analysis in the direction of a softening and a lessening of its frustrations and deprivations. In "The Unwelcome Child and His Death Instinct" (1929), Ferenczi writes of cases of "diminished desire for life," which he recommends be handled in a manner "not unlike the 'pre-treatment' which Anna Freud considers necessary in the case of real children." He adds, "Through this indulgence the patient is permitted—properly speaking, for the first time—to enjoy the irresponsibility of childhood, which is equivalent to the introduction of *positive* life impulses and motives for his subsequent existence. Only later can one proceed cautiously to those demands for privation which characterize our analyses generally." In "The Principle of Relaxation and Neocatharsis" (1929), Ferenczi writes of patients who have "actually remained almost entirely at the child level, and for [whom] the usual methods of analytical therapy are not enough." He adds, "What such neurotics need is really to be adopted and to partake for the first time in their lives of the advantages of a normal nursery." In his last years, Ferenczi experimented with giving this sort of nursery care—what D. W. Winnicott in the fifties came to call "management of regression"—to certain of his very sick patients. Ferenczi's countryman and follower Michael Balint, in his book *The Basic Fault* (1968), recalls one such "grand experiment" of Ferenczi's in which "the patient got as much time from him as she asked for—several sessions per day and, if necessary, also during the night." Balint reports further, "As breaks were considered undesirable, she was seen during the weekends and was allowed to accompany her analyst on his holidays. These details are only a modest sample of what really happened. The experiment went on for some years. The results were still inconclusive when Ferenczi, owing to his illness, had to give up analytical work, only a few weeks before he died."

Freud took an increasingly dim view of his friend's therapeutic zeal, and in his affectionate, if restrained, obituary tribute of 1933, he shook his head sorrowingly over poor Ferenczi's strayings from the fold of regular analysis: "Our friend slowly drifted away from us. . . . We learned that one single problem had monopolized his interest. The need to cure and to help had become paramount in him. He had probably set himself aims which, with our therapeutic means, are altogether out of reach today. From unexhausted springs of emotion the conviction was borne in upon him that one could effect far more with one's patients if one gave them enough of the love which they had longed for as children. He wanted to discover how this could be carried out within the framework of the psychoanalytic situation; and so long as he had not succeeded in this, he kept apart, no longer certain, perhaps, of agreement with his friends."

Just as Ferenczi's insights into analytic hypocrisy, insincerity, and so on had a profound impact on the future conduct of analytic therapy (it led to such concepts as "the therapeutic alliance" and the "non-transference relationship," and to Stone's culminating work on the subject), so did his intuitions about the "childishness" of deeply disturbed patients have momentous implications for psychoanalytic theory. In Ferenczi's fervid and restless and inchoate attempt to help people over whom other analysts had thrown up their hands in despair lie the seeds of all the modern psychoanalytic theories of "schizoid," "narcissistic," and "borderline" disorders. These theories have different terminologies, intellectual styles, and atmospheres (and are tinged, to varying degrees, with the "Kleinian heresy," as Aaron Green calls it), but each is organized around a central and rather simple conceptualization: serious mental disorder is the soul's response to a wound in infancy. Winnicott conceives of a "false self" that an infant develops in despairing defense against the trauma of inadequate maternal care; the analytic task is to give the "true self," which can feel and is cowering behind the "false self," which cannot, the strength to emerge. In an atmosphere of safety and reliability—the "holding environment," of the Winnicottan analysis—the "false self" finally "hands over to the analyst" and the "true self" emerges, like a butterfly liberated from its chrysalis. In Balint's conceptualization, there are two psychic levels on which analytic work may be done: on the verbal level of the Oedipal period and on the preverbal level of the period of the "basic fault." The regular neurotic, whose pathology derives from the Oedipal period, will accept the analyst's interpretations as interpretations and understand their meaning, since he is reliving the events of a time when he could speak and understand; while the patient whose pathology derives from the period of the basic fault doesn't understand what the analyst is saying, since he is reëxperiencing an earlier primitive, non-verbal time. Therapeutic failure is attributed by Balint to the analyst's inability to "click in" to the mute needs of the patient who has descended to the level of the basic fault and to whom interpretations make no sense. He further distinguishes between two types of regression: a nasty "malignant" regression that the Oedipal-level neurotic is prone to, which seeks "gratification of instinctual cravings" in ever-spiralling demands and which the analyst properly gives short shrift to; and the "benign" regression of the basic-fault patient, which is humbly satisfied by the smallest crumbs of responsiveness from the analyst—who does well to heed its plaintive primordial call. Kohut offers essentially the same program in his breathtakingly unreadable *The Analysis of the Self* (1971) and *The Restoration of the Self* (1977). He attributes the narcissistic disorders in which he specializes to a "primary defect in the self," created in infancy by an "unempathic" mother (who in nine cases out of ten is also "shallow," "unpredictable," "bizarre," or a "latent psychotic"). The unenviable offspring of such mothers never experience the "empathic merger with the self-object's mature psychic organization," which would permit them to endure the "optimum (non-traumatic, phase-appropriate) failures of the self-object [that] lead, under normal circumstances, to structure building via transmuting internalization." Like Winnicott's "false-self" patients, these patients develop a shoddy armor (of a "defensive" or "compensatory" character) around their maimed inner core. During analysis, the rage and despair of the "archaic self" are reactivated and, if responded to with proper "empathic resonance" by the analyst, are defused of their terror: infant sorrow becomes adult "joyful self-realization." For Kohut, as for Winnicott and Balint, the Oedipus complex is an irrelevance in the treatment of severe pathology. Where the orthodox Freudian sees sex everywhere, the Kohutian sees unempathic mothers everywhere—even in sex. In *The Restoration of the Self*, Kohut, with quiet pride, cites a momentous interpretation that he gave a woman patient who had come to him after she had been analyzed by an orthodox sex-ridden Freudian analyst: "I added that I thought that her dream of urinating standing up and her wish to see the father's penis were not primarily related to sexual matters, but to her need—familiar from other memories that had emerged in preceding sessions—to extricate herself from her relation with her bizarre and emotionally shallow mother and to turn toward her emotionally more responsive and down-to-earth father." From another direction—that of observation of infants—comes Margaret Mahler's theory of a "separation-individuation process" through whose phases and subphases every infant passes as it negotiates "psychological birth" from a state of symbiosis. Mahler's findings ("findings," to some people) are being applied to adult analysis; serious disturbances of adult life are being traced to disturbances in the "differentiation" or "practicing" or "rapprochement" subphases of infant development.

The members of each of these new schools have developed a kind of horror of orthodox analysis. Kohut's "The Two Analyses of Mr. Z." is but one exhibit in a whole museum of before-and-after analyses, in which the victim of a "rigid" classical analyst's benighted rote methods is saved by a new-school analyst's enlightened exercise of his new theoretical and technical understanding. (The museum extends outward from the world of psychoanalytic discourse to the world of everyday jargon: people speak of going from "cold," "unresponsive," "uncaring" analysts to "warm," "nurturing," "supportive" ones.) Another recent contributor to the before-and-after genre is the Mahlerian analyst Selma Kramer, who pointedly contrasts (in a paper entitled "The Technical Significance and Application of Mahler's Separation-Individuation Theory") two analysts whom she happened to have supervised on the same case. The first analyst —the orthodox heavy—was "unreceptive to a theory of early development, was opposed to my suggestion that one must take cognizance of pre-Oedipal influences, was uncomfortable with any disclosure of countertransference, and was unable to learn from me in supervision"—and so, naturally, "could not engage the patient in analysis." The patient quit and presently found her way to the second analyst, "a much more intuitive young man, more comfortable with his countertransference, able to tolerate and to understand his patient's immature and regressive needs"—and, of course, "able to use separation-individuation theory as a framework for the analysis of the patient's pre-Oedipal conflicts." Winnicott in his late writings castigates himself in no uncertain terms for the harm he feels he did to his patients before he got things straight. "It appalls me to think how much deep change I have prevented or delayed in patients in a certain classification category by my personal need to interpret," he writes in his book *Playing and Reality* (1971), which is dedicated "to my patients who have paid to teach me." He adds, "If only we can wait, the patient arrives at understanding creatively and with immense joy, and I now enjoy this joy more than I used to enjoy the sense of having been clever."

WHEN AARON HAD TOLD ME ABOUT THE PATIENT HE HAD failed with who was false, I immediately thought of Winnicott's "false-self" diagnoses and asked him whether this concept might not have been useful to him in that case. But Aaron had merely remarked irritably, "There's no doubt that I handled the case badly," and looked bored with my description of Winnicott's procedures. He seemed content to leave his own case in a condition of incomprehensibility and muddle. Later, another passage in Waelder's *Basic Theory* helped me understand and "place" Aaron's glum in-curiosity about alternatives to classical analytic technique even in cases of therapeutic failure. Waelder writes:

> It so happens that the therapeutic variations of the "clas-sical" setting usually make it much more difficult to learn more about the patient; whatever their therapeutic merits may be, they are scientifically sterile. The real difference between "orthodox" and "liberal" analysts is therefore not that the former cling to tradition while the latter are open to innovation, but, rather, that "liberals" seem to assume that all problems are already fundamentally solved, so that the structure of a case can, at least in its outlines, be understood in a relatively short time, and all that remains is the task of influencing a condition already properly understood; while the "orthodox" analyst looks upon a new case as a new enigma that will yield its secrets only very slowly and hardly ever entirely. In short, the "orthodox" analyst stands *more in awe of the unconscious.* He is, so to say, less at ease in Zion. . . .

Waelder is upholding the paradoxical view of psychoanalysis that Freud, after making his initial discoveries, adopted and maintained throughout his life—and that Ferenczi was the first to challenge—namely, that the ability of psychoanalysis to alleviate human suffering is contingent upon its being con-ducted strictly as a scientific experiment; the less the analyst tries to help the patient, the more likely is it that he will do so. In a symposium on therapeutic results held in 1948, Phyl-lis Greenacre restated the paradox thus:

> Freud emphasized that his own interest in the truth—in his case, his original interest in the "living pathology" of the

patient—was the greatest therapeutic safeguard to the patient. . . . It seems to be so simply true as to be elusive, that the worker whose goal is the essential verity of his scientific work may in some instances take unnecessary detours of exploration, but by and large will contribute most to the science and to his patients.

This stance has been repeatedly challenged by the analysts who feel that they are healers first and scientists second; on the issue of what comes first—patient or science—analysis has been divided since the nineteen-twenties. The question remains: what do the soft-hearted liberals, the heirs of Ferenczi's therapeutic tradition, actually *do* behind the closed doors of their consultation rooms to implement their desire to heal? As their theories have grown more elaborate, have their kisses grown more passionate, their indulgence of patients' whims more extraordinary? Freud turned out to have vastly overestimated the immoral consequences of Ferenczi's fatherly hugs. In the writings of the liberals one not only finds no evidence of immorality, but one scarcely sees that they are doing anything very different in their sessions from what the orthodox analysts are doing in theirs. In the entire three hundred and twelve pages of *The Restoration of the Self* Kohut offers a single unexciting example of deviation from orthodox analytic practice: he says that in certain situations he thinks it might be better to answer a patient's question first and analyze it later. In *The Basic Fault,* Balint delivers a bit more in his report of a somersault that a woman patient got up from the couch to perform; she had been speaking of her life-long wish to achieve this feat, and he had been inspired to say, "What about it now?" The incident had momentous (favorable) consequences for the analysis.

In a paper called " 'R'—The Analyst's Total Response to His Patient's Needs," the English analyst Margaret Little reports that a breakthrough in a stagnant analysis occurred when she told a patient who was boring her that she was boring her; when the patient went on with her wearisome story, Margaret Little simply insisted that she stop. M. Masud R. Khan cites a number of cases in his book *The Privacy of the Self* (1959), where what he calls his "body-aliveness" or "body attention" sustained the patient during a state of deep regression. In one such case, the patient, an eighteen-year-old boy, didn't speak for several months, as Khan sat behind him conveying "body-aliveness" and occasionally expressing his perceptions of the quality of the boy's silence. Eventually, Khan's reconstruction through countertransference of the boy's traumatic early experiences with a depressed mother (who had made him feel the way he was making Khan feel by his silent withdrawal) broke the silence and propelled the analysis into a new phase.

Kohut's frequent self-satisfied allusions to the fact that he doesn't moralize about his patients' disgusting sexual practices or blame them for their unpleasant personalities have been challenged by orthodox analysts, who point out that this is hardly an innovation of "self psychology," but is a time-honored convention of analytic neutrality: no good analyst moralizes or blames his patients. Kohut, conversely, attributes the curious successes that non-Kohutian analysts sometimes have with narcissistic patients to the analysts' unwitting decency and "empathy." It appears, then, that the vast differences in theoretic outlook dividing contemporary psychoanalysis and placing analysts in sharply uncongenial schools and camps seem scarcely to touch analysis itself, which continues to be conducted by all concerned, somersaults notwithstanding, in much the way Freud said it should be conducted at the beginning of the century. If this is so—if Winnicott, Balint, Kohut, Khan, Mahler, Stone, Brenner, and Aaron Green are all doing the same thing—what is the meaning and point of their enormous theoretic differences? Does it make any difference to a patient whether he goes to a Kohutian or a Mahlerian or a Brennerite?

In his paper "Metapsychological and Clinical Aspects of Regression Within the Psychoanalytical Set-up," Winnicott offers a perspective on this puzzling situation which takes one far in untangling its perplexities. In arguing for the extension of analytic therapy (which Freud had devised for the ego-intact neurotic patient) to the "not-whole" psychotic patient for whom it had not been intended, Winnicott offers a simple and brilliant distinction between the *technique* and the *setting* of analysis. Analytic technique (in this distinction) concerns the understanding and the interpretation of what the patient says and does during the analytic hour, and is something that the analyst learns. The analytic setting in which this work is carried out is, in contrast, something that the analyst, as it were, abides by. Winnicott enumerates the salient features of this unique setting at deliberate length and in deliberate detail:

1. At a stated time daily, five or six times a week, Freud put himself at the service of the patient. (This time was arranged to suit the convenience of both the analyst and the patient.)

2. The analyst would be reliably there, on time, alive, breathing.

3. For the limited period of time prearranged (about an

hour), the analyst would keep awake and become pre-occupied with the patient.

4. The analyst expressed love by the positive interest taken, and hate by the strict start and finish and in the matter of fees. Love and hate were honestly expressed; that is to say, not denied by the analyst.

5. The aim of the analysis would be to get into touch with the process of the patient, to understand the material presented, to communicate this understanding in words. Resistance implied suffering and could be allayed by interpretation.

6. The analyst's method was one of objective observation.

7. This work was to be done in a room, not a passage, a room that was quiet and not liable to sudden unpredictable sounds, yet not dead quiet and not free from ordinary house noises. This room would be lit properly, but not by a light staring in the face, and not by a variable light. The room would certainly not be dark, and it would be comfortably warm. The patient would be lying on a couch, that is to say, comfortable, if able to be comfortable, and probably a rug and some water would be available.

8. The analyst (as is well known) keeps moral judgment out of the relationship, has no wish to intrude with details of the analyst's personal life and ideas, and the analyst does not wish to take sides in the persecutory systems even when these appear in the form of real shared situations, local, political, etc. Naturally, if there is a war or an earthquake or if the king dies, the analyst is not unaware.

9. In the analytic situation, the analyst is much more

reliable than people are in ordinary life; on the whole punctual, free from temper tantrums, free from compulsive falling in love, etc.

10. There is a very clear distinction in the analysis between fact and fantasy, so that the analyst is not hurt by an aggressive dream.

11. An absence of the talion reaction can be counted on.

12. The analyst survives.

Along with being beguiled by this expression of the personal ideal of the analyst (as Winnicott offhandedly concludes, "the whole thing adds up to the fact that the analyst *behaves* himself or herself"), one should also take note of the list's polemical aim of pointing up the resemblance of the analytic setting to the setting of early childhood and infancy—the "very marked similarity between all these things and the ordinary task of parents, especially that of the mother with her infant. . . ." In other words, it is analysis itself, rather than the analyst, that invites regression in the patient; and the significant differences between analysts of different schools lie not in what they do or don't do (in whether they grant favors or not, whether they answer questions first or interpret first, etc.), but in *how they regard and interpret what the patient says and does* when plunged into this potently allusive setting. Whether an analyst views a patient's immutable silence, for example, as "regressive defense" against castration anxiety or sees it as a reënactment of infant trauma will make an enormous difference to the patient. Whether an analyst greets a patient's lapse into a bizarre state of childlike dependency and dysfunction as a long-hoped-for sign that buried layers of self have been reached, or with the sickening feeling that things are getting out of hand and that he had better come up fast with a correct regression-stemming interpretation, will, again, be enormously significant. Psychoanalysis, alone among today's psychotherapies, remains strictly a talking cure. Even the most far-out theorist will confine himself to telling his patients what he believes to be true about them, rather than attempting to manipulate or act on them. But a great many versions of the truth, couched in great varieties of language and emotional gesture, are being offered in today's analytic consultation rooms to patients who have little inkling of the implications (for themselves) of where their analyst stands on issues of which they have never heard.

# II

ONE WEDNESDAY AARON AND I TALKED ABOUT CHEKhov's story "Lady with Lapdog": Its hero, Gurov—a cynical and bitter womanizer, married to a woman he secretly detests, and contemptuous of all women—during a summer vacation in Yalta drifts into yet another affair, with a pretty and innocent young woman who is also unhappily married. The vacation ends, Gurov sees the woman off at the train station and says goodbye to her—forever, as he thinks—and returns to Moscow. He resumes his life of joyless work and dissipation, but gradually finds, to his surprise, that, unlike the other women he had amused himself with, this one has not faded from memory, but has become an ever stronger and more vivid presence for him. He cannot get her out of his mind, and finally, in December, he gets on a train and goes to look for her in the small provincial town where she lives with her weakling of a husband. He finds her, and learns that she, too, has been longing for him. The story ends a few months later in a hotel room in Moscow, where she comes every few months, telling her husband she is seeing a specialist. On the way to the hotel, Gurov reflects on the double life he is leading and ponders the paradox that

> everything that was important, interesting, essential, everything about which he was sincere and did not deceive himself, everything that made up the quintessence of his life, went on in secret, while everything that was a lie, everything that was merely the husk in which he hid himself to conceal the truth, like his work at the bank, for instance, his discussions at the club, his ideas of the lower breed, his going to anniversary functions with his wife—all that happened in the sight of all.

During the bleakly tender meeting in the hotel room, Gurov catches sight of himself in the mirror. He realizes that "it was only now, when his hair was beginning to turn gray, that he had fallen in love properly, in good earnest—for the first time in his life." Then comes this unforgettable passage:

> He and Anna Sergeyevna loved each other as people who are very dear and near, as man and wife or close friends love each other; they could not help feeling that fate itself had intended them for one another, and they were unable to understand why he should have a wife and she a husband; they were like two migrating birds, male and female, who had been caught and forced to live in separate cages. They had forgiven each other what they

had been ashamed of in the past, and forgave each other everything in their present, and felt that this love of theirs had changed them both.

Aaron and I had been talking about the difference between case histories and literature, and I said of the Chekhov story that it illustrated something that case histories don't allow for—namely, the profound effect that people can have on each other, the fateful difference that a meeting between two people can make on the outcome of their lives. "But maybe literature lies," I added.

"Maybe literature doesn't," Aaron said. "It could happen in life as it happened in the story. But the clinician would have to ask himself, 'Well, *has* this man really changed—or has he merely found a slightly different solution to his problem?' That is, to have love only on the condition that it be temporary, intermittent, full of deception, outside of marriage—which is a neurotic solution. His marriage is legitimate, aboveboard, constant, while his love is secret, illicit, occasional, can't be public, can't be shared."

I had to agree. "But tell me, when you read the story, were you moved by it?"

"Yes, I was moved by it. And when a patient tells me his story well, I am moved by it. What Chekhov wrote about is hardly unusual. The analytic literature is full of case histories of moral masochism—cases of men (or women) who cannot establish relationships with women (or men) that are in any way satisfying and act it out by getting involved with people who are already married, whom they can see only rarely, and whose lives consequently are chronically unsatisfying. This is essentially the story of Chekhov's hero. And, put this way, it isn't at all interesting, and certainly not touching. But Chekhov went deeper into his hero. He got his particular, unique, idiosyncratic story, and so it became interesting and touching. There is an important detail in the story. In Yalta, after they make love for the first time, the woman weeps with shame for her fall from virtue, and the man sits down at a table and callously cuts himself a slice of watermelon and eats it. It is an absolutely idiosyncratic, banal, and metaphorically perfect action. It is the same thing with patients—their stories are full of just such arrestingly rich detail, as if a gifted writer had composed them. When you do analysis and get people's particular stories, they stop being cases of this fixation and of that developmental arrest; they become real people. What first attracted me to psychoanalysis was the power and elegance and, yes, even the reductionism of the theory. But the longer I do analysis the less I can generalize and the more I become impressed with the idiosyncrasy of human experience—even of my own! I used to make all kinds of defensive generalizations about myself. It has taken me quite some time to actually find myself a uniquely interesting person." We both laughed at this, and Aaron added, "Freud, by the way, said just the opposite of himself. He said that as he grew older he found himself less interesting. In one of his letters to Jung he said, 'One learns little by little to renounce one's personality.' "

We talked about the classic transference neurosis. Aaron said, "Seeing it happen—seeing the patient's emotional life begin to revolve around the person of the analyst—never ceases to amaze me. Since the only thing that is going on is that the patient comes in four or five times a week and lies on the couch and says whatever comes into his mind and is handed a bill at the end of the month."

"Does it upset you?"

"It used to, when I was less experienced and didn't know the full implication of transference. It upset me because I took it personally. I still take it personally, but I no longer feel the conventional moral obligation so strongly—the obligation to comply with the patient's demand for love. Freud put it very nicely. He said that people are constructed in such a way that when one person exhibits a strong emotional, instinctual attitude toward another, there is a natural tendency to comply with it, to adopt a complementary attitude. Love breeds love. And, similarly, hatred, belligerence, spite, jealousy, rivalry—when they arise in analysis—arouse the complementary hostile feelings."

"Aren't there patients who can't accept the idea that their love or their hatred for the analyst is a reliving of the past?"

"*Most* patients can't."

"But finally you have to convince them—as Freud wrote regarding the case of transference love—that they are not in love with you personally, that their love is an illusion."

"That's become the conventional wisdom on the subject. It's a defense maneuver that many analysts adopt when all of a sudden they find themselves caught within the emotional field of the patient's instincts, when they feel the full impact of the transference beating down on them like hail. But I don't agree with it. No, you don't convince the patient that it's not you she loves. Freud was off base when he wrote that. It *is* you. Who else could it be? There isn't anyone else in the room with her. That isn't the issue. It isn't even arguable. There is only one thing for the analyst to say to the patient who has fallen in love with him—in one way or another—and that is 'Tell me more about it. Say whatever comes into your mind about it. Let's go into it deeper. Let's learn about the nature of your love.' Now, the patient may not listen to him. She may be so overwhelmed by her feelings, so intent on consummating her love sexually, that she will not be willing or able to examine her love, and when this happens the analysis is in trouble—not because the analyst has been forced into a compromised position, but because the patient is no longer attending to her associations. The operation has come to a standstill. The surgeon can go no further with his scalpel."

"But isn't the analyst in a more difficult and ambiguous position than the surgeon, since he is dealing with emotions and passions that belong to all of life and not just to the analysis? Love and hatred are not exclusive to analytic sessions."

"Neither is breathing, neither is blood circulation, neither is digestion exclusive to the operating room. But there is one thing that goes on in the operating room that goes on nowhere else, and that's surgery. And there is one thing that goes on in the analytic session that goes on nowhere else, and that's analysis. If someone outside of analysis came up to me and said 'I'm desperately in love with you,' and I responded by saying 'What comes to mind about that?'—that would be a *horrible* thing to say! Just horrible! But when a patient comes in and says 'I'm desperately in love with you,' and I say 'What comes to mind about that?'—that's absolutely appropriate."

"But what if the patient finds it horrible?"

"She leaves the analysis. There are patients who cannot tolerate the frustration—it calls up too many painful feelings or too much anger—and the analysis breaks off. There are forest fires that get out of control. There are gas mains that blow up. There are buildings that buckle and crumble.

There are wars that break out. There are diseases that kill. Sometimes in regular medicine *the patient dies.* Sometimes in psychoanalysis the analysis doesn't survive an erotic transference."

# 12

ARON AND I DECIDED TO "TERMINATE" OUR TALKS AT the beginning of August—the traditional vacation time and ending time of analysis. When analysis changed from the brief and specific symptom-dispelling therapy it started out as to the extended and ambiguous character-altering process it has become, analysts were faced with an unprecedented question—namely, how do you know when to end the analysis? Attempts to establish criteria for termination have since yielded nothing but the broadest of generalities ("The patient has become capable of love and work") and the vaguest of intuitions ("It feels right to end"). Apparently, no analyst ever knows with certainty when the time has come to set a termination date. However, over the years, the consensus about what constitutes an appropriate length of time for analysis has had a steady upward trend. In the twenties, one to two years was deemed sufficient; in the thirties and forties, two to four years was the norm; in the fifties and sixties, four to six years; today, six to eight. When the limits of allowable time are approached, the analyst is apt to start thinking about termination. Cases that formally terminate—i.e., end by mutual agreement of analyst and patient—are relatively rare. The majority of analytic cases end because the patient moves to another city, or runs out of money, or impulsively quits the analysis, or agrees with the analyst that stalemate has been reached. Even the most experienced and successful analysts acknowledge at least as many cases that run afoul or end prematurely or inconclusively as those that properly terminate.

If a case *does* come through all the dangers of the crossing and enters the (not always calm) harbor of the "termination phase"—the period of weeks or months between the setting of an ending time and its arrival—the analyst is faced with another decision. Shall he treat this phase no differently from any other phase of the analysis, and conduct himself no differently? Or shall he introduce technical modifications that reflect his aliveness to what Leo Stone, in *The Psychoanalytic Situation,* characterizes as "the profound impact of separation following a uniquely intimate human relationship"? To help the patient negotiate "the change from a profound, habitual, and quite unique involvement with another person, to living without this association," Stone recommends that the termination phase be conducted as a kind of weaning period, with the frequency of sessions reduced and with the patient sitting up and facing the analyst—a kind of winding down of transference and countertransference, so that "both participants gain relatively integrated and realistic views of one another." The classical formulation maintains, on the contrary, that "to the very end we continue the analytic process," as the English analyst Edward Glover writes in *The Technique of Psychoanalysis,* first published in 1928 and revised in 1955. Glover sternly continues, "In the first session we laid down the association rule, and this remains in force to the last minute of the last session."

But whichever method an analyst chooses of conducting

the final months and weeks and moments of analysis, there is universal agreement that the subject of termination is a vexatious one. It is an area of analysis that, paradoxically, becomes more murky and mired as analysts' clinical findings grow more precise and refined. For, as analyses grow longer, the necessity that they come to an end grows ever more unpalatable to patients. As Glover writes, in his dry English way:

> If it takes three weeks for a woman to recover from developing a spot on her chin or for a man to recover from shaving off his moustache; if it requires two years or more for the average resilient person to recover from the death of a love-object and five years to recover from being jilted, it is not unreasonable to expect that the process of detaching a patient from an infantile transference-situation in which he has sojourned usually for many months, often for the better part of two years, and occasionally for four years and over, will take some time. . . .

In a paper entitled "On the Termination of Analysis" (1950), the analyst Annie Reich bluntly states that

> even after the transference has been well analyzed and its important infantile sexual elements have been overcome, even after the neurotic symptoms have been given up, the relationship to the analyst is still not a completely mature one. We have to state that the transference is not completely resolved. The analyst is still an overimportant person for the patient, and is still the object of fantasy expectations. . . . In nearly all cases which I have analyzed, there remained a wish to be loved by the analyst, to keep in contact with him, to build up a friendship. . . . The analyst is still seen as a person endowed with special power, special intelligence and wisdom. In short, to a

certain degree he is still seen as partaking in the omnipotence which the child attributes to the parents.

Reich quotes a patient—a candidate in training analysis—telling her of his grief and desolation after the end of a previous analysis:

> "I felt as if I was suddenly left alone in the world. It was like the feeling I had after the death of my mother. I tried with effort to find somebody to love, something to be interested in. For months I longed for the analyst and wished to tell him about whatever happened to me. Then slowly, without noticing how it happened, I forgot about him. About two years later, I happened to meet him at a party and thought he was just a nice elderly gentleman and in no way interesting."

For many patients, termination is an iatrogenic illness for which the only cure is the home remedy of time. As Reich's patient finally stopped grieving for his analyst, so do most patients eventually recover from their loss of an important beloved (or, in some cases, hated) object. (Regarding the latter eventuality, a man from the West Coast told his second analyst here of his unexpectedly severe reaction to the termination of his first analysis, with an analyst he had thoroughly disliked. He had blithely gone off on a camping trip in the desert with his wife, and on the first day was struck with such a profound and devastating feeling of cosmic aloneness that he had had to give up and return to the city. The analyst had been a harsh, strange, ascetic person who took—and gave—only one week of vacation a year.)

Analysts themselves labor under an obstructed view of termination, and thus may have a limited appreciation of its rigors. As the English analyst Marion Milner puts it, "Perhaps we, as analysts, are handicapped in knowing all about what ending feels like, for by the mere fact of becoming analysts we have succeeded in bypassing an experience which our patients have to go through. We have chosen to identify ourselves with our analyst's profession and to act out that identification." If the full experience of termination is a kind of existential rite of passage—a sojourn in the desert, a final stoical acceptance of the uncertainties of adulthood and the inevitability of death—then analysts never grow up and never have to die. The people who instruct others on serious and final things themselves remain Peter Pans, indefinitely staving off adulthood and extinction in the Never-Never Land of analytic practice and institutional politics. It is no wonder that the literature of termination is vague, unfocussed, trivial, off the point, evasive, and uncomprehending.

As I walked into Aaron's apartment building for our last meeting, I thought of another final hour I had experienced. A few weeks before, I had sat with Hartvig Dahl and listened to the tape of the last hour of his six-year-long analysis. I had asked to listen to it, and Dahl had impulsively left his own work and joined me in the auditing room. The patient rambled in his usual (to me) inconsequential and uninteresting way. But he was sad and wistful; the session was punctuated by long and possibly tearful silences. Dahl, sitting beside me, listening, was plainly moved. In the recording, he made wise, fatherly, sometimes folksy interpretations of the patient's halting appreciations of the fact that this was his final meeting with his analyst. At the end of the hour, Dahl said to the patient, "You used the metaphor earlier of a person at a train station waiting fifty minutes to see someone off on a train—I suppose, really, to see him off on his

trip through life. And now it's time to say 'All aboard!' "
Dahl had kept a written journal of the analysis along with
the tapes, and in his entry on the last session he had evidently
felt a novelist's urge to put a proper Ending on his work.
The notebook concludes thus: "I handed him the last bill
and for the first time opened the outer hall door for him as
he left. I choked as I said goodbye, and for the first time our
eyes met in a long look that we both understood."

Another (rare) account of an analyst's emotion on part-
ing with a patient is in the British analyst Harry Guntrip's
memoir of his analysis with W. R. D. Fairbairn:

> As I was finally leaving Fairbairn after the last session, I
> suddenly realized that in all that long period we had never
> once shaken hands, and he was letting me leave without
> that friendly gesture. I put out my hand and at once he
> took it, and I suddenly saw a few tears trickle down his
> face. *I saw the warm heart of this man with a fine mind
> and a shy nature.*

When I asked Aaron about his experiences of termination, he said that frankly he had had no cases of formal ending to speak of yet; most of his earliest patients had quit,
and his subsequent, well-established analytic cases were only
now approaching the termination phase. Even the first case,
which he considered a success, had not ended in a proper termination; victory had been snatched from him by the patient's
premature and abrupt departure in the seventh year of analysis. Like Dora, she took her revenge by leaving, and, like
Freud, Aaron cannot forgive (or forget) her, and keeps going
back to the case and over its particulars like someone picking
at a sore.

Aaron said that, thanks to the analysis, the patient had been able to marry, and that one day she came in and said that because of her new husband's work schedule she would take her vacation in July that year, instead of at the usual time, in August. Aaron reminded her that August was the designated vacation month, and that if she took her vacation in July she would still have to pay for the sessions she missed. She found this intolerable; he wouldn't back down; and she left the analysis.

We had debated this incident many times before, and I had always taken the patient's side. Although Aaron was formally entitled to the money for the missed appointments in July, it seemed to me that he would have done better (morally and strategically) to have been less obdurate. (The choice was his—by this time she was a private patient paying regular fees, rather than a Treatment Center patient.) Aaron agreed that he may not have acted prudently; he acknowledged that his perennial problem about fees, his desire for money, and his anger toward the patient may have caused him to act precipitately. *"But,"* he said, "but. The real issue was not the money itself, and my real blunder wasn't that I charged her for the missed sessions. My blunder was that I didn't understand and interpret the transference soon enough. I didn't point out to her that she was taking flight because she couldn't face her painful feeling of love toward me. I didn't convince her that the money she wouldn't part with was the phallus-child she wanted from me." Before I could protest this outlandish rationalization Aaron leaned forward intently and said, in a new tone of voice, "I know what you're going to say. I can see the derision on your face. And what is happening here is something that never ceases to amaze me— other analysts have commented on it, my analyst has commented on it—namely, that the insights of psychoanalysis are never taken for granted from one generation to the next. Each generation has to make the original discoveries afresh! You can't just say that Freud discovered something and now it will be taught and transmitted as accepted knowledge, the way the findings of physics and biology and chemistry are transmitted. *That doesn't happen in psychoanalysis.* This boggles my mind. Why can't the next generation accept what Freud found out? Because you're challenging me. Thinking, intelligent people like you challenge what Freud found out. Why not challenge the theory of natural selection? What you're challenging, of course, is the centrality of infantile sexuality and of the Oedipus complex in adult psychic life. That's what you're challenging, and that's what thinking, intelligent people challenge.

"Konrad Lorenz noticed that if you walk in front of a little chick at a certain time in the chick's life he'll follow you, and if you do it at other times he won't; there's a particular time when he gets 'set.' And we have found out in psychoanalysis that in human development, too, there is a time that is uniquely formative—and the layman doesn't know this. He can be told it a million times, he can read about it in so many books, he can even 'believe' it, and he still doesn't know it, as, right at this moment, you with your very intelligent skepticism don't know it. I'm not criticizing you. There's something very good about this talk. You are an educated person living in the second half of the twentieth century, and you don't know that the Oedipal period— roughly three and a half to six years—is like Lorenz standing in front of the chick, is the most formative, significant, molding experience of human life, is the source of all subsequent adult behaviors. If you take a person's adult life—his love, his work, his hobbies, his ambitions—they *all* point back to the Oedipus complex. That's a fantastic thing to say. And we have found this out. Freud discovered it, and we use it as our touchstone day in and day out. But what we take for granted the lay public continues to challenge."

"This idea is hard to accept."

"Sure it is. Because do you know what it says? It says, as Freud wrote, that man isn't master in his own house. That he is determined, that his degree of freedom is zero, that he cannot change his destiny, that he is malleable at one formidable time and that everything in his life is settled and preordained ever after. Yes, it's a horrible idea to have to accept. And we analysts take it for common knowledge, and when we talk among ourselves it's a basic assumption derived from a tremendous amount of evidence."

I said, "When you speak of this patient's wish for a phallus-child from you, and of her refusal to admit her love for you—are you talking about unconscious ideas?"

"Yes. When she quit, what she was conscious of was getting her pound of flesh from me for charging for the missed sessions. What she was *un*conscious of was that I was really the center of her life—the most valued, the most cherished, the most beloved person. She couldn't acknowledge that to herself. It was too painful. She couldn't stand it. And when you stop to think about it, very few people can stand it. How does it feel—and this is the tragedy of every child—how does it feel for a little girl to find that the most important person in her life, the person she loves most passionately, and loves in a particular way—namely, that she wants him to give her a phallus-child—*is not going to do it*? No matter what she does and however she tries to maneuver him, he is still *not going to do it*."

"And the wish is reactivated and the attempt is repeated in analysis."

"It is. It can't help but be, and it would be a bad analysis if it wasn't."

"And the two analysts who were stripped of their honors, they did it."

Aaron nodded. "They did it. They bungled the operation. Tell me, what do you think of the surgery analogy now?" he asked, recalling an old debate.

"Why do you like the analogy so much?" I countered.

"Because it's so radical," he said. "Because it indicates how impersonal and intimate analysis is. Because it tells you that it is not a casual procedure, that it is serious and dangerous, that it is dire."

"So you feel that something is done 'on' the analytic patient, the way an operation is performed 'on' a surgical patient?"

"Yes."

"And yet the goal of analysis is insight."

"Yes."

"How do you reconcile the two images—the anesthetized patient on the table to whom something is being done and the person actively and consciously gaining insight?"

"Easily. Because the achieving of insight is as deep and radical and complex a procedure as the cutting out of a tumor. Insight isn't superficial—it isn't simply learning something mildly interesting about yourself. It is *becoming* yourself. It's finding your way to the child in yourself, it is a profound *recognition*. And it takes a tremendous amount of work on the part of both analyst and patient to negotiate

this achievement. In surgery, though the patient is anesthetized his body continues to work as usual: the heart continues
to pump, the blood continues to flow, the lungs continue to
function. Similarly, in analysis a great deal goes on in the
patient that he isn't aware of and that the analyst is cautiously
monitoring. At the end of the analysis, it can happen that
neither the analyst nor the patient knows exactly what happened. There's a story about the analyst Annie Reich, who
once described a very good analysis at a conference. People
were impressed, and said, 'You should write up this analysis,' and she said, 'I'm not ready to write about it, because
I haven't yet figured out what happened.' The analysis had
been finished for several years, and she still hadn't figured
it out.

"Another story tells of an analyst who decided to do some
follow-up work. He telephoned two women patients who had
been in analysis with him five years previously. They were
comparable cases: both had had stormy, tempestuous analyses, with all kinds of *Sturm und Drang* and very emotional,
intense transferences. Now, five years later, one woman said,
'Doctor, every night before I go to bed I thank my lucky
stars that I had you as my analyst. The analysis with you has
changed my life. Not a day goes by that I don't think about
what I learned from you, and apply it. You are an ever-living
presence in my daily life, and I think of you with something
like reverence.' The other woman—who had had just as tempestuous and emotional and intense an analysis—said, 'You
know, every so often I think about you, and I think, Maybe
my life wouldn't be much different if I hadn't been in analysis. To tell you the truth, I don't remember much of the
analysis. You seem to be a nice man. I guess the experience
was O.K. But I can't say what helped me and what wouldn't

have happened anyway.' Right away, he knew who had had the better analysis. When you're through with the operation, you sew up the patient, you hope that the scar isn't too conspicuous, and if everything afterward goes as it should—fine, that's enough.

"At the end of *A Midsummer Night's Dream,* the human characters wake up and rub their eyes and aren't sure what has happened to them. They have the feeling that a great deal has occurred—that things have somehow changed for the better, but they don't know what caused the change. Analysis is like that for many patients."

"The analysts are the fairies, then," I said, taking Aaron's analogy a fanciful step further. "They are Puck and Oberon and Titania and Cobweb. They behave according to the laws of their kind, and they fight the esoteric battles of their kingdom, using the patient as a pawn. They cause strange and remarkable things to happen to him, and they mean no harm."

"No," Aaron said. "No. They mean more than that—and less. Our science isn't harmless. We psychoanalysts play with fire every day, with the possibility of getting burned and of burning someone else. We steeled ourselves to this task long before we became analysts. We steeled ourselves to it in medical school and as interns and residents, when we had to do things that hurt other people. We dealt with it then largely by hurting ourselves: through drudgery, mercilessly long hours, no sleep, endless time spent in the operating room holding retractors—godawful physical self-punishment of every kind. We hurt ourselves while we were hurting other people—sticking them with all kinds of needles, shooting them with all kinds of strong medicines, performing all kinds of painful procedures, letting them die. And by the time we got into psychiatry, and then into analysis, the business of playing with fire was no less dangerous—but we were steeled to it."

Aaron stared with displeasure into the middle distance, and I said nothing. The sound of a door slamming—heralding the patient whose arrival always ended our talks—broke the silence, and ended the final hour of our strange and remarkable encounter.

# Notes

1. *(page 13):* This passage has recently come under attack from scholars. The researches of Henri F. Ellenberger, George H. Pollock, and Albrecht Hirschmüller have shown that Breuer did not abandon Anna O. suddenly but had her put in a sanitorium; that Breuer's "flight" to Venice did not take place at that time; that the child who was supposed to have been conceived during this "second honeymoon"—Breuer's youngest daughter, Dora—was already born; and that she committed suicide not in New York but in Vienna, when the Gestapo knocked at her door.

2. *(page 25):* The unconscious meaning of fees was discussed as follows by Sandor Ferenczi in his paper "The Elasticity of Psycho-Analytic Technique" (1928):

Psycho-analysis is often reproached with being remarkably concerned with money matters. My own opinion is that it is far too little concerned with them. Even the most prosperous individual spends money on doctors most unwillingly. Something in us seems to make us regard medical aid, which in fact we all first received from our mothers in infancy, as something to which we are automatically entitled, and at the end of each month, when our patients are presented with their bill, their resistance is stimulated into producing all their concealed or unconscious hatred, mistrust, and suspicion over again. The most characteristic example of the contrast between conscious generosity and concealed resentment was given by the patient who opened the conversation by saying: "Doctor, if you help me, I'll give you every penny I possess!" "I shall be satisfied with thirty kronen an hour," the physician replied. "But isn't that rather excessive?" the patient unexpectedly remarked.

3. *(page 37):* In her book *Tribute to Freud*, the poet H.D. (Hilda Doolittle) recalls an incredible moment in her analysis with Freud, in 1933–34. In response to something the forty-seven-year-old poet said —she says she doesn't know exactly what it was (!)—the seventy-seven-year-old psychoanalyst furiously pounded the back of the couch on which she was lying and said, "The trouble is, I am an old man— *you do not think it worth your while to love me.*" This caused H.D. to sit bolt upright on the couch in astonishment, one part of her thinking that this might be some device of Freud's to speed the flow of association, and another part of her feeling upset and appalled: "He was a terribly frightening old man, too old and too detached, too wise and too famous altogether, to beat that way with his fist, like a child hammering a porridge-spoon on the table." In evaluating the incident, one should remember that (1) Freud differentiated between his therapeutic analyses and his didactic ones, and considered H.D. a pupil, rather than a patient; and (2) that H.D.'s book is a poetic, fragmented, almost hallucinatory evocation of her analysis with Freud, rather than a literal day-by-day account.

4. *(page 52):* There has been concern in England, and in Europe as well, about the effect of institutionalization on the calibre of the people who enter the profession. Discussing this issue in an essay called "The Becoming of a Psycho-Analyst," in his book *The Privacy of the Self*, M. Masud R. Khan quotes the following disarming passage in a speech given by James Strachey in 1963 at a banquet celebrating the fiftieth anniversary of the British Psycho-Analytical Society:

> From time to time, I receive a copy of what is described as a "Curriculum Vitae," giving the qualifications of a candidate for election. Documents of this kind fill me with blood-curdling feelings of anxiety and remorse. How on earth could I fill up one of them? A discreditable academic career with the barest of B.A. degrees, no medical qualifications, no knowledge of the physical sciences, no experience of anything except third-rate journalism. The only thing in my favor was that at the age of

thirty I wrote a letter out of the blue to Freud, asking him if he would take me on as a student.

For some reason, he replied, almost by return of post, that he would, and I spent a couple of years in Vienna. Now here is the point of all this rigmarole: I got back to London in the summer of 1922, and in October, without any further ado, I was elected an associate member of the Society. I can only suppose that Ernest Jones had received instructions from an even higher authority, and that he had passed them on to the unfortunate Council. A year later, I was made a full member. So there I was, launched on the treatment of patients, with no experience, with no supervision, with nothing to help me but some two years of analysis with Freud. I think you will agree with me that the gradual development of systematic machinery for training candidates and for helping them at the start of their careers has been a necessary condition for the establishment of psycho-analysis as a recognized branch of therapeutics. The curriculum vitae is essential. Whether it is possible for it to become over-institutionalized is an open question. Is it worthwhile to leave a loophole for an occasional maverick? I don't know. But I do know that if the curriculum vitae had existed forty years ago, you wouldn't have had to listen to these remarks tonight.

5. *(page 96):* This activity puts Freud in mind of another "very entertaining episode," in which another patient brought out a small box during a session, ostensibly "to refresh herself with a sweet." Knowing better, Freud writes, "She made some efforts to open it, and then handed it to me so that I might convince myself how hard it was to open. I expressed my suspicion that the box must mean something special, for this was the first time I had seen it, although the owner had been coming to me for more than a year. To this the lady eagerly replied: 'I always have this box about me; I take it with me wherever I go.' She did not calm down until I had pointed out to her with a laugh how well her words were adapted to quite another meaning. The box—*Dose* πύξις—like the reticule and the jewel-case, was once again only a substitute for the shell of

Venus, for the female genitals." In their iconographical study *Pandora's Box* (1956), the art historians Erwin and Dora (!) Panofsky trace the metamorphosis of the original large earthenware jar (πίθος) that Pandora opened in the Greek accounts of the myth to the small box (*pyxis*) with which she has been conventionally equipped in art and literature since the Renaissance, and locate the turning point in a text of Erasmus. In his (on the face of it, gratuitous) use of the Greek word πύξις, could Freud have been signalling his buried awareness of the most famous boxholder of all? Or am I getting a little carried away by my cleverness?

6. *(page 99):* In his essay "The Theme of the Three Caskets" (1913), Freud traces the meaning of Bassanio's choice of the lead casket, in *The Merchant of Venice*, through various mythological and anthropological permutations to a culminating, surprising identification of Cordelia (one of the three choices of Lear) with the figure of Death, and thus to an interpretation of Lear's choice of the bad sisters as an attempt to evade death. Freud writes, "Lear's dramatic story is intended to inculcate two wise lessons: that one should not give up one's possessions and rights during one's lifetime, and that one must guard against accepting flattery at its face value . . . but it seems to me quite impossible to explain the overpowering effect of *King Lear* from the impression that such a train of thought would produce, or to suppose that the dramatist's personal motives did not go beyond the intention of teaching these lessons."

7. *(page 102):* It was under the sway of Alexander's ideas that Harold Searles wrote his audacious paper "Oedipal Love in the Countertransference" (1959), in which he confessed that he not only fell in love with all his patients in the last stages of their analyses —in a sort of glow of Pygmalionesque satisfaction with his work— but thought it a good idea to let them know how he felt. "The patient's self-esteem benefits greatly from his sensing that he (or she) is capable of arousing such responses in his analyst," Searles wrote, and went on to argue, à la Alexander, that Freud had been too pessimistic about the human sexual condition—that if only parents would engage in a "mutual renunciation" of desire with their children, rather than just coldly pushing them away, the Oedipal period would not be traumatic, and neurosis, and even psychosis, might be averted.

# Bibliography

Alexander, Franz, and French, T. M. (1946) *Psychoanalytic Therapy, Principles and Application*. New York: Ronald Press.

————. (1954) "Some Quantitative Aspects of Psychoanalytic Technique." *Journal of the American Psychoanalytic Association* 2:685–701.

Arlow, Jacob. (1972) "Dilemmas in Psychoanalytic Education." *Journal of the American Psychoanalytic Association* 20:556–66.

————, and Brenner, Charles. (1964) *Psychoanalytic Concepts and the Structural Theory*. New York: International Universities Press.

Balint, Michael. (1968) *The Basic Fault*. London: Tavistock.

Bird, Brian. (1972) "Notes on Transference: Universal Phenomenon and Hardest Part of Analysis." *Journal of the American Psychoanalytic Association* 20:267–301.

Brenner, Charles. (1955, 1973) *An Elementary Textbook of Psychoanalysis*. New York: International Universities Press.

————. (1976) *Psychoanalytic Technique and Psychic · Conflict*. New York: International Universities Press.

————. (1979) "Working Alliance, Therapeutic Alliance, and Transference." *Journal of the American Psychoanalytic Association* (Supplement) 27:137–57.

Chekhov, Anton. (1899) "Lady with Lapdog." In *Lady with Lapdog ond Other Stories*, translated by David Magarshak. Baltimore: Penguin, 1964.

Chertok, Léon, and de Saussure, Raymond. (1979) *The Therapeutic Revolution: From Mesmer to Freud*. New York: Brunner/Mazel.

Dahl, Hartvig. (1974) "The Measurement of Meaning in Psychoanalysis by Computer Analysis of Verbal Contexts." *Journal of the American Psychoanalytic Association* 22:37–57.

————. (1978) "Countertransference Examples of the Syntactic Expression of Warded-Off Contents." *Psychoanalytic Quarterly* 47: 339–63.

Doolittle, Hilda. (1956) *Tribute to Freud*. New York: McGraw-Hill.

Eissler, Kurt. (1953) "Remarks on Some Variations in Psychoanalytic Technique." *International Journal of Psycho-Analysis* 39:222–29.

Ellenberger, H. F. (1970) *The Discovery of the Unconscious*. New York: Basic Books.

Erle, Joan. (1979) "An Approach to the Study of Analyzability and Analyses: The Course of Forty Consecutive Cases Selected for Supervised Analysis." *Psychoanalytic Quarterly* 48:198–228.

————, and Goldberg, Daniel. (1979) "Problems in the Assessment of Analyzability." *Psychoanalytic Quarterly* 48:48–84.

Ferenczi, Sandor. (1928) "The Elasticity of Psycho-Analytic Technique." In *Final Contributions to the Problems and Methods of Psychoanalysis*. New York: Brunner/Mazel, 1980.

————. (1929) "The Principle of Relaxation and Neocatharsis." In *ibid*.

————. (1929) "The Unwelcome Child and His Death Instinct." In *ibid*.

————. (1931) "Child Analysis in the Analysis of Adults." In *ibid*.

————. (1933) "Confusion of Tongues Between Adults and the Child." In *ibid*.

Forster, E. M. (1921) *Howards End*. New York: Vintage, 1954.

Freud, Anna. (1936) *The Ego and the Mechanisms of Defense*. London: Hogarth Press; New York: International Universities Press, 1966.

————. (1954) In "The Widening Scope of Indications for Psychoanalysis." *Journal of the American Psychoanalytic Association* 2:607–20.

Freud, Sigmund, and Breuer, Josef. (1895) *Studies on Hysteria*. Standard Edition,* 2.

* *The Standard Edition of the Complete Psychological Works of Sigmund Freud*, published in 24 volumes by the Hogarth Press, Ltd., London.

Freud, Sigmund. (1900) *The Interpretation of Dreams*. Standard Edition, 4 and 5.

———. (1901) *The Psychopathology of Everyday Life*.

———. (1905) "On Psychotherapy." Standard Edition, 7.

———. (1905) "Fragment of an Analysis of a Case of Hysteria." Standard Edition, 7.

———. (1909) *Five Lectures on Psycho-Analysis*. Standard Edition, 11.

———. (1910) " 'Wild' Psycho-Analysis." Standard Edition, 11.

———. (1912) "Recommendations to Physicians Practicing Psycho-Analysis." Standard Edition, 12.

———. (1913) "On Beginning the Treatment." Standard Edition, 12.

———. (1913) "The Theme of the Three Caskets." Standard Edition, 12.

———. (1914) *A History of the Psycho-Analytic Movement*. Standard Edition, 14.

———. (1914) "Remembering, Repeating, and Working Through." Standard Edition, 12.

———. (1915) "Observations on Transference-Love." Standard Edition, 12.

———. (1917) *Introductory Lectures on Psycho-Analysis*. Standard Edition, 16.

———. (1918) "Lines of Advance in Psycho-Analytic Therapy." Standard Edition, 17.

———. (1918) "From the History of an Infantile Neurosis." Standard Edition, 17.

———. (1923) *The Ego and the Id*. Standard Edition, 19.

———. (1925) "Some Psychical Consequences of the Anatomical Distinction Between the Sexes." Standard Edition, 19.

———. (1925) *An Autobiographical Study*. Standard Edition, 20.

———. (1926) *The Question of Lay Analysis*. Standard Edition, 20.

———. (1932) "The Acquisition and Control of Fire." Standard Edition, 22.

———. (1933) "Sandor Ferenczi." Standard Edition, 22.

———. (1937) "Analysis Terminable and Interminable." Standard Edition, 23.

———. (1939) *Moses and Monotheism*. Standard Edition, 23.

————. (1940) *An Outline of Psycho-Analysis*. Standard Edition, 23.

————. (1954) *The Origins of Psychoanalysis—Letters to Wilhelm Fliess. Drafts and Notes: 1887–1902*. New York: Basic Books.

————, and Jung, Carl G. (1974) *The Freud/Jung Letters*. Princeton: Princeton University Press.

Friedman, Leonard J. (1975) "Current Psychoanalytic Object Relations Theory and Its Clinical Implications." *International Journal of Psycho-Analysis* 56:137–46.

Fromm-Reichman, Frieda. (1950) *Principles of Intensive Psychotherapy*. Chicago: The University of Chicago Press.

Glover, Edward. (1928) *The Technique of Psychoanalysis*. New York: International Universities Press, 1955.

Greenacre, Phyllis. (1948) "Symposium on the Evaluation of Therapeutic Results." *International Journal of Psycho-Analysis* 29:11–14.

————. (1954) "The Role of Transference: Practical Considerations in Relation to Psychoanalytic Therapy." *Journal of the American Psychoanalytic Association* 2:671–84.

Greenson, Ralph R. (1967) *The Technique and Practice of Psychoanalysis*. New York: International Universities Press.

————, and Wexler, Murray. (1969) "The Non-Transference Relationship." In *Explorations in Psychoanalysis*. New York: International Universities Press, 1978.

————. (1972) "Beyond Transference and Interpretation." In *ibid*.

Guntrip, Harry. (1975) "My Experience of Analysis With Fairbairn and Winnicott." *International Review of Psycho-Analysis* 2:145–56.

Hirschmüller, A. (1978) *Physiologie und Psychoanalyse in Leben und Werk Josef Breuers*. Jahrbuch der Psychoanalyse Beiheft 4. Bern; Verlag Hans Huber. (Hirschmüller's untranslated findings are summarized by Else Pappenheim in a Letter to the Editor of the *American Journal of Psychiatry* 137 [December 1980]: 1625–6.)

Jones, Ernest. (1953–57) *The Life and Work of Sigmund Freud*, in three volumes. New York: Basic Books.

Kernberg, Otto. (1975) *Borderline Conditions and Pathological Narcissism*. New York: Aronson.

Khan, M. Masud R. (1959) "Regression and Integration in the Analytic Setting." In *The Privacy of the Self*. New York: International Universities Press, 1974.

———. (1963) "Silence as Communication." In *ibid*.

———. (1970) "The Becoming of a Psycho-Analyst." In *ibid*.

Klein, Melanie. (1957) *Envy and Gratitude*. London: Tavistock.

Kohut, Heinz. (1971) *The Analysis of the Self*. New York: International Universities Press.

———. (1977) *The Restoration of the Self*. New York: International Universities Press.

———. (1979) "The Two Analyses of Mr. Z." *International Journal of Psycho-Analysis* 60:3–27.

Kramer, Selma. (1979) "The Technical Significance and Application of Mahler's Separation-Individuation Theory." *Journal of the American Psychoanalytic Association* (Supplement) 27:241–61.

Kris, Ernst. (1956) "On Some Vicissitudes of Insight in Psychoanalysis." *International Journal of Psycho-Analysis* 37:445–55.

Limentani, Adam. (1972) "The Assessment of Analyzability: A Major Hazard in Selection for Psychoanalysis." *International Journal of Psycho-Analysis* 53:351–61.

———. (1977) "Affects and the Psychoanalytic Situation." *International Journal of Psycho-Analysis* 58:171–82.

Little, Margaret. (1957) " 'R'—The Analyst's Total Response to His Patient's Needs." *International Journal of Psycho-Analysis* 38:240–54.

Loewald, Hans. (1971) "The Transference Neurosis: Comments on the Concept and the Phenomenon." *Journal of the American Psychoanalytic Association* 19:54–66.

Mahler, Margaret; Pine, F.; and Bergman, A. (1975) *The Psychological Birth of the Human Infant*. New York: Basic Books.

Marcuse, Herbert. (1955) *Eros and Civilization, a Philosophical Inquiry into Freud*. New York: Vintage, 1962.

Milner, Marion. (1950) "A Note on the Ending of an Analysis." *International Journal of Psycho-Analysis* 31:191–93.

Orwell, George. (1949) "Reflections on Gandhi." In *The Collected*

*Essays, Journalism, and Letters of George Orwell*, vol. 4. New York: Harcourt, Brace, and World, 1968.

Panofsky, Erwin and Dora. (1956) *Pandora's Box*. Princeton: Princeton University Press.

Pollock, G. H. (1968) "The Possible Significance of Childhood Object Loss in the Josef Breuer–Bertha Pappenheim (Anna O.)–Sigmund Freud Relationship." *Journal of the American Psychoanalytic Association* 16:711–39.

Proust, Marcel. (1928) *The Past Recaptured*. New York: Random House.

Reich, Annie. (1950) "On the Termination of Analysis." In *Psychoanalytic Contributions*. New York: International Universities Press, 1973.

Rieff, Philip. (1966) *The Triumph of the Therapeutic*. New York: Harper and Row; Harper Torchbook, 1968.

Searles, Harold. (1959) "Oedipal Love in the Countertransference." In *Collected Papers on Schizophrenia and Related Subjects*. New York: International Universities Press, 1965.

Stone, Leo. (1954) In "The Widening Scope of Indications for Psychoanalysis." *Journal of the American Psychoanalytic Association* 2:567–94.

———. (1961) *The Psychoanalytic Situation*. New York: International Universities Press.

van der Leeuw, P. J. (1968) "The Psychoanalytic Society." *International Journal of Psycho-Analysis* 49:160–64.

Waelder, Robert. (1960) *Basic Theory of Psychoanalysis*. New York: International Universities Press.

Winnicott, Donald W. (1954) "Metapsychological and Clinical Aspects of Regression Within the Psychoanalytical Set-up." In *Collected Papers: Through Pediatrics to Psychoanalysis*. New York: Basic Books, 1958.

———. (1954–55) "The Depressive Position in Normal Emotional Development." In *ibid*.

———. (1955–56) "Clinical Varieties of Transference." In *ibid*.

———. (1969) "The Use of an Object and Relating Through Identifications." In *Playing and Reality*. London: Tavistock, 1971.

# READING CHEKHOV
## A Critical Journey

'An excellent book . . . it is a pleasure to read, and it sends you
straight back to Chekhov, as it should'
A. S. Byatt, *Guardian*

'It is literary pilgrimage, homage, travelogue, biography, literary
criticism and a restrained love letter all rolled into one'
Neel Mukherjee, *The Times*

'One of the most consistent non-fiction writers of our time.
Certainly, she is one of the most brilliant'
Sebastian Smee, *Spectator*

'It is impossible to put this book down and not feel that one
knows Chekhov much better – and impossible not to want to go
and re-read him' Anne Applebaum, *Sunday Telegraph*

# IN THE FREUD ARCHIVES

Who will inherit the secrets of Sigmund Freud? Who will protect his reputation? Who may destroy it?

Janet Malcolm's investigation into the personalities who clash over Freud's legacy is a classic story of seduction and betrayal, love and hatred, fantasy and reality.

'From beginning to end it has the coolly accomplished excitement of a thriller' *Sunday Times*

'One of the most consistent non-fiction writers of our time. Certainly, she is one of the most brilliant' Sebastian Smee, *Spectator*

# THE JOURNALIST AND
# THE MURDERER

*with an introduction by Ian Jack*

'One of the best journalists writing in English anywhere'
John Lloyd, *Financial Times*

*Every journalist who is not too stupid or too full of himself to notice
what is going on knows that what he does is morally indefensible.*

Janet Malcolm begins this book with the words above, which have
become famous (and infamous), and then sets out to demonstrate
the charge with the story of the lawsuit between Jeffrey MacDonald,
a convicted murderer, and Joe McGinniss, the author of a book
about the crime. As a study of the uneasy relationship between a
journalist and his subject it has no equal.

# Birthdays & Biscuits

## LINDA CHAPMAN

Illustrated by Kate Hindley

Orion
Children's Books

First published in Great Britain 2015
by Orion Children's Books
an imprint of Hachette Children's Group,
a division of Hodder and Stoughton Ltd
Orion House
5 Upper St Martin's Lane
London WC2 9EA
An Hachette UK company

1 3 5 7 9 10 8 6 4 2

The paper and board used in this paperback are natural and
recyclable products made from wood grown in sustainable forests.
The manufacturing processes conform to the environmental
regulations of the country of origin.

A catalogue record for this book is
available from the British Library.

Printed in Great Britain by Clays Ltd, St Ives plc

ISBN 978 1 4440 1194 4

www.orionchildrensbooks.co.uk

To two great dog-training teachers –
Helen Green of Companion Dog Training,
who taught me so much about dog training,
and to Anne Bull at AMK9 for being so
encouraging and for being such a great
source of doggy advice. And also to
three special dogs who were very willing
tasters of dog-biscuit recipes – Freddie the
Labradoodle, Simba the Golden Retriever,
and Candy the Cockapoo!

## MY BAKING BOOK (and other stuff)

Name: Hannah

Age: ~~10³/₄~~ 11

Birthday: 1st August

Likes: baking, drawing, swimming, seeing my friends

Dislikes: spiders and slugs

This is my journal. It's for all sorts of important things – lists, cake designs, cookery facts, a few other things, but most of all for RECIPES!

Blonde

Greeny blue

ME

# 1

Has anything ever happened to you that at the time feels like the worst thing in the world, but afterwards you realise maybe it wasn't such a disaster after all? My experience on *Junior Brilliant Baker* was just like that.

Actually, before I tell you about *Junior Brilliant Baker*, I should probably tell you a bit about me. My name's Hannah Hallett and I'm eleven years old (my birthday was two weeks ago). I live in Ashingham with my mum, my stepdad, Mark, and my four-year-old stepsisters Molly and Ella. My dad lives in America and I don't see him much – he and Mum split up when I was a baby. The most important thing you need to know is

that I'm baking-mad, which gets me back
to *Junior Brilliant Baker*. It's my favourite
TV show ever! It's a competition for young
bakers between the ages of eight and thirteen,
and when I decided to apply for it, out of all
the thousands of people who auditioned, I
was actually one of the few invited to be on
the show! It was a dream come true ... well,
at first.

It started off brilliantly. In the first round,
we baked bread and the judges liked mine so
much they made me Junior Brilliant Baker of
the week. It was amazing!

But in the second round, everything fell
apart. Literally. My lemon meringue pie
collapsed and the pastry on my chocolate and

raspberry tart came out
tough and chewy.
I ended up being
one of the two worst
bakers that week and was knocked out of the
competition. At the time, it seemed like the
biggest disaster in the world, but the strange
thing is, now, just two weeks later, it doesn't
feel as awful as I'd thought.

You see, my friends and family held a big
party for me and made me realise how lucky
I am and how well I did just to get on the
show. And now I'm not in the competition
any more, I've been able to enjoy the summer
holidays. Instead of practising
and getting stressed, I've
been seeing my friends,
helping at Mum's bakery
(more about
THAT in a
moment) and
just baking
for fun. My
mum often says

that every cloud has a silver lining, and in this case she is SO right.

So, Mum's bakery. She opened it four months ago, after she and Mark got married and we moved to Ashingham. It's called the Sugar and Spice Bakery and it's my favourite place in the whole world! I help out behind the counter and Mia, my best friend, does too. We're not old enough to work there properly so we talk to the customers and wrap up the cakes, pastries and bread. I really love the bakery, but when Mum first told me that opening it would mean moving house and going to a new school, I was pretty worried. It had been Mum's dream for as long as I could remember, and I wanted to support her – I just didn't want to change schools and leave all my old friends. It didn't help that in Ashingham most people don't go to a primary school for Year Six, they go to a middle school. My new school, King William's, takes pupils from Years Five to Eight, and it's much bigger than I'm used to – more like a secondary school – which made

4

moving even more scary. Luckily, I met Mia at the bakery before term started, as well as my other new friends Alice, Misha and Lara, and I've fitted into King William's just fine. I've still got my old friends but now I have new ones too – and I LOVE Mum owning the Sugar and Spice Bakery. And basically that's me!

Mia is coming round any minute. We're meeting Mum at the bakery. It's almost closing time, and Mum is staying on to decorate some biscuits she's made for the launch party of her friend's new beauty shop tomorrow – Friday. Mia and I are going to help. (And hopefully we'll get to eat some of the biscuits too!) My perfect way to spend a day!

MIA

SOURDOUGH

LARA

MISHA

Big silver linings about moving to Ashingham

ALICE

SUGAR & SPICE BAKERY

the BEST bakery in the WORLD!

6

# 2

The doorbell rang. I shut my journal and ran downstairs. Mia was standing on the front step. She had two cupcake-shaped clips holding back her chin-length strawberry blonde hair. The freckles on her nose had come out over the summer and they made her eyes look even greener.

"Hi!" she said. "Are we still going to ice biscuits?"

"Yep." I turned and called over my shoulder. "Mark! Mia's here. We're going to walk to the bakery to meet Mum."

"OK," yelled Mark from the kitchen, where he was supervising the twins painting pictures. "See you later."

Outside, our neighbour Mrs Rees was watering the hanging baskets in her front garden. Her three little pug dogs were snuffling at her feet. They ran to the fence to say hello and Mia and I tickled their noses. They're really cute, with enormous eyes and squashed-up faces.

Mrs Rees smiled. "Hello there! Where are you two off to?" Mrs Rees is in her seventies. She has tightly curled blonde hair, and is big, jolly and welcoming. If she was a cake, she'd be a custard slice.

Oh yes, that's something else about me – I compare people I know to different types of bakes. It's a bit weird, but  can't help it. Mum is a hot cross bun – sweet and a bit spicy: she's kind and warm but she does have a temper; Mark is a fresh farmhouse loaf – solid, comforting

8

and reliable; Mia's like a loaf of my mum's sourdough bread – you might not notice her in a crowd, though she's the nicest person when you get to know her. As for me, well, I guess I'm like a sugar-coated Eccles cake: nothing too showy, but nice inside and liked by most people.

"Hi, Mrs Rees," I said.

"We're going to the bakery," Mia said. "We're helping Hannah's mum ice biscuits for the launch party of Sarah's new beauty shop."

Mrs Rees nodded vaguely. I had a feeling she hadn't heard Mia properly, because she is quite deaf. "Are you going to Sarah's launch party tomorrow night, Mrs Rees?" I asked loudly.

"The launch party?" Mrs Rees repeated. "Do you mean for Sarah King's new shop? Yes, I am, dear. Lots of people seem to be going."

"I hope they like the biscuits," said Mia. Mrs Rees frowned. "What biscuits, dear?"

I hid my grin. "Mum's making biscuits for the launch," I said. "We're going to help her ice them now. We could bring you some back for your tea."

"A bee?" said Mrs Rees, looking round in alarm. "Where?"

"No, not a bee. I said tea!" I shouted. "We'll bring you some biscuits for your tea."

Mrs Rees beamed. "How very kind. Now, why did you say you were making biscuits again?"

It was a lovely warm afternoon as we made our way to the bakery. Wisps of cloud floated across the sky and birds chirruped in the trees. We turned into the quiet little side street, and spotted Sarah's new shop. It used to be a grocery, but now it's been redecorated ready for its big opening as Natural Beauty. There's a new sign above the door, freshly painted in pink, peppermint green and gold. Inside, the shelves and tables are filled with pretty bottles, pyramids of bath bombs and handmade soaps.

The bakery is further down the street. Mum and I used to imagine what our perfect bakery would be like – and the Sugar and Spice Bakery is everything we hoped for. There are cherry blossom trees outside and it has a big curved front window. There's a counter filled with cream cakes, doughnuts, sponge cakes, macaroons and meringues; a stand of bread baskets with slate labels where Mum writes the names of the different types of bread; and a hot cabinet where sausage rolls and meat pies are kept. And there are displays of special-occasion cakes Mum makes, and a coffee machine for people to get takeaway coffee.

When we arrived, the lights were off and the sign on the door was turned to 'Closed'. I knocked and Mum came to let us in.

I took a deep breath as we walked inside. The delicious smell of baking mingled with the faint scent of coffee and cinnamon. Mmm.

THE SUGAR AND SPICE BAKERY

Posh Wedding cake display

Cakes & doughnuts

KITCHEN

ME

SUGAR & SPICE

FRESH BREAD

Pictures of mum's cakes

PASTRIES

"So, are you ready to help me ice more than a hundred biscuits?" Mum said, locking the door behind us.

We both nodded. "Definitely!" I said.

# 3

Mia and I washed our hands and put aprons
on. We aren't allowed to help in the kitchen
during the day because the kitchen is quite
small. It's only really big enough for Mum
and her assistant, Dylan – and they have a lot
to do! But in the evenings and on Sundays,
when Mum bakes the special-occasion cakes
that people order, Mia and I always love to
help. Mia is as mad about baking as I am,
which is one of the things that
makes her the best friend ever!
When we're older we're going to
have a bakery together and live in
a flat above it. Oh, and we'll
have two pugs and a cat.

Mum had already baked the biscuits. She'd shaped them to look like different beauty products. They looked brilliant.

"The biscuits just need to cool," Mum told us. "If we put the icing on while they're warm, it won't set properly."

"What type of biscuits are they?" I asked.

"Plain vanilla, but it's a special recipe for biscuits that are going to be iced. You don't want a crumbly biscuit for something like this – you need it to be firm and keep its shape while it's being baked. Try one."

Mia and I took a biscuit each. They were crunchy instead of crumbly, but still really sweet and nice.

"These are delicious! Can I have the recipe?" Mia asked.

"Of course. I'll write it down for you," Mum said. "First, though, let's get the icing ready. And let me show you what I want the biscuits to look like."

Mum got out her design book (which is kind of like my journal) and showed us some sketches. First, we were going to pipe the designs on the biscuits with white icing and then we would fill the sections in with different colours – peppermint green, pink and white to match the Natural Beauty brand.

MUM'S BISCUITS FOR NATURAL BEAUTY

"Won't the different colours run together?" Mia asked.

"That's why we're piping the design on with a stiff white icing," Mum said. "Once that's dried, it will act like a little barrier to keep the other colours separate. You spoon the coloured icing into the separate sections, wait for that to set and then pipe on any

16

extra detail. I'd like to add the words 'Natural Beauty' in tiny letters on each biscuit, but I'll probably wait until tomorrow to do that. Tonight we'll get the basic piping and icing done."

We helped Mum make the white icing and then got out the piping bags. Mia and I had to pipe a steady outline around the biscuits, before Mum filled in the tricky details. Even though we had the easy job, it was still hard work! We practised on spare biscuits (ones that were broken or that didn't turn out quite right) until we could pipe steadily without lots of lumps and bumps.

"What will you do with the rest of these?" I said, eating half a broken biscuit. "They're yummy."

"I thought we could take them home and make a cheesecake," Mum said. "Broken biscuits are great for a cheesecake base."

"Or we could eat them all tonight!" I said, with a grin.

"You'll pop! Come on, I think you're ready to start icing the proper biscuits now."

## TOP TIPS FOR ICING BISCUITS

1. Mum uses proper royal icing made with whipped egg whites, but you can use normal sugar icing powder mixed with water too. You won't get as perfect results but it's much easier and the biscuits will still taste yummy! If you're going to pipe on a design, you need to make the icing really stiff and thick. The icing for spooning on can be a bit runnier.

2. If you don't have piping bags, you can get little squeezy craft bottles with a nozzle from a craft shop and fill them with icing instead.

By the time we'd finished, I was beginning to think I would happily never ice another biscuit again, but when we looked at what we'd done, it was amazing! We'd made

18

perfume bottles, lipsticks, bath bombs and bubble bath bottles – all beautiful biscuits in the Natural Beauty colours.

"Phew!" Mum said, wiping her forehead. "I think that's it. Thanks so much for your help, you two."

"I bet people will love them," said Mia.

I nodded. My thoughts were full of my own biscuit design ideas. I was thinking of a different biscuit for each of my friends. I was itching to get my journal and do some sketching. Mia could have a cupcake, Misha, a microphone (she loves singing) and for Alice and Lara I would do horses or a riding hat or horseshoes …

"Earth to Hannah!" Mia waved a hand in front of my face. "It's tidying time." I blinked, then sighed. The last thing I felt like doing was loading the dishwasher and wiping the surfaces, but I knew the bakery had to be clean so that Mum could come in and work as usual first thing in the morning.

I picked up a cloth. Baking is the most fun thing in the world – clearing up definitely isn't!

## MUM'S PERFECT BISCUITS FOR ICING

Ingredients:

225g salted butter at room temperature, cut
   into cubes
225g caster sugar
1 large egg, lightly beaten
450g plain flour
Royal icing sugar, to decorate

What to do:

1. Preheat the oven to
   180°C. In a bowl,
   cream butter and
   sugar together until
   just combined, then
   gradually beat in the egg
   using a wooden spoon
   or electric whisk.

2. Whisk in the flour a
   little at a time until a
   dough forms. Tip out
   the dough onto a clean

20

surface and bring into a ball with your hands. If it's too crumbly at this stage, add a little drop of milk.

3. Put the dough in a large freezer bag and flatten into a rectangle about 2cm deep, then place in the fridge for an hour.

4. Take the dough out of the fridge, divide into two and start rolling on a floured surface until each  piece is about 5mm thick.

5. Use biscuit cutters to cut shapes and place on a greased baking tray. It's best if you cut out shapes that are roughly the same size because then the biscuits will need the same amount of baking time.

6. Bake for 6-10 minutes until golden brown.

7. Leave to cool on a wire rack. The biscuits should be crisp and dry.

Ice or decorate however you want! I like white icing and hundreds and thousands.

# 4

As we finished clearing up, Mum's mobile rang. It was Sarah, the owner of Natural Beauty. She and Mum had first met when Sarah had started coming to the bakery with her son, George, on his way to tennis practice. Mum and Sarah are really good friends now, and when Natural Beauty opens they want to run party events together so people can be pampered with beauty products and decorate cupcakes and biscuits at the same time.

George and I are good friends too. At first,

I didn't like him much because he was always really moody. But when I got to know him better, I found out he was unhappy at having to play tennis all the time and hated all the pressure. In the end, he told his mum how he felt and now he just plays tennis for fun. Sarah has a lot more free time, which is how she's been able to follow her dream of opening her own beauty shop. It's like Mum says: there are ALWAYS silver linings to everything!

Sarah asked if we would call in on the way home so she could see the biscuits. We boxed up a selection, checked with Mia's mum that it was OK she stayed out late and then set off. The King family live in a big house just outside Ashingham. George is a year older than me. He doesn't go to my school; he goes to the posh boys-only school outside the town. His house is huge. It has a big sweeping circular drive with a fountain, a massive garden and a tennis court. It's like something from a magazine. I'm not sure I'd want to live there, though – I like being near my friends and being able to walk to their houses. George has to get his mum to drive him whenever he wants to go anywhere.

Mum, Mia and I piled out of the car as Sarah opened the front door. She greeted us with a big smile. She reminds me of a neat, pretty macaroon. She's always very tidy, her clothes and make-up just perfect.

"Hi, everyone. Come in. I can't wait to see these biscuits."

We followed Sarah into the enormous kitchen. Mum put the boxes of biscuits on the table and opened them.

Sarah caught her breath.

"Oh, these are wonderful! Like little works of art. They're perfect! Thank you!"

The kitchen door opened and George came in. His hair was a tousled mop as usual. He had three other boys with him.

"Hi," he said. His friends gave us quick grins.

"Hannah, Mia – these are Alec, Callum and Joe. They're George's friends from school. They're staying over tonight," Sarah said.

I'd met Alec and Callum before, but not Joe. George spotted the biscuits.

"They look good, Mum. Can we have one?"

"No! They're far too nice to eat," said Sarah.

"You're seriously weird," George said, rolling his eyes at his mum.

"We probably should do a taste test," my mum said. "Biscuits are no good if they just look pretty."

"Oh, all right then," said Sarah. She offered them round.

I took a lip balm-shaped one with
pink and green icing. It was crisp
and sweet and the icing was thick
and hard. Delicious.

"So, what have you been up to?"
I said to George, as Sarah boiled the kettle
to make her and Mum some coffee.

"We've been rehearsing. You know we're
in a band, right?" George said. "I play drums,
Alec and Callum play guitar and now Joe
sings too."

"We're called Mission Possible," said
Alec, who has brown hair and very blue
eyes. Callum is shorter with dark hair and a
cheeky smile, and Joe has red hair and
freckles.

"Why don't you come and hear us play?"
George said.

Mia and I followed the boys to one of the
garages. George's dad had soundproofed it so
George and his friends could practise there.
The boys' instruments were propped against
the wall and there was a sofa in the corner.

"This is cool," I said, looking round.

Mia and I sat down and the boys started to play. I recognised the song – it was by one of Misha's favourite singers, Ellie B.

"They're good," I whispered to Mia.

She nodded. "Really good."

Joe's voice was amazing. He didn't sound anything like Ellie B, but that didn't matter. He was great. The others played their instruments really well – they all seemed to know exactly what they were doing.

"So? What did you think?" George asked.

"It was brilliant!" I said.

"Have you performed anywhere?" Mia asked.

"Not yet," said Alec. "But we'd like to."

"Yeah, it would be awesome to be on stage," said Callum.

"We need to find somewhere we can do a gig," said Joe. "We've been practising loads."

"It's much better since Joe joined us," said George. "The rest of us aren't too good at singing."

Mia and I listened to a few more songs before we went to find Mum and Sarah.

Sarah had brought some of her
new beauty products into the
kitchen and we spent the next
hour as the sun went down
trying out hand lotions and
body lotions, perfumes and face masks.

"It's lovely having you all here," Sarah said.
"George is no fun when it comes to stuff like
this. He's just not interested."

I grinned. "I can't see George wearing a
face mask."

Sarah chuckled. "No, strangely enough, he
runs a mile whenever I suggest it!"

"Well, anytime you need guinea pigs, let
us know," Mum said. She was sitting with
her feet up, wearing an eye mask. "This is
wonderful."

"That's my Time-to-Relax lavender and
cucumber eye mask," Sarah said.

Mum sighed blissfully.

"How many people are coming
tomorrow evening?" I asked Sarah.

"Well, I've had replies from at
least eighty people saying yes.

It's going to be quite a squash! There are a few journalists from the local paper and some local magazines, as well as lots of my friends. Actually, that reminds me. I was wondering if you two girls could do me a favour."

"Of course," I said. "What is it?"

"Some friends of mine, who've just moved into a rented house in town, will be there. Their daughter, Abi, starts King William's in September, in your year. Her mum, Natalie, says Abi's really not looking forward to going to a new school. If I introduce you, would you have a chat with her at the party, make her feel welcome?"

"Of course!" I said. I remembered just how nervous I had felt when I first started at King William's.

"Which school was she at before?" Mia asked.

"St Leonard's," said Sarah.

St Leonard's High is a girls-only school in a grand old house with big gardens and sports courts outside Ashingham, near George's school. I had a feeling Abi was going to get a shock coming to King William's. It's not a dump or anything, but it's not what you would call beautiful. It's a modern red-brick building, with a leisure centre next door and lots of concrete around it.

"We'll talk to her," I said. "And try and help."

"Thanks, girls." Sarah smiled. "I knew I could count on you."

There was a faint snoring noise beside her. Mum had fallen fast asleep!

"Looks like my Time-to-Relax eye mask really does its job!" said Sarah, laughing.

IDEA FOR A CAKE FOR GEORGE

"Watch your backs! Sausage rolls coming through!" Dylan called, walking out of the bakery kitchen next morning. Dylan is Mum's apprentice. He's always full of energy. He's tall and skinny with spiky blond hair. He makes me think of a long, thin breadstick.

I pulled open the cabinet door for him. Paula, who works behind the counter, was saying goodbye to a customer.

"How's it going out here?" Dylan said,

32

as I helped him put the sausage
rolls into the cabinet.

"Busy," I said. "We've had
lots of customers already and
it's only ten o'clock."

"Good, good, good," he said.

Paula picked up a newspaper from beside
the till. "It's going to carry on being busy too.
It says so in my stars." Paula loves reading
horoscopes. "Listen," she went on. "For
Sagittarius, 'Make the most of the action-
packed day ahead of you!' See! The stars
never lie."

Dylan looked over her shoulder. "So how
come it says for my star sign, 'Make the most
of a quiet day, chill out like a popsicle'?"

"Does it?" Paula frowned and looked
closer. "Oh, it doesn't say anything of the
sort!" She tutted. "Get back to the kitchen!"

"Yes, ma'am!" said Dylan, mock-saluting
her and winking at me and Mia. "Laters,
slackers! Some of us have work to do!"

"Of all the cheek!" huffed Paula, but her
eyes twinkled so I knew she didn't really

mind. Paula reminds me of a fruit scone. She's small and round, with dark eyes and short black spiky hair. She's in her fifties (Mum says), but she doesn't act old at all. She usually wears black jeans, polo necks and Converses, and she's far more into music than Mia and I are.

"What are you two girls up to today?" she asked. "Are you staying here or off doing things?"

"We'll be here most of the day, then we're meeting Alice, Misha and Lara at Harry's this afternoon," I said.

Harry's is the ice-cream parlour in the town centre.

I remembered what Sarah had said last night and turned to Mia. "We should tell the others about this new girl, Abi. Maybe she can come to Harry's with us one day.

It would be so much nicer for her to know some people before school starts."

Mia nodded. "Good idea. We'll have to wait a bit, though – Alice, Misha and Lara are off on their riding holiday next week, remember?"

Paula looked interested. "What new girl's this?"

Mia and I told her about Abi.

"Ah, I wonder if they're the family who have moved into Brooksby Close," Paula said. "I noticed they had a daughter about your age."

Just then the door opened and Miss Harris came in. She teaches at our school and runs the Baking Club that Mia and I go to. "Hi, Paula. Hi, girls. I was hoping you two would be here," she said.

Miss Harris

"Us? Why?" I asked.

"I have a problem I need help with. Have you heard of PAWS?"

We both looked at her blankly. "It's a small dog-rescue centre on the edge of town," said Miss Harris. "I've been going there a few times a week to help exercise the dogs. It's an amazing place. Dawn, the owner, will take in any dog that needs a home. Provided they're not dangerous and she has a kennel free, she'll take them."

"It sounds cool," I said. I would love to have a dog, but Mum says it wouldn't be fair because she and Mark are out all day working. "What do you need us for? Walking the dogs?"

"No – though I'm sure Dawn would be delighted if you did want to do that," Miss Harris said. "What I was really hoping was that you might help me with a fundraising

day, a sort of family 'Fun Day' that Dawn is trying to organise. The vet's bills and food costs are turning out to be much higher than she'd anticipated when she first

opened PAWS, and though
she gets some money from
rehoming the dogs, and she has a
regular income from renting out
the surrounding fields to a local
farmer, it's still not enough. She needs to do
some serious fundraising or she thinks PAWS
might have to close."

"But … what would happen
to the dogs then?" I said.

"Another rescue centre
would probably take most of
them, but the bigger centres
are often full to capacity and
many will only take in young,
healthy dogs. Some of the older dogs at
PAWS would almost certainly have to be put
down."

I was shocked. How could a rescue centre
do something so horrible?
"That's awful."

"We can't let that happen,"
said Mia quickly.

Miss Harris sighed. "I know.

The amazing thing about Dawn is that she takes all dogs, no matter how old. She feels every dog deserves a chance. This Fun Day is the launch of her fundraising plans, so it's really important it goes well. It's not just about the money raised on the day – if people come along and become more aware of the work PAWS does, it will hopefully inspire them to get involved in the other fundraising events Dawn wants to organise."

"We'd love to help," I said, glancing at Mia, who nodded.

"Yes, when is the Fun Day?" said Mia. "Do you have any plans for it so far?"

"Ah, well, you see, that's the problem. It's supposed to tie in with PAWS' first birthday, on Bank Holiday Monday in ten days' time.

 Dawn has booked a band and a bouncy castle, and planned a dog show, hoping to encourage people to come along, but she's been so busy looking after the dogs that she hasn't had time to get things properly organised or to advertise it."

"Why doesn't she just cancel and do it in a few months' time?" I asked.

"She could, but it would be so much better to have it while the weather's good," said Miss Harris. "It would also mean cancelling the things she *has* booked. Which is why I've said I'll help – and why I wanted to ask you two to get involved."

"Sounds like a great plan," said Paula. "You two are brilliant at organising things."

"Well, Hannah is," said Mia.

"You are too," I said.

"You're much better than me," she said.

"Ah, that's because Hannah's a Leo," said Paula. "Leos are the world's natural organisers. But being a Pisces, Mia, you're creative and artistic – you make the perfect team."

Mia and I grinned at each other.

"That's great! We have a lot of work to do in under two weeks," Miss Harris said.

"That's OK; we're not doing much else," said Mia.

"Yes, there must be lots more we can do to raise money on the day," I said.

"What about a cake stall?" said Mia. "Ooh! Everything could be decorated with paw prints and dog faces."

"Yes!" I said. "And a stall to buy drinks, and a doggy lucky dip with prizes for people's dogs ..."

"And a treasure map, where people have to guess where the bone is buried," said Mia.

Miss Harris beamed. "I *knew* I could rely on you two for good ideas. I'm going to PAWS to see Dawn tomorrow morning for a planning meeting. Would you both like to come too if your parents say it's OK?"

We nodded. "Yes please," I said.

"Wonderful," said Miss Harris. "I'll pick you up here at half past nine then. Now," she rubbed her hands together, "I think I'll have a custard slice and a coffee to celebrate!"

40

# THE PAWS FUN DAY AND DOG SHOW

Day: Monday, 25th August
Place: PAWS
Ideas:

Cake stall - dog themed?

Doggy lucky dip

Stalls selling things - a pet shop?

Other stalls?
Coconut shy - make coconuts look like dogs'
heads with ears and noses? But might feel
mean to be knocking dogs'
heads off stands, even if just
coconuts?? Maybe not a good
idea.

Treasure map - guess where the hidden bone
is.

41

# 6

Mia and I talked about nothing but PAWS
for the rest of the day. Mum said she would
make biscuits and cakes to sell there and
donate any profits she made to the centre.
She, Paula and Dylan offered to help run the
cake stall on the day. I was really excited.
The Fun Day sounded like a perfect summer
project and it was for such a good cause.

Just before three o'clock, Mia and I walked
to Harry's to meet the others. We were the
first to arrive and sat at our favourite table in
the window.

"Look, there they are," Mia said, spotting
the girls, who were spilling out of Lara's
mum's car. Misha spotted us and waved wildly

with both hands. Alice and Lara grinned.

"Hannah! Mia! Woo-hoo!" Misha whooped as they walked in, making the other customers look round. She skipped towards us and tripped over a handbag on the floor next to one of the tables.

Best ice cream in the World!

"Whoops, sorry!" she gasped. She gave the bag a pat, as if it were a dog. "It's not hurt, it's fine. There, there," she said. "You're fine, aren't you?" I giggled at the slightly alarmed expression on the ladies' faces.

Misha reached us and high-fived me. "Hannah! Is that a new T-shirt?"

"Yes, Mum bought it for me."

"I like." Misha grabbed a straw from the table and held it as if it was a microphone. *"You're so beautiful, in every single way ..."* she sang.

I rolled my eyes. "Sit down."

"Yes, sit," said Alice, pressing her hands on Misha's shoulders. She cast an apologetic look at the ladies. "Sorry."

Misha grinned at them over her shoulder. "I don't get out very often."

I giggled. Misha is very loud and always likes to be the centre of attention, but she is funny.

"So, how it's going? What have you been up to? We haven't seen you for ages," Misha said.

"Yes, *three whole days*," I said.

"That's, like, *forever*!"

"We've been helping at the bakery and doing some baking with Mum," I said, glancing at Mia. She tends to be quieter when we're all in a group together. When I first met her she was so shy, she didn't have any friends at school, and she found it quite hard to fit in with Misha, Alice and Lara, who are definitely one of the popular groups in our year. She's started to relax around them now, but she still doesn't talk as much when we're with them.

44

"We iced some biscuits," she said. She showed the girls a picture of the biscuits for Sarah's launch party on her phone.

"They look yummy," said Alice.

"They were!" I said. "Sarah loved them – we took them over yesterday and she let us try some of her beauty products."

"Luck-y!" said Lara enviously.

Misha nudged me. "So, was *George* there?" she said.

"Yes," I said.

"He and his friends from school have started a band," said Mia. "They're really good."

"Maybe he'll write you a love song, Hannah," Misha said.

"Ha ha," I said. I knew better than to let Misha's teasing get to me.

Luckily the waitress came over to take our order so Misha was distracted. I decided on a

banana split, Mia had
a strawberry sundae,
Lara and Misha had
knickerbocker glories,
and Alice chose a toffee
fudge sundae.

"What have you three been
up to?' I asked. "Have you been
riding much?" Misha, Lara and
Alice often spend time at their riding
school during the holidays.

"Yes. We've been at the stables every day,"
said Alice. "Yesterday we helped give pony
rides at a fete. That was fun."

I gasped. "Pony rides!" I said to Mia. "That
would be perfect!"

She knew straight away what I was getting
at. "Oh yes! For the Fun Day!"

The others looked confused. "Is this some
new language that only the two of you
speak?" Misha asked.

I explained. "You could all help too," I said.

"It sounds amazing, but we go away on our
pony holiday next week," said Alice.

"We can help on the day, though," said Lara. "We could run some stalls if you tell us what to do."

"Do you think your stables might bring ponies for doing pony rides?" I said.

"We can ask," said Alice. "And we could definitely help with that."

"I could do a song and entertain people," said Misha. She started to sing. "*How much is that doggy in the window …?*"

"Or maybe you could just help with the pony rides," I said. "You might make people run away!"

"Thanks!" she huffed.

I grinned. "You're welcome!"

Just then the ice creams and drinks arrived.

"Here's to a very fun Fun Day!" Alice said, lifting her spoon.

"To a very fun Fun Day," we chorused.

# 7

That evening, Mark had booked a babysitter for the twins so that he, Mum and I could go to the Natural Beauty launch. Mum had gone straight there after the bakery closed to help Sarah set up.

When Mark and I arrived, the shop was brightly lit and there were already lots of people inside. The air was scented with essential oils from the bath bombs and handmade soaps piled high on the display units. Mum had arranged the biscuits on tiered cake stands around the shop, and packed others into little gift bags tied with ribbon for people to take home. She'd also baked a special cake, which looked just like the Natural Beauty sign outside. The cake had pride of place on the main counter and the biscuits looked perfect! I felt very proud.

Sarah's husband, Richard, was serving drinks with George in one corner, while Sarah welcomed people and encouraged them to go through to the back room where they could try out products and buy any if they wanted. I spotted Paula and Dylan, and Miss Harris and Mark's friend Stefan. He and Miss Harris had just started dating. There were quite a few people I didn't know, too – smartly dressed ladies wearing lots of jewellery, and men in suits, who had obviously come straight from their offices.

"Hannah! Hi!" George waved. I squeezed my way through the crowd towards the drinks table.

"There are so many people here!" I said.

He nodded. "Yes, Mum's really pleased. What can I get you? I'm in charge of soft drinks." He pointed to a tray of glasses. "There are elderflower and apple mocktails, or just plain orange juice, or fizzy water."

"Mmm, elderflower, please," I said. He handed me a tall thin glass with a slice of apple over the edge, a twirly green straw and a white umbrella. "Is Mia here?" I asked, looking round.

"I'm not sure. I haven't seen her, but she might be in the back room," George said.

"OK, thanks, I'll go and find her. See you later," I said, as more people came over for drinks.

As I headed towards the back room, I bumped into Sarah. "Hi, Hannah!" she said. "Don't the biscuits look fantastic? Thank you so much for helping." Her eyes were sparkling and she looked happier than I had

ever seen her. "Are you going to go and
try some products? Or ... hang on." She'd
spotted someone. "Do you remember I told
you about Abi, the girl who's coming to your
school? She's over there with her mum and
dad. Can I introduce you?"

"Sure," I said, looking to where she was
gesturing. I saw a lady with short, dark hair,

and a tall man beside her,
talking to some of Sarah's
other friends. The girl with
them had the same dark hair
as her mum, tied back in a
high ponytail. She was fiddling
with the straw of her drink,
looking bored, but as if she
was politely trying to hide it.

I followed Sarah, with a
feeling of anticipation. I was
looking forward to meeting
Abi and reassuring her about
school and everything. I love
helping people and being
friendly.

"Hi, everyone," Sarah said. "Sorry to interrupt – I wanted Abi to meet Hannah. Hannah, this is Abi and her parents, Natalie and Michael. Hannah goes to King William's," she explained. "She'll be in Year Seven in September too. Her mum is my friend Rose, who owns the bakery down the street."

The grown-ups nodded in recognition. "Oh, I was there just the other day," said Natalie. "Their sourdough is amazing."

"Thank you – I'll tell Mum." I turned to Abi and gave her my best friendly smile. "Hi."

"Hi," she muttered. She looked at the floor. I wondered if she was shy. Well, that was OK. When I first Mia, she'd been very shy and had hardly spoken at all, but I'd kept trying and in the end she had come out of her shell. If Abi was shy, I would just do the same.

"So, I hear your mum made all the biscuits here tonight, Hannah?" Michael, Abi's dad, said.

"Yes, and the cake," I said. "I helped decorate the biscuits. I love baking."

"And she's brilliant at it," said Sarah, with a smile.

"How long have you lived in Ashingham, Hannah?" Michael asked. He and Abi's mum seemed really friendly, but Abi was still avoiding looking at me.

She was focused on twirling the straw in her drink.

"We've only been here since Easter," I said. "I was really worried about starting a new school, but everyone's been really friendly." I glanced at Abi. "I can tell you all about it if you like?"

Abi shrugged, not looking up from her drink.

Sarah beamed. "That sounds great. Why don't you two girls go and get to know each other? You could go and try some of the

54

products. You don't want to hang around with us adults."

Abi glanced at her mum. I knew that look. It clearly said, *I don't want to go.* Natalie gave her arm a gentle push. "Go on, sweetie."

There was a pause.

"Should we go, then?" I said to Abi, feeling a bit awkward. She obviously didn't want to come with me, but she also didn't really have a choice with all the adults looking at us.

She nodded and followed me to the back room where people were milling around the counters, trying out moisturisers, and sniffing the bubble baths and essential oils.

We stopped in the centre of the room. I looked around, hoping to see Mia. It would be good to have someone else to try and get Abi to talk. There was still no sign of her, though.

"So," I said, "you're coming to King William's."

"Yep."

Abi glanced towards the door, as if she wanted an escape route. I didn't get it. I was being friendly. Even if she was shy, wouldn't she *want* to try and find out something about the school she was going to – to make friends with someone who would be in her year?

"Uh, is there anything in particular you want to know about it?" I asked.

"Not really." Her voice was off-hand – rude, almost. I felt a prickle of irritation. I was trying to be friendly here; I didn't *have* to talk to her. Part of me wanted to walk off and leave her, but I'd promised Sarah I would make an effort, so I tried again.

"You've just moved into town, haven't you? Whereabouts are you living?"

"Brooksby Close."

"Oh, that's near me."

I paused, waiting for Abi to ask where I lived, but she looked in the opposite direction. The silence lengthened. Wow, she *really* didn't want to talk. Now I was the one who wanted to escape! I gave it one last try.

"What do you like doing when you're not at school?"

Abi shrugged. "Nothing much. I'm going to go back to Mum and Dad now. Bye." She turned and walked away.

I stared after her. Well, that was friendly – NOT. I didn't know whether to feel relieved she had gone or cross. I couldn't believe how rude she'd been. Well, if she didn't want to be friends, that was her problem. I decided to go back to the front room and get another drink.

George swapped my empty glass for a full one. I took a gulp. Elderflower and apple mocktails were yummy!

"Did you find Mia?" George asked.

"No, she's not here yet," I said. "But your mum just introduced me to that new girl, Abi. Do you know her?"

"Oh yes, she's cool," George said. "I didn't realise she was here. I used to see her at the tennis club. Her mum and dad and mine are friends so we hang out sometimes."

"So she's usually quite nice, then?" I said in surprise.

"Yes." He looked at me. "She's fun. Why?"

"She wasn't very friendly with me just now. I could hardly get her to say anything."

"Oh." He shrugged. "Never mind." And he turned to serve someone a drink.

Typical boy, I thought, rolling my eyes. I wandered off to try and spot Mia again. She would understand why I was feeling cross. As I looked round the room, I saw Abi was back with her parents, picking at a fingernail and answering only when her parents' friends spoke to her. Well, at least I knew it wasn't just me.

"Hannah!" I heard Mia's voice. She was coming into the shop with her mum. I pushed Abi to the back of my mind, waved and hurried over.

While her mum went to talk to mine, I told Mia what had happened with Abi.

"Maybe she's just shy," Mia said.

I frowned. "I thought that at first but she didn't seem shy and George said she's usually good fun."

"Well, sometimes people find it hard to be friendly straight away," said Mia. "She might just need time to get to know us."

"Maybe," I said. I wasn't convinced.

"Should we go and try and talk to her again?" Mia said.

I shook my head. "No, let's go and try out the products."

At seven o'clock, Sarah clinked her glass and made a speech about how delighted she was to open Natural Beauty and how she hoped everyone would call in lots and tell people about it. Then she cut the cake and we all had a piece. After that, people carried on chatting until around eight o'clock, before starting to drift off home.

Abi's parents brought her over to say goodbye. "It was great meeting you, Hannah," said Abi's mum. "Maybe you could come round sometime before school starts."

"OK," I said, though I really didn't want to. And it was clear Abi didn't want me to either. Her parents were smiling at me, but she was staring at the floor again.

"I'll get your number from Sarah, if that's all right?" Abi's mum said.

I nodded. "Or just call in to the bakery. I'm there most days, and so's Mia. She's my best friend from school."

Mia smiled shyly at them all. "Hi, Abi," she said. "You should come in to the bakery one day and see us – we can tell you all about school."

"Yeah," Abi said briefly. She scuffed her shoe along the ground. I saw her mum and dad exchange looks.

"Well, hopefully we'll see you soon," said Abi's dad, speaking a bit too heartily as he tried to fill the silence. "After those delicious biscuits and cake, I have a feeling you might be seeing quite a bit of us in the bakery."

"Come along then, Abi," said her mum, and they left.

"I see what you mean," Mia whispered. "She's not friendly, is she?"

"Not at all," I said. I didn't know what to make of Abi at all.

Miss Harris came over to say goodbye with Stefan. "We're off now," Miss Harris said.

Stefan held up his goody bag. "I must get the recipe for these biscuits. I have already eaten two and they are delicious. I will swap you the recipe for German iced gingerbread."

"It's a deal," I said, with a smile.

"And I'll see you and Mia at the bakery in the morning," Miss Harris said. "I told Dawn you offered to help and she's delighted. Now we just have to come up with a plan to make this day a success."

"We'll do everything we can," I promised.

Miss Harris and Stefan left arm in arm.

"I'm so glad they got together," I said.

"With a little help from us," said Mia, grinning.

# ELDERFLOWER AND APPLE MOCKTAILS

## Ingredients:

1 litre cloudy apple juice

75ml elderflower cordial

Sparkling water or lemonade

Small handful of mint leaves

3 lime or lemon wedges

20 ice cubes, crushed

1 apple, sliced

## What to do:

1. Fill a jug with the ice cubes, then add the apple juice and elderflower cordial. Squeeze in the lime or lemon wedges and stir in the mint leaves.

2. Pour into glasses until glasses are half full, then top up with sparkling water or lemonade.

3. Decorate with a slice of apple on the side and a straw. Enjoy!

# 8

On the way to PAWS the next morning, Miss Harris told Mia and me a bit more about the rescue centre.

"Dawn inherited the old farmhouse eighteen months ago when her uncle died. She'd always dreamed of running a dog rescue centre, so this seemed like the perfect opportunity. She has kennels for twenty-two dogs at the moment and three part-time members of staff. The place is always full." Miss Harris smiled. "The dogs really are gorgeous. I bet you'll love them."

"Why did you start volunteering?" I asked.

"I've always loved dogs, so when I moved here, I looked to see if there were any local dog rescue centres that needed volunteers to walk the dogs. I wish I could have a dog myself, but it's just not fair when I'm out of the house all day during term-time. PAWS means I still get my doggy fix. And it's a beautiful place. There are fields all around it – a farmer rents some of them, but the ones closest to the centre are used for exercising the dogs. They'll be the perfect setting for the Fun Day. The band is going to play there after the dog show, and I thought we could try and organise a barbecue too. I've also been in touch with the local pet shop – Pet Heaven – and they're going to run a stall and donate a percentage of their takings to PAWS."

"That's a great idea. Mum's offered to run a cake stall – and provide the cakes too," I said.

"That's really kind of her," said Miss Harris.

"Maybe Sarah could run a Natural Beauty stall?" Mia suggested. "We could ask her."

I nodded. "Oh, and the owner of Willow Stables has said they'll organise pony rides."

Alice had texted me that morning to confirm.

"That all sounds fantastic, girls," said Miss Harris. "And here we are!"

She turned into a driveway. There was a big sign beside it with a paw print: *PAWS – every dog deserves a home!*

At the end of the drive was a large car park. Set a little way back from the car park, and reached by a pathway lined with purple lavender bushes, was a stone farmhouse. The house had old-fashioned diamond-paned windows. It was a bit ramshackle, but very beautiful, with pale pink climbing roses growing around the front door.

There were also a couple of modern buildings beside the car park. I could hear dogs barking inside one of them. It had a sign over the door saying RECEPTION. Behind the buildings, I could see a paddock with fenced-off exercise areas and a wildflower meadow with paths cut through the long grass.

"Come along in and meet Dawn," said Miss Harris.

We followed Miss Harris into the reception area. It was a light, airy room, with photos of dogs all over the walls. A lady was standing behind the desk. She was small and slim with short, dark hair. She was talking into a mobile phone, her tanned face etched with worry.

"But this is awful! The Fun Day is nine days away. You can't cancel!"

She saw us and gave a quick, anxious smile and then turned her attention back to her phone conversation.

Dawn would be
a bread roll –
small, practical,
not showy;
essential.

"All right, fine," she said. "I understand. Thank you for letting me know." She hung up, and with a shake of her head, turned to us. "Hi." She was smiling but I could see the strain in the lines around her eyes.

"Hi, Dawn. Everything OK?" Miss Harris said.

"Not really. The band I booked for the Fun Day have pulled out. They were one of the main attractions," Dawn said.

"Oh no!" Miss Harris said. "That's a blow."

"Yes." Dawn took a deep breath. "But there's nothing I can do."

"Look, don't worry," said Miss Harris. "I'm sure we can think of other things to make the day a success – Hannah and Mia have already had lots of good ideas."

Dawn smiled, and this time her smile was more relaxed. "Hi, girls. It's lovely to meet you. So, which of you is Hannah and which is Mia?"

"I'm Hannah, and this is Mia," I said.

"We do really want to help," Mia added.

"Thank you," Dawn said warmly. "Why don't you come and meet the dogs? Then we can go up to the house and talk."

Dawn led us through some double doors. We entered a wide corridor, which had kennels on either side. Each kennel had a name-plate, a metal front, a dog bed, water bowl and rubber chew toys. There were all shapes and sizes of dogs inside – some big, some small, some with long hair, some with short, some with yappy barks, others with deep, booming barks. The dogs pressed their noses against the kennel doors and stood on their hind legs, tails wagging in greeting. I wanted to cuddle them all!

There was a large room at the end which had feed bins and kennel supplies. Two women were working there. One, who had light brown hair in a ponytail, was cleaning an empty kennel, while the other, whose hair was dyed dark purple, was at a sink washing food bowls. They smiled and came to say hi. The one with the light brown hair was called Rachael, and the other was Jess. They were both in their early twenties, I guessed, and Dawn told us they worked at PAWS part-time, along with a boy called Rob.

"Not me, though," Dawn said. "I'm on duty day and night. I never know when I'll get a phone call saying a dog needs a home, or when a dog might be ill. But I love it." She looked round at the dogs and smiled. "There's nothing that makes me happier than finding these dogs new homes. I just wish we had more money so we didn't have to worry about what might happen to them if we can't keep going."

"Well, the Fun Day should help with that," said Miss Harris. "If we make it into a really great day, lots of people will get to know all about this place and the amazing work you do. Maybe we'll even be able to start a fundraising committee so that you can stop worrying and concentrate on looking after the dogs."

"I like that idea," said Dawn, smiling.

Miss Harris crouched beside a nearby kennel. "This is Freddie, my favourite dog. Hello, boy." She was talking to a curly-coated black dog. He had floppy ears and lovely chocolate-brown eyes. "He's a Labradoodle," she said. Freddie jumped up at the mesh and Miss Harris tickled his nose.

"He was half-starved and dehydrated and riddled with fleas when he was brought in," said Dawn. "His owners had left him tied up outside because they couldn't be bothered to house-train him and didn't want him soiling the house. They shouted at him and smacked him whenever he barked. Poor thing had every right to be scared of humans after the way he'd been treated, but when I went to see him, he just licked my hand and looked at me, as if to say 'Please take me away'. We nursed him back to health and now he's bouncing around. His experiences don't seem to have dented his trust in humans."

She opened Freddie's kennel and he bounded over to us. Dawn caught him by the collar so he couldn't jump up. His tail thwacked against our legs as he nudged us with his nose and licked our arms. He was gorgeous! I couldn't believe anyone had been cruel enough to mistreat him.

"And this is Tilly," said Dawn, pointing to a black-and-white spaniel in the next kennel. "We think she was used for breeding at a puppy farm. When she got too old, they dumped her on the roadside. Her pads were red raw from running around trying to get home when we found her. She's getting on a bit, but she would make someone a lovely pet."

"What about this little one?" said Mia, going over to a kennel where a small brown-and-white dog with floppy ears and big brown eyes was lying in his bed looking up at us and wagging his tail.

"This is Brandy, he's a Cavalier King Charles spaniel. His owner was in her eighties when she died and I took him in. He's a poppet, but he's twelve now – which is eighty-six in human years. He has a heart condition and is slightly blind, so he's not going to be easy to rehome. I'm hoping the right person will come along looking for a loving companion."

Dawn opened Brandy's kennel and Mia and I went in. The little dog got up stiffly and came to greet us. I kneeled down and he put his front paws on my knees, licked my face and made a snuffly sound. Mia stroked his head and tickled him behind the ears. I remembered what Miss Harris had told me; Brandy and Tilly probably wouldn't get the chance to go to new homes if PAWS was forced to close. They would have to be put down. My heart twisted. Suddenly helping make the Fun Day a success didn't just seem like something fun to do in the summer holidays; it seemed the most important thing in the world.

I gave Brandy a final stroke and got  to my feet. "Shall we go and talk about the Fun Day? There's a lot to do."

"Good idea," said Dawn. Miss Harris helped her shut the dogs in their kennels. She told Rachael and Jess what she was doing and then led us out of the kennel block and into the car park. "What's that building there?" I asked, pointing to another modern building on the far side of the car park. It had a fenced-off paddock behind it, just like the main kennel block, but there were no dog runs or exercise areas and the windows and doors were all shut and locked up.

"It was going to be another kennel block, once I'd got this one up and running," Dawn said. "To be honest, though, I'm so rushed off my feet as it is that I'm not sure if I'll ever do it. One day I'd love to rent it out – maybe to someone who wants to have a doggy grooming parlour or something – but it needs decorating and plumbing and everything first. Anyway, come on up to the house."

Dawn unlocked the front door of the farmhouse and we followed her into a big hallway. There were several large rooms leading off the hall, all containing furniture covered in dust sheets. Dawn took us down a corridor and into a separate, self-contained part of the house. It had a small cheerful lounge with a bright stripy rug and red sofa, a kitchen to one side, and a bedroom and a bathroom to the other.

"My uncle had a carer to look after him and this was her flat," Dawn explained, as we sat in the lounge and she fetched us some cans of lemonade. "I find it easier to live here than in the whole house. I don't need all that space with it just being me! So, anyway, I'm dying to hear your ideas for the Fun Day."

We talked and talked and, by the end of the meeting, we had a long list of things to do. Mia and I were going to organise a decorating biscuits stall, make a PAWS birthday cake that could be raffled, organise a treasure map competition and ask Sarah about running a Natural Beauty stall. We'd also try to find more volunteers to help on the day. Miss Harris was going to organise a barbecue and a drinks tent, and hunt for another band, while Dawn was going to finalise the details of the dog show. There were apparently all sorts of things to do for that: rosettes and competitors' numbers to order, entry forms to be typed up and printed, prizes to buy, and she'd need people to be stewards on the day. She showed us the programme of events. There were lots of fun classes like 'Dog Who Looks Most Like Its Owner' and 'Best Trick' that people could pay to enter. She was hoping people would bring their dogs along and then stay and spend money on the stalls.

"We also want to try and get people to visit the kennels. Some of them might be interested in offering a home to one of the dogs. We need to make sure they're all looking their best. Here's the poster I've made."

Dawn's poster was OK, but quite plain. It didn't really make the day sound fun for the whole family, more like a small dog show. I volunteered to make an extra leaflet that we could put in shops and post through people's letterboxes. We needed to make sure the whole of Ashingham knew about it. After all, there was no point making the day amazing if no one came.

After we had finished our meeting, Miss Harris, Mia and I took some of the dogs for a walk. Miss Harris took Freddie, Mia took Brandy and I took Tilly.

Freddie and Nell bounded through the long grass, while Brandy ambled along and snuffled at buttercups. They looked so happy and relaxed.

Determination filled me. Whatever we had to do to stop PAWS closing, we would do it!

# 9

Mia was going to see her grandparents for lunch so Miss Harris dropped her at home and took me back to the bakery. I told Mum, Dylan and Paula all about PAWS and showed them the pictures of the dogs I'd taken on my phone.

"I'm going to design some flyers, but I also told Dawn I'd put up a notice here about PAWS, asking for volunteers," I said. In the short time I'd

spent there, it was obvious how hard everyone at PAWS worked and that they needed more help.

77

"Sounds like a good idea," said Mum. "You could do it on my laptop now, if you like?"

"OK, thanks, I will," I said. I stopped in the doorway of the office and thought about little Brandy. "*We* couldn't adopt a dog, could we?"

"No," Mum said firmly. "Absolutely not, Hannah. You know we're out of the house too much. It wouldn't be fair."

I sighed. I knew that tone of voice. Arguing was pointless. Oh well, at least I could try to help the dogs in other ways. I sat in the office and designed a notice to go on the bakery wall.

# PAWS

### WHERE NO DOG IS EVER TURNED AWAY!

Do you love dogs?
Do you have a few hours spare to walk and
cuddle dogs who don't have owners?
Then we need YOU!

PAWS desperately needs volunteers to walk the
dogs, play with them and groom them. If you
think you can help, please contact Dawn.

PEDRO

LADY

BREWSTER

At the bottom, I added some photos of the dogs, along with their names and a brief history about them. Then I printed a copy of the notice and stuck it up on the bakery wall near the door.

Just then the shop bell tinkled and two people came in. It was Abi and her dad, Michael.

Abi's dad gave me a friendly smile. "Hello, Hannah. We thought we'd come and pick up some of that delicious sourdough bread and something for dessert." He came up to the counter. Abi hung back.

"What sort of thing would you like?" I asked. "We've got lemon drizzle, Victoria sponge, chocolate fudge – or there are the different fruit tarts you can see."

"Wow, it's hard to choose," Abi's dad said. "I think maybe a strawberry tart."

"Good decision," said Paula, taking one and putting it into a cardboard box. "These are my favourite. I'm Paula, by the way."

Michael smiled. "Pleased to meet you. I'm Michael and this is my daughter, Abi. We've just moved into town."

"Brooksby Close?" said Paula.

He nodded.

"I thought I recognised you," Paula said. "Where did you move from?"

"Oh, not too far away. We used to live just outside Ashingham, but we sold our house and we're now renting. It's a bit of a change," Abi's dad said, with a glance at Abi, who had come to stand beside him. "Our new house is smaller, for a start. But I have to say I'm rather enjoying not having such a big garden to look after. And no animals to manage either – we used to have chickens, a goat, a dog and a retired horse!"

81

"What made you move?" asked Paula.

"Oh, this and that," said Abi's dad vaguely.

I noticed Abi wander over to the wall and start reading the PAWS notice. I didn't feel overly enthusiastic about talking to her again, but her dad was so nice, I thought it couldn't hurt to make an effort.

"Hi," I said.

"Hi," she said briefly.

"I've just put that up." I gestured to the notice. "Mia and I went to PAWS this morning – we're helping organise a Fun Day to raise money. You should come along," I said. "Do you like dogs?"

She nodded.

"Me too. If you have time over the summer, you should go and walk some of the dogs there. They're so lovely, and Dawn, the owner, could use a bit of help." An idea struck me. I couldn't adopt a dog, but maybe she could! "You had a dog in your old house, didn't you? Maybe you could rehome one of PAWS' dogs?"

Abi looked at me as if I'd slapped her. "No. No, I couldn't." She turned away, her face full of misery.

"Are you OK?" I said. I'd only suggested she rehomed a dog. What was the big deal?

She swallowed. "I'm fine."

But she obviously wasn't fine because she hurried out of the shop, banging the door behind her.

My mouth dropped open. Whoa! What was THAT about?

"Abi?" Her dad looked round. "What happened?"

"I … I'm not sure," I said honestly.

"I'll be right back," he said. Abi was outside, her arms folded round her body. I saw him speak to her.

I didn't hear what they said, but I saw her wipe her eyes and wave her hand at me in the shop. They had a brief conversation before he came back in. "Sorry about that," he said. "You just touched a nerve, Hannah. It's not your fault," he added. "You weren't to know. Abi's going through quite a lot at

83

the moment. Thanks for trying to chat to her. Maybe another time, eh?"

I nodded uncertainly. Whatever had I said?

He turned to Paula. "We'd better get going. Could I have a loaf of sourdough as well as the tart, please?"

"Of course." Paula served him quickly.

"Thanks." He smiled, and left. I watched as he and Abi walked down the road together.

"What happened there?" Paula asked me.

I told her what I'd said. "I don't know what happened, to be honest. I was just trying to be friendly. It was weird."

"Hmm," said Paula. "Just remember, it can't be easy moving house and thinking about starting a new school. She's probably feeling quite upset. She might just need another chance."

"I've already given her two chances," I said.

"Sometimes people need more than that," Paula said.

I sighed. I knew Paula was right. I remembered how Abi's dad had said she was

84

going through a tough time. Maybe I was being too harsh. It might be that she was like George when I'd first met him and just really miserable about stuff going on in her life. I decided that, when I saw her again, I'd keep trying to be friends. I don't like the idea of anyone being unhappy.

"Well?" Paula said, looking at me.

I nodded. "OK, I'll keep trying," I said.

## TO DO FOR THE FUN DAY

- Design flyer and take copies to local shops when Dawn has them printed
- Design and bake cake for raffle
- Design and bake biscuits for people to decorate
- Ask Sarah if she wants to run a Natural Beauty stall
- Recruit volunteers for the day!

## PAWS BIRTHDAY CAKE DESIGNS

Birthday Candles

sugar paste dog

Next morning – Sunday – when Molly and Ella woke me at six, I didn't groan for once, but jumped out of bed and headed straight for the computer. The sooner I got the flyer done, the sooner we could get it printed and put up in places where people would see it!

A couple of hours later, I finally had a design I was happy with. The word "FUN!" was repeated over and over at the top, and then PAWS' 1st BIRTHDAY FUN DAY was in big letters in the centre, above the date and times. There was a list of things that would be going on and I'd added a photo of Freddie with a speech bubble coming out of his mouth, saying, "Please support us. It's going to be a grrrrr-eat day!" I also included a few more pictures of dogs along the bottom and wrote, "Come and have fun and help PAWS carry on the good work!"
I emailed a copy to Dawn, who replied almost immediately to say she loved it and would get them printed as soon as she could. I printed a copy too and took it downstairs

to show Mum and Mark. Mum was cooking breakfast and the delicious smell of bacon drifted out of the kitchen. Mark was setting the table and the twins were playing in the garden.

"Ready for a bacon sandwich?" Mum asked.

"Yes, please," I said. "What do you think of this?"

Mark came over to look too. "It's really good," he said.

Mum nodded. "It is. Well done, sweetie. You've done a great job. Hopefully you'll get lots of visitors."

"I hope so. Miss Harris says PAWS might have to close if Dawn doesn't find a way to raise money."

"I can take some in to work, if you like. It sounds like it should be good fun," Mark said.

After breakfast, feeling full of bacon sandwich, I decided to take advantage of the lovely sunny day. "Can I go for a walk?" I said. "I thought I could see if Mrs Rees wants me to take the pugs out."

"Sure, just take your phone," Mum said. "Then when you get back, maybe we can go fruit picking and make a cheesecake with those leftover biscuits from the launch. I fancy a strawberry cheesecake, I think."

"Mmm," I said. "Or raspberry."

"Or both!" Mum said, with a grin.

I put my shoes on and went next door. Mrs Rees was happy for me to take Billy, Benny and Bobby out.

"They do love their walkies," she said fondly, helping me clip on their leads.

It was a beautiful day and there were lots of people in their front gardens. The three pugs pulled madly, excited to be out, but luckily they were small and I could easily keep hold of them. Or so I thought. I got into trouble when they each went a different way around a lamppost and got tangled up.

I was trying to untangle the leads and had
just freed Bobby and Billy, when I saw Abi
come out of a nearby house with a letter in
her hand. She stopped briefly, so I knew she'd
seen me too, but then she put her head down
and hurried up the street to the postbox.

I wanted to go after her but I had other
things to deal with right at that moment.

"Billy, Bobby, stop it!" I said, tugging their
leads. Benny had managed to wrap his lead
twice round the lamppost. "Oh, come here,
you silly thing. You're all tangled!"

Just then, a cat jumped down from a fence. Bobby saw it and started yapping and pulling even more. He leaped forward and his lead slipped through my fingers.

"Bobby!" I cried.

Abi heard my cry and looked over her shoulder to see Bobby hurtling towards her. Quick as a flash, Abi reached out for his lead and caught it in one hand. With a strangled yelp, the little dog was pulled up short.

"Thank you!" I called in relief.

Bobby forgot the cat and trotted towards Abi to say hello. She kneeled and scratched him under his chin.

When I'd finally sorted out Benny and Billy, I went over. "Thanks so much for catching him," I said again. Bobby had his paws on her knee and was snuffling at her face. "He's called Bobby," I said.

"He's lovely," she said wistfully. She sniffed and stood up.

"Here you go!" she said, thrusting the lead in my hands. She turned and hurried back towards her house.

I jogged after her, the dogs bounding beside me. "Wait! Abi! What's the matter? Are you OK?"

She stopped at the gate and looked at me. "No." The words burst out of her. "No, I'm not." She ran to the front door and went inside.

I stood for a moment, not knowing what to do. I wanted to go after her, but I couldn't with Billy, Bobby and Benny.

On the way home, I couldn't stop thinking about what had happened. For some reason, stroking Bobby had made Abi miserable. And when I'd mentioned dogs yesterday, that had upset her too.

What was it her dad had said? *Abi's going through quite a lot at the moment. It's not your fault. Thanks for trying.*

By the time I reached Mrs Rees's house, I had made up my mind. I was going to go back. I had to try and find out what was wrong.

# 10

Standing at Abi's front door for the second time that day, my heart thumped loudly in my chest. She hadn't wanted to talk earlier. Would she just tell me to go away? Before I could change my mind, I rang the bell.

Natalie, Abi's mum, opened the door. "Oh, hi, Hannah," she said.

"Hello," I said. My lips felt dry. "Um, is Abi here? I saw her coming in earlier and I thought I'd pop round and say hi."

"That's nice of you. She's just in her room. I'll give her a shout. Abi!"

"What?" Abi came halfway down the stairs and stopped abruptly when she saw me.

"Hannah's called in to say hello. Why don't you take her up to your room?"

The house was neat and tidy, and there were cardboard packing cases in the hall. I followed Abi up the stairs. She didn't say anything until she'd shut her bedroom door behind us.

"What do you want now?" she said flatly.

I felt very awkward. "Look, if you don't want me to stay, I'll go, but you seem really sad, and I thought you might need a friend. I don't think you're the horrible person you're making yourself out to be."

Abi sank onto the bed. She tilted her head away from me and hid her face in her hair.

I glanced around the room. There were cardboard boxes filled with stuff that still hadn't been unpacked, and the walls were scuffed from where other people's pictures had been taken down. Abi had put up a cork board on one wall, which had lots of photos of a brown-and-white spaniel and a name spelled out in big letters: ROSIE.

"Abi?" I said, as the silence dragged on.

"Please. Just go," Abi said, her voice tight. "No one can help."

Despite what I'd said, I knew I couldn't leave now. I just couldn't. I sat down beside her on the bed and tentatively put a hand on her shoulder. Suddenly, she burst out, "I can't bear it! I hate this place. I hate everything about it – this house, changing schools. *Everything*." She buried her head in her hands.

I didn't know what to say.

She gave a sob. "I haven't even got Rosie any more!"

"Is that your dog?" I said, looking up at the cork board.

"Was." Abi gulped. "She had to be put down five months ago. She was really old, so it was the right thing to do, but I loved her so much and I really miss her. Mum and Dad said we could get a new puppy and I was all ready to choose one, but then everything went wrong with Dad's business and we had to sell the house and move here."

"I'm sorry," I said. "Couldn't you get a puppy anyway?"

Abi rubbed her eyes with the bottom of her T-shirt. "No. We rent this house, you see, and the landlord won't let us have pets."

So, *that* was why Abi had been so upset when I'd mentioned adopting a dog yesterday. It was probably the worst thing I could have said.

She wiped her nose with the back of her hand. "I'm sorry," she said shakily. "I don't usually cry so much."

"It's OK." I spotted a box of tissues on her desk and handed them to her. "Here."

"Thanks." She wiped her eyes and blew her nose. "Why did you come round?" she said. "I was so rude earlier – and Friday too. I wouldn't have wanted to talk to someone like me."

I shrugged. "You seemed like you needed a friend."

She managed a small smile. "Well, thanks, I appreciate it." She twisted the tissue in her fingers. "I just haven't wanted to make friends with anyone. Mum and Dad keep trying to make out that this is all some big adventure, but I can't see it that way. Dad's got a new job, which is good, and he says at least he's home more and not travelling so much. But Mum's had to get a job too because we need the money and she hasn't worked since before I was born. She was a veterinary nurse and now she's working in a boring office, which I know she hates. She misses our animals and the garden and being outside. And now I've got to go to a new school where I won't know anyone and everyone has made their friends already. This isn't a big adventure; this is horrible."

"You'll know me at school," I said. "And Mia. And we can introduce you to our other friends. They're really nice."

"Thanks," Abi said in a small voice.

I longed to be able to help her with her problems. I couldn't magically conjure up more money for her family and a house with a big garden, where she could have a puppy and other animals. Still, maybe I could do *something*.

"Look, don't shout at me," I said slowly. "But why don't you come to PAWS one day? Not to adopt a dog, but they're always looking for people to walk the dogs and give them fuss and attention. I know it's not the same as having your own, but at least you'd get to be around dogs again."

She swallowed. "I can't."

I didn't get it. "Why?"

"I just think it would hurt too much to see them and know we're not allowed to have one."

I sighed. I was sure Dawn would have loved someone who loved dogs as much as Abi to help her. "OK, well, how about helping with the Fun Day? PAWS is having a fundraising event to celebrate its first birthday, and also to raise awareness about the money it needs to stay open. Me and Mia, my best friend, and Miss Harris, one of the teachers from school, are pitching in with the organising. There's loads to do – leaflets to give out, biscuits and cakes to make. Are you interested?"

Abi glanced at me. "You don't give up, do you?"

"Not usually," I said, giving her a quick smile. "How about it?" I was sure that getting involved with the Fun Day would be the perfect way to make Abi feel better. It would take her mind off feeling miserable, and she'd get to meet lots of people too.

"I guess I could," Abi said slowly. "I haven't got anything else to do – Mum and Dad are both working for most of the week." She nodded. "Yes, OK. I will."

I beamed. "That's brilliant. Thank you!"

I told her all about the Fun Day and the plans we had for it.

"It sounds really good. How about making dog biscuits to sell as well?" said Abi. "My mum used to make them for Rosie and she loved them. I've still got the recipe somewhere."

She jumped up and started leafing through some papers on her desk. "Yes, here it is!"

I took the paper from her. I'd never made dog biscuits before, but the recipe looked very easy, just like human savoury biscuits. "This is great – we should definitely make them." I put on an advertising-type voice. *"Homemade organic biscuits – why treat your pooch to anything less?"*

Abi smiled. "We could design labels saying that. And package the biscuits in cellophane with ribbons."

"Perfect! Shall we go to my house now and try out the recipe?" I said.

Abi hesitated. "All right," she said. "Let's do it."

We went downstairs and found Abi's mum and dad in the kitchen.

"Of course," Abi's mum said, when we asked her. "Abi's been spending far too much time inside since we moved."

"Yes, go and enjoy yourself," said her dad.

As Abi and I walked over to my house, I texted Mia.

"I'll just see if she wants to come along too," I explained to Abi. "She loves baking and I'm sure she'll want to know how to make dog biscuits."

By the time we'd reached mine, I had a reply from Mia saying she was on her way. I was glad she could join us. Now I was starting to get to know Abi a bit better, I wanted Mia to meet her and see that she wasn't horrible after all.

"Hi," Mia said, when she saw Abi.

"I bumped into Abi while I was walking Mrs Rees's pugs," I said. "She's offered to help with the Fun Day."

I could tell from the way Mia's eyes widened that she was surprised, but she hid it well. "That's great," she told Abi.

"I've got a recipe for some dog biscuits," said Abi. "I thought we could sell them to make money." She looked at Mia. "I'm … uh … I'm sorry about Friday," she said in a rush. "I know I wasn't very friendly then. Things have been kind of tough at home."

"It's fine," said Mia, giving her a warm smile. "No worries."

That's one of the things I love about Mia. She's shy, but if people want to be friends with her, she's always happy to make the effort.

"Let's get started then," I said.

Mum said that she would send Mark and the twins fruit picking and we could make the cheesecake later.

Mia, Abi and I cleared the kitchen table and got out all the ingredients – flour, cornflour, butter, a chicken stock cube, an egg, milk, cheese and Marmite. Mia and I were a bit surprised at the Marmite, but Abi told us that dogs love Marmite. Apparently lots of them love peanut butter too! How weird is that?

The French doors at the end of the kitchen were open and the afternoon sunshine streamed in as we set to work. Mia rubbed the butter into the flour, Abi grated cheese and I greased some baking trays and covered them with a light coating of flour as the recipe said. Then while the dough chilled, I found some dog-bone-shaped cutters in the cupboard. Mum has just about every type of cookie cutter you could imagine!

"How about these?" I said, holding them up.

"Those would be good," said Abi. "We could also make some really tiny biscuits if you have small cutters – they could be used as training treats." Abi really seemed to know about dogs!

"We should take some to PAWS," Mia said. "Do you want to come with us, Abi? We're going with Miss Harris tomorrow morning for an update on the Fun Day and to help with the dogs for a few hours."

I saw Abi tense. "I … I don't think so."

"Oh, OK, don't worry. You can always come another time." Mia obviously thought that it was because Abi had other plans.

I quickly changed the subject.

"Dawn said she would have the flyers printed by tomorrow. If we do go to PAWS we can pick them up and you could help us give them out when we get back."

"Sure," said Abi, smiling gratefully.

When the dough was chilled, Mia and I rolled it out. Abi didn't want to because she hadn't done much baking before – it was her mum who always used to make the dog biscuits. She did help us cut out the shapes, though.

Soon the kitchen was filled with the smell of baking. When the biscuits were ready, we tasted them. They were surprisingly nice –

quite strong: you could definitely taste the chicken stock and Marmite, and they were harder than normal biscuits – but I could imagine dogs loving them.

We cleaned up and then sat on the step outside with cans of lemonade. "I'm tired!" I said, pushing my hair back from my forehead.

"It was fun, though," said Mia, holding the cold can up to her cheeks.

I nodded.

Abi lay back on the step, lifting her face to the sun. I noticed her let out a contented sigh. I was pleased she looked so much happier.

"I can't wait to see the PAWS dogs again tomorrow," Mia said.

"I know! I bet they'll love our biscuits," I said.

"You know," Abi said, her eyes still closed as she lay back in the sun. "Maybe I *could* come with you."

"Oh, do!" said Mia.

"Are you sure?" I asked, more cautiously.

Abi sat up. "Yes." She gave me a small smile.

I smiled back feeling very glad I'd gone and knocked on her door today.

## CHEESE AND MARMITE DOG BISCUITS

Ingredients:

150g plain flour

1 heaped tbsp cornflour

60g margarine or butter at room temperature, cut into cubes

1 chicken stock cube

1 egg, lightly beaten

1 tbsp Marmite

Handful of finely grated cheese

A little milk

What to do:

1. Heat oven to 150°C, then grease two flat baking trays and scatter with flour.
2. In a large bowl, mix the flour and cornflour together, then crumble in the stock cube and mix again.
3. Now rub in the butter or margarine until it looks like breadcrumbs. Then stir in the egg, Marmite

and cheese and bring together with your hands to make a dough. If the mixture is too crumbly, add a splash of milk. If you add too much milk and it gets too sticky, just add a bit more flour.

4. Put the dough in a freezer bag and squash into a rectangle then chill in the fridge for 15 minutes.

5. Flour a surface and roll out the dough until it's about 3mm thick all over, then cut out shapes using a cookie cutter

6. Lay the biscuits on the baking trays, leaving a little space around each one, then put in the oven for around 15 minutes, until golden.

7. Ask an adult to help you take the biscuits out and transfer to a rack to cool.

P.S. Abi says dogs also like bacon or ham-flavoured biscuits. For training treats, just use small cutters about 1-2cm in size.

# 11

Mia and I met at the bakery next morning
– Abi was going to join us at eleven o'clock
when Miss Harris would take us all to PAWS.
After the early morning rush,
the bakery was quiet and we
sat down to eat some chocolate
cupcakes. I showed Mia my
designs for the PAWS birthday cake.

"This one is my favourite," she said,
pointing at the cake that looked like a kennel
with a dog sitting in the doorway.

"That's my favourite too," I said.

"It could have a chocolate sponge roof,"
Mia suggested, "decorated with chocolate
buttercream and chocolate buttons."

"Good idea!" I picked up my pencil and labelled it so I would remember.

"OK, the design for the birthday cake is done and the flyer's sorted," Mia said.

I nodded. "Dawn is getting three hundred printed."

"What next, then?" asked Mia. I turned to my list of 'things to do' on the back page of my journal.

"We need to talk to Sarah about running a stall," I said. "Why don't we go to Natural Beauty now and ask her?"

We licked the last of the delicious chocolate icing off our fingers and went up the road.

Sarah was serving a customer when we arrived. We waited until she had finished and then explained why we were there.

"That's a fab idea," she said. "Count me in. It'll be good advertising too – I can hand out leaflets and show people my products. I'll happily give any profit I make on the day to PAWS. It's for a great cause. Have you thought about getting a band to play? People always like to listen to music."

"There was one but they pulled out," I said. "Miss Harris is trying to find another."

"What about George's band?" Sarah suggested. "They've been practising a lot, and I know I'm biased, but they are actually pretty good."

I thought about it. It wasn't a bad idea. They *were* good and, if they came, their friends and family would probably come along too. "OK! I'll ask Miss Harris this afternoon," I said.

Later, in the car on the way to PAWS, Miss Harris asked Abi lots of questions, like which school she had been at before, and where she lived now. I knew Miss Harris was trying to be friendly, but I could tell Abi didn't want to talk about it. All the questions seemed to make her shrink inside herself. I'd told Mia this morning about Abi, but of course Miss Harris didn't know any of that.

"Do you think you might join Baking Club when you start school, Abi? It's brilliant," Mia said, when Miss Harris stopped talking to concentrate on a roundabout.

I gave her a grateful look. I was sure she was trying to steer the conversation away from Abi's home life.

"I … I haven't done much baking before, but it sounds fun," said Abi.

Miss Harris smiled. "Don't worry. There are lots of people there who don't know much about baking – Hannah and Mia are quite unusual."

"Are you saying we're odd, Miss?" I teased.

"Only in a good way!" she said.

Mia's change of subject had worked, and we talked about baking and Baking Club until we arrived at PAWS. I could hear the dogs barking as we got out of the car. I glanced at Abi. She looked as if she wanted to get straight back in and drive away again. I knew it was going to be hard for her to see all these dogs who so badly needed homes, when she couldn't offer them one herself.

Dawn was waiting for us in reception.

"Hi, Dawn, this is Abi," said Miss Harris said. "She's offered to help with the Fun Day too."

Dawn smiled at her. "That's really kind of you."

"Can we see the dogs?" Mia asked.

"Of course." Dawn took us through into the kennels.

"Hello, Brandy," I said, going over to tickle the spaniel's ears. "Look, Abi. Isn't he sweet?"

"And this is Freddie, my favourite," Miss Harris told her, going to the cage next door.

"I like all of them!" Mia said, stroking Tilly through the wire door of her kennel.

Abi hung back by the double doors.

Dawn looked at her inquisitively. I think she thought Abi was scared. "Do you like dogs, Abi?"

Abi swallowed. "Um … yes."

"Why don't you come and say hello to Freddie?" Miss Harris said. "He's lovely."

112

Abi walked over hesitantly as Dawn unlocked Freddie's cage. I joined them.

Freddie bounced out, whining in delight when Miss Harris scratched his ears. "Oh, yes, you know I wish I could take you home," Miss Harris said. "But you really wouldn't like it when I'm at work all day."

Freddie galloped over to me and Abi. "Easy, boy," I said, laughing as he jumped up and almost sent me flying.

He leaped at Abi too, but she quickly turned her body away. For a moment I thought she was going to run out of the kennels, but then I heard her talking to him firmly. "No, feet on the ground before I say hello. There's a good boy. Now, sit."

Freddie plonked his bottom on the ground and wagged his tail. Abi stroked his head, giving him her full attention. "That's better. Good boy."

"Wow! He's never usually that well-behaved," Miss Harris said to her. "You've obviously got a knack with dogs."

Dawn nodded, looking impressed. "That

was exactly the right thing to do when he jumped up, Abi. He's lovely but he's still young and needs to learn some manners. Thank you."

Now Freddie collapsed on his back, showing Abi his tummy, and she bent her head, tickling him, making one of his back legs scratch in the air.

Miss Harris laughed. "I think he likes you, Abi."

"He's lovely," Abi said, sighing. "They all are." I heard the wistfulness in her voice, but the grown-ups didn't seem to notice.

"Well, there's plenty to do if you have time to stay and help," said Dawn. "You could help me groom some of them. They could all do with a good brush – a bath too. Rachael, Jess, Rob and I often run out of time for the fun things like that. It's hard enough to keep on top of the essential maintenance, like nail clipping, ear cleaning and running health checks."

"My mum might be able to help with that sort of thing," Abi said suddenly.

"Really?" said Dawn.

"Yes. She used to be a veterinary nurse. I'm sure she'd be happy to do some grooming too. We haven't got a dog any more, and I know she misses her."

"Well, if your mum could spare a couple of hours, please tell her that I'd be very, very grateful," said Dawn.

"I will," Abi said. She lapsed into silence and carried on patting Freddie.

When we had finished saying hello to the dogs, we had a quick meeting about the Fun Day and then loaded the boxes of leaflets into the boot of Miss Harris's car. Abi had to go home after PAWS but Mia and I planned to give some out that afternoon.

Then, while Dawn and Jess worked in the kennels, answering the phones and clearing up the runs, Abi, Mia, Miss Harris and I groomed the dogs and played with some of them in the huge garden. They all loved our biscuits!

Miss Harris got a phone call about the Fun Day when we were about to leave. It was clear from the way she smiled and nodded and said "thank you" a lot that it was good news.

"That was Tom at the butcher's," she told us, as she hung up. "He's said he'll donate sausages and burgers for the barbecue," she went on.

"Brilliant!" said Dawn.

"We'll give out loads of flyers in the next few days," I said. "By the end of the week everyone in Ashingham will know about the Fun Day!"

"Oh, I hope you're right," said Dawn. "My bank manager has given me three months to turn things around."

"Three months," said Miss Harris. "That's not long."

"I know," said Dawn. "But hey," she took a breath, "let's be positive. Maybe the Fun Day will change things for the better."

Abi was quiet on the way home. Miss Harris dropped her off first. She was sitting in the middle of the back seat so I jumped out to let her past.

"Thank you for taking me today," she said to Miss Harris.

"No problem. Thanks for coming, and if your mum does have time to help, Dawn, that would be great."

"I'll ask her," Abi said. "Thank you. Bye, Hannah. Bye, Mia." She turned away. I went after her.

"Are you OK?" I whispered. "Did you have a good time?"

Abi nodded. "Yes. You were right. PAWS is an amazing place. I just wish …" She trailed off.

She didn't need to finish her sentence for me to guess what she wished for. I knew how much she wanted things to be different, how much she wanted a dog of her own.

I squeezed her arm. "At least you made some of the dogs at PAWS happier today," I said.

She managed a smile. "I guess that's true. Thanks for inviting me. I'll see you tomorrow to give out leaflets."

"Yep. Ten o'clock at the bakery," I told her.

I went back to the car.

"Everything all right?" Miss Harris asked.

"Fine. We were just arranging to meet tomorrow." I wished I could help Abi more. Still, at least she had enjoyed going to PAWS – I knew that inviting her along had definitely been the right thing to do.

# 12

Later that night, Abi texted me:

> Mum says she'll help Dawn with
> dogs. She's going 2moro after work.

I texted back:

> *Gr8! Are u going with her?*

Abi's text came back quickly.

> Yes. I think so.

I smiled. This was good.

> *The dogs will be pleased! C u tomorrow at the bakery 2*
> *give out leaflets! Mia and I posted some through doors*
> *this afternoon but we still have loads left.* ☺ *Night! X*

I put down my phone and opened my journal. What was left to do for the Fun Day? I decided to write out a day-by-day plan.

## Tuesday

Put more leaflets through people's doors/find places we can put the leaflets up in town.
Try and get people to help with the stalls – tea and coffee, face painting, treasure map, dog show, raffle.
Make dog biscuits and labels.

## Wednesday

Deliver/put up more leaflets.
Make more dog biscuits?

## Thursday

Go to PAWS and see if we can help.
(Misha, Alice and Lara home – yay!!!)

## Friday

Make the biscuits for decorating.

Saturday

Make and ice PAWS
birthday cake.

Sunday

Help get dogs and PAWS ready?

Monday

THE FUN DAY!!!!!!

I had just finished when I got a text from
George.

*Hey! Mum says Miss Harris asked if my band can play
at the dog Fun Day! Awesome!*

I smiled to myself.

*I know. I suggested you!* ☺

His reply pinged back.

*Thx!!!! Only prob is Joe's on holiday.*

I stared at the text. Hang on, wasn't Joe the
only one who could sing? How was this
going to work? I typed a quick text:

*Don't you need Joe???*

George replied:

*I reckon we'll be fine. We can all do the singing.*

There was a few seconds' pause then another text came.

*Want 2 come & listen some time this wk?*

OK. If Mum can drop me. When?

*2moro afternoon? Alec and Callum are here 4-7.*

I went to ask Mum, who said she could take me after the bakery had shut, then texted George back.

Mum said that's OK. C u 5ish. ☺

"Time for bed," Mum said, sticking her head round my bedroom door.

"OK," I said. I put my phone down and took one last glance at my journal.

Mum came and looked over my shoulder. "Wow, a day-by-day plan. You're working really hard on this, aren't you?"

"Yes, I really want it to go well. We need to

get as many people there as possible – visitors as well as people to help."

"Well, you know I've said I'll run the cake stall with Paula and Dylan," Mum said. "And Mark will help with the barbecue. Some of the bakery regulars might like to come along too. Why don't you write 'Help Wanted' on the top of the flyers in the bakery and see if anyone offers? It's short notice but you might get a few people."

It was a good idea. Next morning, I put a pile of Fun Day flyers on the counter and wrote a sign next to them with an arrow saying, "HELP NEEDED. PLEASE ASK HANNAH!"

"These look really good," said Paula, picking one up. "I'll take a stack and give them out at my belly-dancing class."

"I can drop some through letterboxes near me," said

Dylan, bringing a tray of
doughnuts in from the
kitchen.

"Thank you! Mia and I
are going to run the decorating
biscuits stall. Abi's going to organise the dog
biscuits stall with her mum. Sarah will be on
her Natural Beauty stall, and Misha, Alice
and Lara are going to help with the pony
rides. Oh yes, and Miss Harris says Stefan
has offered to supervise the bouncy castle and
help Mark with the barbecue later on."

"So many people are getting involved!"
said Paula, as the shop door opened and a
lady dressed in a long skirt, with beads and
scarves around her neck, came in.

It was Harmony, one of our regular
customers. She has a shop called Utopia on
the high street, which sells crystals and
wind chimes, and she also works as a
reflexologist.

"What's everyone getting involved with?"
she asked.

Paula showed her the leaflet.

"This sounds like a very good cause," Harmony said. "I've never heard of PAWS, but I love dogs. I used to have a rescue dog when my children were growing up. He was called Barney and was so lovely. He used to follow the children everywhere. I'll take some leaflets for my shop, and if you want I could take a tent up there and do fifteen-minute reflexology sessions? I'd be happy to donate the funds to PAWS."

"That would be brilliant!" I said. "Yes, please!"

Over the course of the morning, I was amazed at how many other customers wanted to help. Most of them had never heard of PAWS.

Then Dennis Hopkinson came in. He's an elderly gentleman, who's always really gloomy. I think of him as being like a sponge cake that has sagged in the middle.

"What's this, then?" he said, looking at the flyers.

He snorted. "A dog show and Fun Day? They should know better than to have a Fun

Day on the bank holiday – it always rains on bank holidays."

"Well, even if it rains, it will still be fun," I said, putting his cherry pie into a bag.

He looked at the flyer again. "I like dogs. It says here you need help. What with?"

"Um, well, all sorts of stuff – selling raffle tickets, being a ring steward, helping on the barbecue and showing people the way to the toilets, the dog show and the kennels," I said.

"And you're helping organise all this?" he said.

I nodded. "Me, Mia and our friend, Abi. Well, with Miss Harris."

"I like to see young people getting involved with good causes," he said. "Well done, you.

Put my name down to help with showing people where to go. I'll do that."

"Thank you, Mr Hopkinson!" I said.

"Well, well, well," said Paula, as he left. "I never thought I'd see the day when Dennis Hopkinson offered to help." She winked at me. "He must have a soft spot for you, Hannah."

I rolled my eyes, but I was delighted we had another volunteer. And by the end of lunchtime, five other customers had offered to help too.

"The whole town's going to be there at this rate!" Mum said, when I told her.

"That's the idea," I said, grinning. "Mia, Abi and I are going to give out some flyers later – just to make sure that there's no one in town that *doesn't* know about it. We also need to bake the dog biscuits."

Mum nodded. "Mark's working at home today. Try not to disturb him because he'll be busy. How many biscuits are you going to make?"

"Loads and loads!" I said.

# 13

Mia and Abi and I walked all around the town centre asking shops if we could leave flyers with them for their customers to pick up. When we got back to my house, it was time to bake the dog biscuits.

We made a huge quantity of dough, and while it chilled, we designed little bone-shaped labels. We were going to package the biscuits in cellophane and attach the labels with ribbons. We wrote all the ingredients on one side of the labels, because Mum had said people needed to know exactly what was in the biscuits in case their dogs were allergic to anything.

"I wonder what your mum will think of PAWS," I said to Abi, as we worked.

"I bet she'll love it," Abi said. "She loves all animals, but especially dogs."

"Why did your mum choose an office job, then?" Mia asked. "Why didn't she go back to being a veterinary nurse or another job with animals?"

"She says it's really hard because lots of people want to work with animals," said Abi. "She needed a job quickly so she took the first one she was offered."

"It's a pity she couldn't work with Dawn," I said. "It's not as if PAWS doesn't need the help. They just can't afford it."

"I know," Abi said. "I think Mum would love to work there. Though, to be honest, I wish Mum didn't have to work at all. I liked it when she was at home all the time."

I gave her a sympathetic look.

"At least starting at King William's won't be quite so scary now you know me and

Mia," I said. "And we'll make sure you get to meet Misha, Alice and Lara when they're back from their holiday too. And at least you know you can go to PAWS and see the dogs there."

"You say that a lot, don't you?" Abi said.

"What?"

"At least."

I shrugged. "I suppose it just makes me happier when I think *at least* and look for stuff to be positive about rather than thinking about the stuff that isn't good. If you think about the stuff that isn't good, you just stay miserable all the time."

Abi frowned. "I hadn't thought about it like that."

I checked the time. "Hey, we should roll out the dough," I said.

"Can I have a go at doing some rolling and cutting out the biscuits?" Abi said.

"Of course," I said.

We divided the dough into three and each started rolling and cutting biscuit shapes before putting them on the baking trays.

Abi's biscuits didn't work out very well.
She'd rolled her dough unevenly; some
biscuits were very thin
and stuck to the counter
when she tried to get
them up, and others
were too thick.

"Oh dear," she said. "I don't think I'm
doing this right."

"Don't worry," I said. "We've got
plenty more dough and the dogs at PAWS
can always have any that aren't good enough
to sell."

"Let's bake the ones we've got, then roll out some more and this time we'll help you," said Mia.

We put the biscuits in the oven and started rolling out the second round of dough, showing Abi how not to press too hard or roll the dough too thinly. When we took the first round of biscuits out of the oven and inspected them, Abi giggled. "Oh dear, I don't think even the dogs at PAWS will want mine. Look!"

Because her biscuits were all different thicknesses, they had cooked unevenly: the thin edges were almost burned, the middles were not quite cooked, the thinner biscuits had crumbled into pieces and the thicker ones looked stodgy and pale. As she tried to transfer them to the wire rack, they fell apart.

We all started to giggle then. "OK, these are officially a disaster," said Abi. "They'd better go in the bin."

"No, wait," I said, as she started to sweep them up with her hands. "I'm sure we can do something with all the little bits."

I remembered the delicious strawberry, raspberry and blueberry cheesecake Mum had ended up making with the leftover broken biscuits from Sarah's launch party. Could we do something like that with Abi's broken biscuits to make a yummy dog treat?

"Here. Put them in this bag," I said, passing Abi a large freezer bag, "and bash them with the rolling pin. I'll heat up some butter. Mia – do you want to chop some ham?"

Abi looked at me as if she thought I was a complete nutter. "Do what?"

But Mia nodded. She understood what I was thinking. "Good idea," she said. "We could make something with the broken biscuits, can't we? A kind of doggy traybake."

"Exactly!" I said. "We can mix the biscuit crumbs with the melted butter then press them into a tray and chill in the fridge. It should set hard enough for us to be able to cut up into small pieces. I bet the dogs will love it as much as the biscuits!"

I melted the butter in the microwave for twenty seconds, then we mixed everything together and added the ham Mia had chopped. We pressed it into a tray and put it into the fridge to set.

← no-cook doggy traybake

"There!" I said. "The perfect doggy treat! You could take it up to PAWS tonight. I bet they'll love it."

"Wow," said Abi. "And I'd have just thrown those dodgy biscuits away!"

"Baking disasters don't always have to stay as disasters," said Mia. "You just need to change your plans." Then, almost as an afterthought, she added, "Like in life, really, I suppose."

"Yes," I agreed. "You should always try to make cheesecake out of broken biscuits."

Mia nodded at me. "And remember that every batch of broken dog biscuits is really a delicious doggy traybake in disguise."

We both giggled.

Abi shook her head. "You two are nuts."

I nudged her. "But you like us."

Abi smiled, and for the first time since I'd met her it was a whole face, eyes-lit-up kind of smile. "Yes," she said happily. "I do."

# 14

Abi's mum collected her at five o'clock to go to PAWS. Soon after that, Mum got home from the bakery and she drove me and Mia over to George's house.

"Do you think the band will be any good without Joe?" Mia said, as we got out of the car.

"Not sure. I hope they sound OK."

Unfortunately, they didn't sound OK. Neither George, Alec nor Callum was as strong a singer as Joe. They weren't totally rubbish, but they didn't sound anywhere near as good as they had done when we'd first heard them play, and definitely not good enough to entertain the whole of Ashingham.

"Well? What did you think?"
George asked, when they'd finished
their first song.

Mia and I exchanged looks. How
could we possibly tell him and the
others the truth?

"Well … um …" I bit my lip.

Mia blushed and didn't say
anything.

Callum groaned. "It was terrible,
wasn't it? I knew it."

"I told you we sucked without Joe," said
Alec.

"You don't *suck*," I said, trying to be
diplomatic. "It was just better with Joe."

"What are we going to do?" said George.

"I guess we'll have to cancel," said Alec.

"You can't!" I said. "There's no time to find
another band. It's in all the flyers!"

"Yes, this is our first proper gig," said
George. "We can't cancel."

"How about you just play the music and
don't sing?" I said.

"That'll be rubbish," George said.

"It won't. You're all really good musicians."

"I'm not sure. Let's keep practising for now," said George. "Maybe the singing will get better."

By the time Mia and I went home, we both had headaches from listening to the boys. They'd played a lot more songs but they hadn't really improved. They could all sing a bit, but none of them was good enough to be the lead singer. Sometimes they didn't even hit the right notes!

"What can we do?" Mia said to me on the way home.

"I think we have to try and persuade them just to play their instruments," I said.

"But how?"

I didn't have an answer for that.

I was still thinking about the band problem when Abi called. Her mum had loved PAWS.

138

"We bathed and groomed the dogs," she said, her voice bubbling with happiness. "Then Mum helped clip their claws and stuff like that. Dawn's asked us to go back at the weekend to make sure all the dogs are looking their best for Monday."

"Wow, that's great!" I said.

"I know," Abi said. "She and Dawn are like new BFFs. We ended up staying for dinner. Mum says that Dawn should run dog-training classes at the weekends, and go ahead with her idea of renting the spare space in the other building to a dog groomer or something."

"And then Dawn would have regular money from the rent and she wouldn't have to worry so much all the time," I said. "It would be perfect!"

"Exactly! The trouble is that the second building still needs quite a lot of work and Dawn just hasn't got the money to do it."

"Maybe we can raise enough at the Fun Day?" I said.

"I hope so. Mum told Dad all about PAWS and he said he'll contact the local radio station. He used to put adverts on there when he had his own business. He thinks there's a chance they'll do a feature about PAWS and the Fun Day on one of their programmes. We should also go out again tomorrow and post some more flyers through people's doors. There are still some streets we haven't done." It was brilliant to hear Abi sounding so excited. "I can't believe there are just five days left!" she said.

"Oh, I hope it's a success," I said.

"It *has* to be!" Abi said.

Wednesday and Thursday flew by. Mia, Abi and I baked more dog biscuits and delivered more flyers, while Miss Harris persuaded businesses to donate prizes for the raffle and helped Dawn organise the dog show. I wanted to get started on the biscuits for decorating and the birthday cake, but knew if I baked them too early they would be stale. Mia and I helped at the bakery too, of course. Everyone there was excited about the Fun Day.

Sarah called in to show us some special hand cream she'd adapted for dog walkers who suffered from cold, chapped hands. Harmony came to tell us she'd asked a friend to come and sell dog collars with healing crystals attached. Nearly all of our regular customers asked how the preparations were going. Best of all, when Abi's dad contacted the local radio station and told them how lots of people were getting involved, they decided to run a feature on the Fun Day and arranged to go to PAWS to interview Dawn on Saturday. The only problem was the band – I still couldn't work out what to do about the boys' singing.

On Thursday evening, Misha, Alice and Lara got back from their riding holiday, so

we all arranged to meet at Harry's on Friday.
I asked them if Abi could come too. They
said it was fine.

As Abi, Mia and I walked from the
bakery, I felt a bit nervous. I hoped Misha,
Alice and Lara would like Abi. I needn't
have worried, though. Abi was very
relaxed and easily joined in with the
conversation.

"What sort of music
do you like?" Misha
asked her.

"All kinds," said Abi.
"Ellie B is my favourite."

Misha smiled. "Mine
too." She held her spoon as if it was a
microphone and sang a few lines from one
of Ellie B's latest songs. *Think I'm falling –
falling in love with you ... "*

Alice threw a balled-up serviette at her.
"Shut it, Mish!"

"But it's good," Abi protested.

"You haven't just spent a week with
her singing day and night," said Lara, also

throwing her serviette at Misha. Misha
ducked and carried on.

Abi clapped. "Wow, you're
brilliant!"

"Don't encourage her," Alice
said, rolling her eyes.

"Oh, I really should be on
stage," said Misha, standing and
bowing to an imaginary audience.

I stared at her. Misha was an amazing
singer. I had the solution to the band problem
right in front of me. "Of course!" I swung
round to Mia. "Misha! George's band!"

"Yes!" she gasped. "You're right!"

"Um … earth to Hannah and Mia. You're
talking in your own language again," said
Misha.

"You'd like to perform on stage, wouldn't
you?" I said. "Sing with a band to lots of
people?"

"Yeah," said Misha, looking puzzled. "You
know I would. I've always wanted to."

"Then, Cinderella," I said, grinning, "I
think your wish is about to come true!"

George wasn't sure when I spoke to him on the phone and told him my idea, but he said Misha could come over that evening to try out with the band.

I waited anxiously to hear how it had gone. Just before dinner, two texts pinged on to my phone, one after the other. The first was from George:

Misha rocks. She's in! Awesome! ☺

The second text was from Misha:

*OMG! That was SOOOOOO much fun. Gonna sing with them at the wkend. Move over, Ellie B, it's my turn 2 b a STAR!!!!*

I grinned. Perfect! Now that was sorted, I could turn my attention to what I liked doing best – BAKING! If Mia and I wanted to have enough biscuits for kids to decorate and a birthday cake that everyone would want to win in the raffle, we were going to have to have a serious bake-a-thon. That suited me just fine!

# 15

Mia and I spent most of the weekend, when we weren't helping at the bakery, at my house, baking biscuits, and making and icing the PAWS birthday cake. After her failed attempts with the dog biscuits, Abi decided it was best if she left the baking to us and she spent Saturday and Sunday at PAWS with her mum.

On Saturday lunchtime, Dawn was interviewed by the local radio station. Mum had the radio on in the bakery kitchen and brought it through to the shop so we could all listen when the interview was broadcast.

Dawn was brilliant. The DJ asked her to tell some of the dogs' stories and explain how

she had started the centre. She talked about
Freddie and Brandy, and how worried she
was that the centre might have to close. She
finished by mentioning the Fun Day.

"It's going to be a wonderful day," Dawn
said. "There are going to be all sorts of stalls
selling human and doggy presents, delicious
refreshments made by the Sugar and Spice
Bakery, a reflexologist, a dog show, a bouncy
castle, a barbecue, a raffle with great prizes
and a chance to meet the dogs at the centre.
Or people can just come and walk and
picnic in the grounds if they prefer. I want
to thank everyone who has been involved
in supporting the day, but particularly, Jane
Harris, a teacher at King William's, and

three wonderful eleven-year-olds, Hannah, Mia and Abi, for all the hard work and effort they've put in. This day wouldn't be happening without them."

Mum hugged Mia and me. "You two should be very proud of yourselves."

"I just hope the day raises lots of money and lots of people get to know about PAWS," I said.

Paula smiled. "Well, I saw your weekend horoscopes this morning, and it's looking good. Listen to this!" She fetched her newspaper. "Leo," she said, nodding at me.

"'Big trees grow from small seeds. This bank holiday weekend, you shall see hard work come to fruition', and Pisces," she said, with a look at Mia, "'The weekend is the time to enjoy a period of good luck and good fortune: all you touch shall turn to gold.' See," she said. "The Fun Day will be a success. It's written in the stars!"

Oh please, I thought, please let the stars be right!

The Fun Day was due to start at half past twelve, but Mum and I arrived at seven o'clock on Monday morning. We were the first people there. We had packed all the cakes and biscuits into her car in airtight containers, along with tablecloths, cake stands, napkins, paper bags and cardboard boxes.

We were just starting to unpack the car when Dawn came out.

"Hi!" I called. "Dawn, this is my mum, Rose."

"Hi!" Mum called.

Dawn lifted her hand in greeting. "Pleased to meet you." As she came closer, I saw she looked pale, as if she'd been crying, and she had grey shadows under her eyes.

"Is everything OK?" I asked her.

Dawn shook her head. "No. I had some really bad news last night."

"What is it?" said Mum in concern.

Dawn swallowed. "Jack Collington – he's a farmer who rents some fields from me – rang up. He doesn't want to renew the lease when it ends in three months' time. That means I won't have any regular income apart from the money I get from rehoming the dogs, which is very little. Without the rent from the fields, I just don't see how we can stay open. We're struggling enough as it is."

My heart sank. This was awful news.

Mum put a hand on her arm. "Oh, Dawn. I'm sorry."

Dawn bit her lip. "Just when I thought things were looking up, that this Fun Day might really help, this goes and happens."

"Maybe someone else will want to rent the fields," Mum said. "This doesn't have to be the end. Don't lose hope."

Dawn took a breath. "You're right. There's nothing I can do about it now anyway. I just have to get on with things. Would you mind not mentioning it to anyone else?" She cleared her throat and looked in the car boot. "What have you got here?" she said, putting on a bright voice. "Do you need a hand carrying things?"

"Thanks," said Mum.

We picked up the boxes and carried them to the paddock where the stalls were going to be. My thoughts were racing. I thought of cute little Brandy and friendly Freddie, Nell who loved her walks and Tilly who had had such a hard life till she came to PAWS. What would happen to them all? I didn't want to think about it. I couldn't bear it. We had to do something. But what?

Dawn helped us unload, and then went off to set up the dog-show ring with rope and metal posts.

Abi and her mum and dad arrived.

"So, this is the place I've heard so much about," Michael, Abi's dad, said, getting out of the car.

"What do you think?" Abi asked him.

"It's beautiful," he said. "And with all the dogs here, I can see why you love it!"

I looked around. He was right. The house and gardens *were* beautiful. The grass and trees twinkled with an early morning dew and the house was framed against a clear blue sky.

"There's just so much Dawn could do with this place if she had the money," said Abi's mum.

Abi wanted to show her dad the dogs. Her mum and I went with them.

"This is Brandy, and this is Tilly, Dad," Abi said, after Jess had let us in. "The terrier over there is Esme – she's really bouncy. And this is Freddie."

We stopped at Freddie's cage. He stuck his nose through the wire and Michael tickled his cheek. He seemed to like dogs just as much as Abi and her mum did. "You're a handsome chap."

"He's Miss Harris's favourite," I said. "She'd love to adopt him, but she can't have a dog because she works full-time."

"There should be doggy nurseries," Abi said. "There must be lots of people like Miss Harris who would like a dog but need someone to look after it in the day."

"That's a really good idea, you know, Abi," said her dad.

"It is," said her mum. "I'm sure Dawn could rent the other building to someone who could run a doggy daycare business."

"That would be great," I said. That would definitely make up for the loss of rent on the fields, I thought.

"It could be a grooming parlour as well," said Abi. "And luxury holiday boarding kennels. Dawn could run training classes for the clients and make even more money that way."

"Yes, a proper doggy centre for all doggy needs," agreed her mum.

"It would be a really good business opportunity for someone. Dawn should look for an investor," said Michael.

"Is there anyone you know who might be interested, Dad?" Abi asked. "You have lots of friends who invest in local businesses, don't you?"

Her dad looked thoughtful. "Let me think about it. I might just have a solution."

"Really?" I gasped, my heart leaping.

"It's possible," he said. "But look, today's about the Fun Day and we should get on with setting up. Those stalls aren't going to build themselves. Let's go outside and get started."

I nodded. I hoped Abi's dad would have a solution for PAWS but, for now, we had more important things to do.

# 16

Over the next hour, lots more people arrived to help and the gardens were soon a hive of activity.

I tried to push thoughts of PAWS' future to the back of my mind and concentrate on the day ahead. Mum, Paula, Mia and I set out the cake stall and the tea and coffee stall. It looked lovely with the lacy tablecloth and tiered cake stands showing off the cakes and biscuits, pretty cupcake bunting and the Sugar and Spice Bakery bags to one side.

We put the PAWS birthday cake on its own raffle table where people could see it before they bought their raffle tickets. It had turned out as well as I'd hoped. We'd slathered it with buttercream icing and made a fondant icing figure of a dog that looked just like Freddie! Mrs Rees was there to sell the tickets.

When Mia and I had finished doing everything for our biscuit decorating stall, we went to check how everyone else was getting on.

Abi and her mum's dog-biscuit stand looked great! The bone-shaped biscuits were wrapped in shiny cellophane and the handmade labels tied on with ribbon.

Next to them was a face-painting stand run by two of Miss Harris's friends, and another stand with a Find-the-Bone treasure map competition that was being run by Mrs Patel, a teacher from school. There was also a big stall run by the local pet shop, Pet Heaven, selling leads, brushes, chews and bowls. Sarah's Natural Beauty stall was there and Harmony's reflexology tent was in a quieter spot next to a table where her friend was selling crystals and wind chimes. Rachael was organising the dog-show entries, while Jess and Rob manned the kennels.

Stefan and Mark were busy putting up the bouncy castle, with the twins running around them in excitement. Abi's dad was hammering in signs directing people to the toilets and the refreshments and the dog show, and George's dad was helping George and his friends set up the area for the band. Misha would arrive later with Lara and Alice and the people from the stables. Everything was going to plan.

Now all we needed was lots of people to come and have fun!

And people did come! More people than I ever could have imagined. All the advertising – the flyers, talking to people, the radio interview – seemed to have worked. It was lucky that Abi's dad had guessed it might get busy and organised an overflow car park in one of the fields. We needed it! The usually quiet grounds were filled with people and dogs, all smiling and having fun.

I didn't have a chance to see the dog show in the end – I was too busy running the Decorate-a-Biscuit stand with Mia. Mum was super-busy on the cake stall too. Our cash boxes quickly filled as people handed in notes and coins, often telling us to keep the change and put it towards PAWS.

The afternoon raced by. We had almost run out of cakes and biscuits when the classes in the dog show finished, and Dawn announced over the loudspeaker that there would now be a grand prize-giving where she  would cut the birthday cake and draw the winning raffle tickets. After  that, George's band would play and the barbecue would start serving.

Everyone gathered in front of the large table covered with trophies and prizes. It was set to the side of the stage where the band would be performing. Misha was there with George, Alec and Callum.

I went over. "Are you feeling nervous?" I asked.

"A bit," she said. It was strange. I'd never seen Misha this anxious before.

"You'll be fine," I told her.

"I can't believe how many people there are," she said.

"Just imagine you're in Harry's," I said. "You never mind singing there, even if the other tables are full."

It was time for the prize-giving to begin. Dawn had to use a microphone as there were so many people gathered around. She announced the dog-show prizes first and, one by one, the winners of each class went up to receive their prizes. Everyone smiled and clapped. After that, Miss Harris pulled out the winning raffle ticket. The cake was won by Paula! She was very pleased.

"The stars told me I would reap rewards today," she said, nudging me as she came back with the cake in a big box. "You'll have to help me eat this!"

"Yes, please!" I grinned.

Dawn started to speak again. "Before we get on with the barbecue and listening to the band, I just want to say thank you to you all for coming along and making the day such a success. As most of you know, I started PAWS a year ago and this is our first birthday, and it's lovely being able to celebrate it with so many people." I saw Dawn swallow and I knew she must be wondering whether PAWS would ever see its second birthday.

"Thank you to everyone who has helped out," she went on. "In particular, I would like to thank Hannah, Mia and Abi. Can you come forward, girls?"

Mia, Abi and I exchanged embarrassed looks and went up to the table at the front.

"These three girls have been amazing," Dawn told everyone. "They've worked so hard – whether it's been baking biscuits or washing dogs. I've got a little present for you all." She presented us each with a small bag. Inside, we found a silver chain with a little silver dog on. "Thank you!" we chorused.

Inside my heart felt heavy. The Fun Day was supposed to be the start of a big fundraising push, but without the rent from the fields, Dawn might not be able to carry on at all. All our hard work might have been for nothing. I kept thinking about the dogs in the kennels – Freddie, Tilly, Brandy and all the others. What would happen to them?

Mia smiled at me. "Today's gone really well, hasn't it?" she whispered.

I took a deep breath and nodded. "Yeah," I said, forcing myself to smile.

Dawn called Miss Harris up to thank her and presented her with a bouquet of flowers and everyone clapped and cheered. She blushed.

"I love coming here," she told everyone. "Please, if any of you love dogs and have time to spare, dog walkers are always needed. Do come and help out if you can!"

"And now it's time to welcome the entertainment!" said Dawn. "Please put your hands together for Mission Possible – George, Alec, Callum and, for today, a special guest appearance by Misha Shameli!"

George counted everyone in with his drumsticks, Alec and Callum played their guitars and Misha started to sing. It was a well-known Ellie B track, but Misha slowed it right down and it sounded completely different. It was brilliant!

I spotted Mum standing near the barbecue with Molly and Ella as Mark cooked burgers and sausages. I went over to her.

"Misha's really good," Mum said.

"She's always wanted to sing in a band," I said.

"I can see why," said Mum. "Look how much everyone's enjoying it."

I glanced around. People were swaying and listening to the music or settling down on picnic blankets on the grass.

Mum put her arm round my shoulders. "Today's been fantastic, Hannah."

I sighed. I was glad I could finally talk about the thoughts that had been weighing me down all day. "It's not enough, though, is it?"

"It might be. Dawn could find someone else to rent the fields. The current farmer's lease runs for another three months, so she's got time. And the money raised today will help her get PAWS onto a better financial footing. The other thing to remember is that now so many more people know about PAWS, I think she'll have lots more volunteers and people willing to run a fundraising committee. You've made the day a real success."

"It's only been this good because so many people have got involved," I pointed out. "It's not just me."

"You were the one who encouraged people to help," said Mum. "You spoke to everyone at the bakery and you persuaded people to join in who might not have otherwise. I'm proud of you, sweetie. Really proud."

I felt a bit better. Mum was right – there was still a chance things would work out, and everyone *was* really enjoying themselves. Abi and her mum and dad were talking to Dawn, Paula was dancing with Dylan, Mrs Rees was feeding Billy, Bobby and Benny dog biscuits, and Mark and Stefan were doing a roaring trade at the barbecue.

Mum and I sat down on the grass. I leaned my head against Mum's shoulder and wished with all my heart that things would turn out all right for Dawn and PAWS.

"Hannah!" I looked round. Abi was running towards me, beaming from ear to ear. What was going on? I got to my feet and went to meet her.

"You're never going to guess what's just happened," she gasped. She looked as if she was about to burst with excitement. "Oh, there's Mia!" she said, waving. "I've got to tell her too! Mia, come here!"

"Tell us what? What is it?" I said.

"Yes, what's going on?" Mia said.

"Only the best thing ever!" Abi's eyes shone. "Do you remember this morning Dad mentioned he might know someone who would want to invest in this place, turn it into a proper doggy centre with daycare and training classes and all that?"

My heart leaped. "Does he know someone?"

"Yes – him!" Abi said.

Mia and I stared at her.

"When we sold our house, he and Mum had some money left. They've been saving it to use as part of the deposit on a new house, but they've decided we should invest it in PAWS instead!"

"Oh, wow!" I gasped.

"And that's not even the best thing. When they were talking to Dawn, they said it would mean they couldn't buy another house and she offered us the main house here to live in! She says it's too big for her and she likes the little flat, so she's going to rent us the main house for not much more money than we're paying now!"

"That means you can live here and have a dog!" Mia said.

"I'll have lots of dogs," Abi said, with a grin. "And yes, I'll be able to have one of my own too. Mum's going to run the doggy daycare business, Dawn will run training classes, and Dad will stay in his current job for now and oversee the business side of things. He's sure he can find someone else to rent the fields, so there will still be money from that too. There's a lot to sort out but I think it's going to be perfect."

"Totally one hundred per cent perfect!" I said. I hugged her. "Oh, Abi, I'm so pleased!"

"I can't believe it," she said. "When we first moved, everything just felt so awful, but now it's even better than it was. Mum's going to be able to work with animals again, and I'm going to have loads of dogs to look after, not just one." She turned to me. "Thank you. If you hadn't made such an effort to be friends – well, none of this would have happened."

Mia grinned. "It's the Hannah effect. Things happen when she's around!"

"Shut up!" I said, blushing.

Abi giggled. "She's right, though. Thank you." She looked round. "Mmm, that barbecue smells good. Do you two want a hot dog?"

We bought hot dogs and cans of Coke from the barbecue, then went to sit with Alice and Lara, who were listening to the band on two large picnic rugs. We all chatted for a while and then I lay back. I could hear Alice and Lara trying to decide whether Callum or Alec was cuter, and Mia and Abi talking about how Miss Harris should adopt Freddie now he could go into doggy daycare while she was at work.

I gave a happy sigh. It's funny how sometimes things change and it all seems like a disaster, but then it turns out to be a new and exciting opportunity. I guess the one thing that's certain in life is that you never know exactly what's around the corner, but whatever it is, it's better not to fight it – just try and make the best of it and look for silver linings.

"You're very deep in thought."

I opened my eyes. Mum was standing over me.

I propped myself up on my elbows. "I'm just thinking about being happy," I said.

"Really? And what conclusions have you come to?" Mum asked, kneeling beside me.

"That if you end up with broken biscuits, you should just make cheesecake instead," I told her.

Mum's eyes twinkled. "Very wise. If you're lucky, the cheesecake will end up tasting even better than the biscuits would have done on their own."

"Exactly!" I said.

Mum gave me a sideways look. "So? Are you feeling happy then?"

I smiled as I looked around at everyone I knew, chatting and relaxing in the golden rays of the setting sun. "Yes," I said. "I really am."